Conversations with Women Showrunners

Featuring over forty interviews with America's leading showrunners, this book provides unique perspectives and insights into the TV industry and demystifies the craft, backbone, skill, strategies, challenges, and persistence it takes to succeed in Hollywood and internationally.

These conversations are part master craft lesson, part backstage pass, part career guide from the geniuses who create TV. This book shines a light on what it truly means to be a showrunner working in the television industry today and reveals how to navigate a career and a future in the global marketplace.

Interviews include showrunners who work in animation, comedy, drama, family, kids, "genre" – sci-fi, horror and more, plus procedurals, late night and multi-camera sit-com including: Angela Kang (*The Walking Dead*), Aline Brosh McKenna (*Crazy Ex-Girlfriend*), Barbara Hall (*Madam Secretary*), Charlotte Brown (*Rhoda*), Chris Nee (*Doc McStuffins*), Dailyn Rodriguez (*The Lincoln Lawyer, Queen of the South*), Elizabeth Berger (*This is Us*), Gloria Calderón Kellett (*One Day at a Time*), Ilene Chaiken (*The L Word, Empire*), Janine Sherman Barrois (*Claws, Self-Made, The Kings of Napa*), Jo Miller (*Full Frontal with Samantha Bee*), Julie Plec (*The Vampire Diaries*), Krista Vernoff (*Grey's Anatomy, Station 19*), Liz Meriwether (*New Girl, The Dropout*), Liz Tigelaar (*Tiny Beautiful Things, Little Fires Everywhere*), Marta Kauffman (*Friends, Grace and Frankie*), Meg DeLoatch (*Family Reunion*), Michelle Nader (*2 Broke Girls*), Monica Macer (*Queen Sugar*), Nkechi Okoro Carroll (*All American*), Tracy Oliver (*Harlem, First Wives Club*), Sierra Teller Ornelas (*Rutherford Falls*), and many more.

Ideal for professional and aspiring television writers, as well as students of screenwriting, film and TV, this book is essential reading for anyone interested in the art, craft and business of creating television.

Marygrace O'Shea is an Associate Arts Professor at NYU's Tisch School of the Arts Undergraduate Film and Television Department. She has also taught at Columbia University's Graduate Film Program, has been a Visiting Professor of the Arts at Sarah Lawrence College, an instructor at the Media Arts and Technology Department at BMCC, and has led master classes for students from La Femis. She has worked on shows for ABC, PBS, NBC, HBO, and FOX including *Law and Order: Criminal Intent, Law and Order: SVU*, and HBO's *In Treatment*. She is an active member of the WGA East.

Conversations with Women Showrunners

Marygrace O'Shea

LONDON AND NEW YORK

First published 2024
by Routledge
4 Park Square, Milton Park, Abingdon, Oxon OX14 4RN

and by Routledge
605 Third Avenue, New York, NY 10158

Routledge is an imprint of the Taylor & Francis Group, an informa business

© 2024 Marygrace O'Shea

The right of Marygrace O'Shea to be identified as author of this work has been asserted in accordance with sections 77 and 78 of the Copyright, Designs and Patents Act 1988.

All rights reserved. No part of this book may be reprinted or reproduced or utilised in any form or by any electronic, mechanical, or other means, now known or hereafter invented, including photocopying and recording, or in any information storage or retrieval system, without permission in writing from the publishers.

Trademark notice: Product or corporate names may be trademarks or registered trademarks, and are used only for identification and explanation without intent to infringe.

British Library Cataloguing-in-Publication Data
A catalogue record for this book is available from the British Library

Library of Congress Cataloging-in-Publication Data
Names: O'Shea, Marygrace (College teacher) author.
Title: Conversations with women showrunners / Marygrace O'Shea.
Description: London ; New York : Routledge, 2023.
Identifiers: LCCN 2023032195 (print) | LCCN 2023032196 (ebook) |
Subjects: LCSH: Women television producers and directors--United States--Interviews.
Classification: LCC PN1992.4.A5 O84 2023 (print) |
LCC PN1992.4.A5 (ebook) | DDC 791.4502/320820973--dc23/eng/
20230816
LC record available at https://lccn.loc.gov/2023032195
LC ebook record available at https://lccn.loc.gov/2023032196

ISBN: 978-1-032-28720-1 (hbk)
ISBN: 978-1-032-28719-5 (pbk)
ISBN: 978-1-003-29822-9 (ebk)

DOI: 10.4324/9781003298229

Typeset in Optima
by Taylor & Francis Books

For my ever-inspiring mother and child

Contents

Acknowledgements	xi
Introduction	1
ALINE BROSH MCKENNA I'm Here to Tell You That You're Qualified	3
ANGELA KANG Permission to Go After What I Love	9
BARBARA HALL We're All on the Side of the Show	15
CHARLOTTE BROWN The First Woman in The Room Who Wasn't There to Take Lunch Orders	22
CHRIS NEE The World as I Hope it Will Be	28
DAILYN RODRIGUEZ Be An Advocate for Yourself	35
DAYNA LYNNE NORTH Be Your Own Hype Girl	40
DEE JOHNSON I Climbed Every Rung of the Ladder	46
ELIZABETH BERGER We Loved the Way Television Made Us Feel	52

viii *Contents*

ERICA KODISH
You Girlfriend, Are Going into Battle, You Have to Get
Ready for That   57

FELICIA D. HENDERSON
Sometimes, You've Got to Put on Your Sasha Fierce   62

GILLIAN HORVATH
I'm a Lot of Things and Only One of Them is a Woman   69

GLORIA CALDERÓN KELLETT
They Don't Know I'm Superman   76

ILANA PEÑA
Let's, Like, Do Big Things   81

ILENE CHAIKEN
You Have to Believe that You Know Best   87

JANINE SHERMAN BARROIS
I'm Going for the American Dream Daily   92

JENNY BICKS
In a Good Room, It's Magic   99

JO MILLER
People Want to Hear an Angry, Menopausal Woman
Screaming, So Here I am   105

JULIE PLEC
I Moved Here with No Experience and No Skills   111

KRISTA VERNOFF
The Key to Longevity in This Town is Knowing Yourself
Really Well   115

LINDA YVETTE CHÁVEZ
Me, Fully and Without Fear   120

LISA HANAWALT
A Little Room to Play   126

LIZ MERIWETHER
People Feeling Safe is, as a Showrunner, Your Responsibility   132

Contents ix

LIZ TIGELAAR
I Had to Stop Myself from Being So Wide-Eyed and Grateful
All the Time 137

MARTA KAUFFMAN
I Wanted to Prove it to Myself 145

MARTI NOXON
Let Go of Being Liked by Everybody 150

MEG DELOATCH
I'm Authentically Telling My Story 156

MELINDA HSU
Foster an Atmosphere of Possibility 163

MICHELLE NADER
Open Your Mind to All the Possibilities of What Could Be 170

MONICA MACER
You Gotta Be the First One Out on the Dance Floor 178

NATALIE CHAIDEZ
My Lane is Transgressive Women 184

NKECHI OKORO CARROLL
Everyone Deserves the Right to Dream 190

RAELLE TUCKER
Is This a Net Positive for the World? 197

SARAH GERTRUDE SHAPIRO
Fear is the Enemy of Creativity 206

SHOSHANNAH STERN
Trusting Your Gut is The Only Way To Go 213

SIERRA TELLER ORNELAS
I Come from Storytellers 221

SOO HUGH
Ideas are Your Insurance 227

SUSANNAH GRANT
A Deeply Joyful Way to Spend Your Life 233

x   *Contents*

TANYA SARACHO
    We Have Been Excluded from the Narrative for So Long   238

TRACY OLIVER
    Know What You're Worth   244

VEENA SUD
    Blasting Away the Sacred Cow of Motherhood   250

WINNIE HOLZMAN
    See the Beauty of It   255

Acknowledgements

This book has been generously supported by Dean Allyson Green and the Dean's Faculty Grants from NYU's Tisch School of the Arts. Without Dean Green's leadership in the area of creative research, this book would not have been possible.

Enormous thanks to Jeff Melvoin and Jackie Reingold, both of whom were instrumental in connecting me early on with many women portrayed in this book. Without their trust and outreach, the conversations might never have begun. Huge thank yous to all the women who took the time to speak with me, their assistants and staff, and their publicists, in particular Alison Rou.

To my students, thank you for the inspiration. I hope this work shines many paths for you. To my fellow union members and the staff at the Writers Guild East and West, thank you for the community, home, support, inspiration and fierce advocacy.

To my generous, wise, and supportive colleagues Maggie Greenwald, Shari Rothfarb, Charlie Rubin, Susan Shapiro and Heather Winters, thank you for cheering me on, and for all your support and advice throughout the long process of bringing this book into the world. To my colleagues in my department at Tisch, thank you for your continued enthusiasm and encouragement. Thanks also to Jill Rothenberg for your fresh eyes and additional editing and to all my friends who did early reads on the book proposal. Leslie, Neelima and Dara, thank you too! A special thank you to my editors and the staff at Routledge, particularly Rachel Feehan, Claire Margerison and Sarah Pickles.

For your endless hours of dedicated transcription, research, proofreading, and support – thank you to the many, many student interns and researchers who helped this project. I want to especially thank the loyal and dedicated former students who stayed with the project for several years, working weekends and summers in crunch times, in particular Caroline Beegan, Isobel Houseman, Annie Morrisun Hsu and Zazie Sales.

My love and gratitude to friends and family for their support and patience, particularly Luca, Joanie O, Madrina, Iobel, Merritt, Margie and Jen.

Introduction

This book grew out of two needs that my students and I both shared – a need to bring the voices of women showrunners into the classroom because the literature is still largely silent on them, or worse, continually erases them and their achievements, and a need to see the variety of possible paths to build a career in an industry that is still largely hostile to women.

No matter what it may feel like, or what you've been told, women have been creating and running shows since the start of television. The wisdom and experiences of the women in this book, gathered in one place, is meant to illuminate the many paths others have taken, so you can find yours.

To collect these voices, I followed a trail of breadcrumbs and contacts through friends, colleagues, and sometimes directly from one interviewee to the next. Many times it took me over two years to secure an interview. Eventually momentum built, and with the combination of the Agency Action removing some layers of gatekeepers, the shutdown in production during the pandemic giving people more time to speak, as well as more people feeling comfortable speaking remotely, the project blossomed. Many of these interviews took place in that moment and its spirit of openness and vulnerability. A project that started out as a lament and became a celebration.

While not a complete list of all women showrunners, this collection is a broad sampling of the women I spoke to. Their careers start from the 1970s on, in different narrative scripted genres, including comedy and drama, kids tv and late night, network, cable and streaming. As these interviews evolved from a Q + A format into "as told to portraits," the flow became most compatible to individual writers rather than pairs, though there are many showrunners who have built successful careers writing as teams.

Each chapter evolved from a conversation, and retains the flavor of spoken words, the path of our conversation, and the individual point of view of the woman portrayed with minimal editing for ease of reading. Each participant had the opportunity to make corrections or to take a pass on their chapter. Each showrunner approved her own chapter as written.

Over the course of research for this book, there have been some improvements in the industry, but there is still a long way to go before there is parity or equity in representation, opportunity and compensation. The dirty

DOI: 10.4324/9781003298229-1

2 Introduction

little secret is, though the quantity and variety of shows has grown – more shows, more jobs – the percentage of representation of women and women of color in those jobs and on those shows has remained virtually the same for the past 20+ years. To repeat, there are more jobs and shows numerically, but the *percentage* of women getting those jobs is constant. You will see a greater number of shows by women, but those shows are not a greater percentage share in the marketplace. This is how we can easily believe things are "better" when a showrunner graces the cover of a trade publication, but things are in fact systemically unchanged. How that plays out in individual careers is a disconnect between what you and the culture are asked to believe, and what you experience on an individual level. Most often budgets, conditions, work hours, compensation and pace of career advancement are in no way equitable.

My hope is that the stories of these women will accompany you on your journey and help move those numbers to something more representative of us all, for us all, the sooner the better.

ALINE BROSH McKENNA
I'm Here to Tell You That You're Qualified

Figure 1.1 Aline Brosh McKenna
Source: photo by Kit Karzen

Aline Brosh McKenna wrote the films *The Devil Wears Prada, 27 Dresses, Morning Glory,* and *We Bought a Zoo,* among others. Her films have grossed over $860 million, so far. She showran and co-created the CW's *Crazy Ex-Girlfriend* with writer, performer, and star Rachel Bloom, which ran from 2015 to 2019. Aline makes her debut as a feature director with *Your Place or Mine,* starring Reese Witherspoon, Ashton Kutcher, and Steve Zahn, for which she also wrote the screenplay. Aline grew up in New Jersey and graduated *magna cum laude* from Harvard.

DOI: 10.4324/9781003298229-2

4   *Aline Brosh Mckenna*

Mentoring has been a huge part of my life since *Crazy Ex-Girlfriend*. I didn't have a lot of employment opportunities for folks when I was a feature writer. But as a showrunner, finding people, promoting women, especially, but just writers in general, has been one of the great joys of the job. I think I'm better at mentoring than I was at being mentored. Most of my mentors were male. I'm not a hundred percent sure why but that is, but that definitely was true for me. When I think of a mentor, I think of someone who says to you, "You're meant to do this, and you're going to do well. And don't mind the vicissitudes because I'm here. I've been in this world, and I'm here to tell you that you're qualified," because that's really the thing you need to hear.

"Female Filmmaker Friday" came about because I was on Instagram, and I saw that director Tamra Davis had posted this wonderful picture of herself and said, "We need more images of women directing." I thought, "Wow, that's a really good idea." I emailed Tamra and I said, "What do you think if we started a hashtag and get people to put these up?" It really is true that if you can't see it, an image of that person doing that job, you can't imagine yourself doing it. A director skews to a lot of male stereotypes. It's just bossing people around and pointing at things. It's such a power role. I think just seeing all shapes, sizes, races, ethnicities, backgrounds, pregnant, short, fancy dress, jeans, cargo pants, all the different ways of being a female director is powerful. One of the things that really moved me was that somebody had posted on Facebook, "My daughter looked at these when she was deciding what to wear to school for career day." That killed me.

I have a lot of women I mentor. The most notable success in that area would be Rachel, obviously. Because when I first met her, I just thought, "Well, maybe I can help this young woman somehow, introduce her to some people, or help her with her idea," and it kind of became being partners and doing the show together, but it really started from, you know, I'm a fan. I had seen her videos on YouTube. And I know how meaningful it has been in my life when people have reached out to me.

Rachel had this handbag that she was carrying when we met, and it was a little bit tatty. She had no money. And so, I said to her, "If we sell this pilot, I'm going to buy you a nice handbag." We got the pilot ordered by Showtime. I took her to Beverly Hills, and I bought her a blue Prada tote bag she still carries, a beautiful bag. I remember we went to lunch after that, and she said, "I don't understand. Why are you doing this for me? Why are you so nice to me? Why are you doing this for me?" And I said, "Because people did it for me. And I know how meaningful it is and how great it feels to have somebody choose you and mentor you." As great as it feels to be the person who is being mentored, to me it's even more of a thrill to try and mentor and help other people.

I'm always in meetings with producers where they're saying, "We can't find any female directors. We're looking. We can't find them." Like, please. Guys. You're not looking. Well, look at the AFI program. Look at women in other departments. There are women in every single department who are capable of doing this job. But again, you know people are used to looking in the more male departments to elevate people, and so you have to be looking at the jobs that have more women in them where those people are just as capable. You have to be more entrepreneurial about finding people. They're just not thinking. The other thing is you have to be aggressively seeking these people out. You can't just wait for them to wander over to your door. You have to say, "Oh, I notice a woman's name on that. What's she doing? What's she like? What else has she directed?" You have to be proactive. It's the same way you're hiring diverse people. You can't wait for the system to filter them over to you. You have to go and find them and invite them into the process.

For me, being in an environment in TV where the writer is the most listened-to voice is some sort of crazy, lovely dream. A lovely fantasy. Every showrunner does it differently. Everybody has their own system. When we got the show, I realized that we were going to have to figure that out. I hadn't worked in television in 15 years before *Crazy Ex*. I did a couple of pilots when I was starting, and my old writing partner and I had written nine pilots and shot three of them. So, I have experience being EP on set. But it hadn't been in many years, and it was only a pilot. When we got ordered to series, I have a lot of friends who run shows, so I called a lot of people and got their advice, all super conflicting.

You have to find the thing that works for you. I think in the beginning, I had been in rooms before, and my ambition was to find people who could run the room while I was on set in some way. That actually turned out to not work for us. What I personally learned is that I'm in the room 89 percent of the time. That's the engine room. That's where I needed to be, and we have other wonderful people with great on set experience, and they're able to cover me there. Having other experienced people who could cover set was critical because I needed to be in the room for our show to function.

What I'm really focused on in my day is sitting and typing. Some showrunners don't want to do that because it sucks. It's hideous. Writing's the worst. There's some showrunners who abandon the room very early so they can hang out on set, which I get because it's way more fun to be on set, you know, hanging out and sitting in the chair kibitzing, hanging out with the actors, way more fun. But if you neglect the engine room, you're going to run out of steam. I spent most of my time in the room, and I know that is different for different people. Other showrunners have other writers who can cover them in the writers' room, but that's not how we did our thing.

We had the same staff since the beginning, since the first day. We didn't change any writers. We promoted two writer's assistants. We had no turnover. We had very good hours. We wrote from ten to six. One day I said to the writers, "I can't remember. How many times have we stayed late in three years?" And somebody said, "Five!" I couldn't remember, but they certainly did. Because they're used to being hostages. They're used to being in a situation where the showrunner is going to keep them there. They're sort of at the

6 *Aline Brosh Mckenna*

whim of somebody who may not want to go home for their own personal reasons. It happens frequently. When they understood that we were going to have very good hours and that I was very organized and I was going to stick to that, that was extremely meaningful in terms of gaining people's trust.

I've been in other kinds of writers' rooms. From my early TV experiences, when the guy comes in, and you start unraveling a perfectly salvageable story, you're thinking like, "Oh, my night's done. I guess I'm not having dinner with my roommate or my husband or my children because I'm going to sit here and watch this guy stare into space and try, instead of fix this thing, rethink this thing." And I think one thing that happens is that people think that you're solving for X, but there isn't an answer. There's only your vision of the show. It's not a mathematical equation where you're seeking some sort of ultimate answer. I also am extremely, and I think pathologically, decisive. So, they're not looking at someone staring into space, which is another awful thing when you have a showrunner who can't decide, and you're just literally watching that guy go through his mental paces. We're always doing and deciding, and I would rather go ahead and make a decision and then see if it pans out. I am just a very decisive cat.

But that doesn't mean I've never doubted myself. I mean, that's what being a writer is. It's like, pick yourself up off the ground. It's like the resilience of getting up every day and opening up your Final Draft. As I said, wouldn't you rather hang out on set? What's worse than writing? It's awful. When people say, "I love writing," I'm like, "Something's wrong." I don't know what you're doing. It's miserable. Every morning, every morning that you open up Final Draft. One of the things I truly love about a writers' room is that it is so hard to get that document open, but when I have 10 really smart, funny, awesome people that I care about looking at me, and we need to get going, we get going. The way that we do it is most of the rewriting happens in the room, so the writers will write their draft and turn it in. A lot of showrunners will take your draft and rewrite it. Really early on I was like, "What am I doing with these people then?" I have these smart funny people. Why would I not take advantage of their expertise? We do it more like a traditional comedy room. I throw it up on the screen, and I rewrite it with them sitting there. That process took a little while because they had to see that I was an equal opportunity deleter, that I would delete anyone's stuff just as easily as my own. You know that everybody was being rewritten equally. Once we established that, it works great, and as someone who has written solo for 20 years, when I write solo now, man, I miss a roomful of smart funny people calling out jokes and thoughts and suggestions because it's great.

I've also really loved directing on *Crazy Ex*. I've done all the season finales. I'm so lucky because by the time I directed my first episode, I had done 17 episodes with this crew. I think for women in terms of being the captain of a crew, that's intimidating. But I had been sort of the captain of the whole enterprise for 17 episodes along with Rachel. I was already very accustomed to working with these folks and giving them feedback and getting feedback from them. It was a very comfortable place to start directing. I always wanted to direct. I wasn't ever able totally to figure out how I was going to do it with my family. But now that my kids are a little older, it's a little bit easier to see the path there. I think that all showrunners should direct because you get a perspective on your show and on your set that you can't get any other way. You work with your department heads in a completely different way. I would recommend it to anyone who runs a show, male or female. It's easy to ask, "Why didn't we get that?" But when you're standing there, it's like, "I'll tell you why we didn't get it. We didn't have time. This didn't work. This location was funky. This was harder to light than you thought. An actor was having an issue. The scene wasn't working." You just have a much more specific idea of how this whole thing functions. Your ass is on the line, and it's great for everyone to see that and experience that together. It's also great for the crew because normally if they're on set and a director is saying, "I think Aline would want this," or people are wondering what we would want in the editing room, if I'm standing there, and I'm directing it, that takes that piece of the equation out.

By the way, the other thing is women have this obsession with wanting to have technical mastery over all the technical components of a set before they go direct, and men don't even think about it. They don't even concern themselves with it. They just wander over, and they'll figure it out when they get there. Part of the reason for that is that women are penalized, and people roll their eyes, but what's important is that you understand the story and how the show is photographed and how to talk to people and how to communicate the vision of the show. Those are not gendered activities. By the way, it annoys those people when you walk over and try to tell them what lens or what filter to use. Just go over to them and tell them what you want it to look like. Cite some comps. Be articulate about what you want it to look like and why. The DP (Director of Photography) doesn't want you to pick out their lens.

When we first pitched the show, I already had a ton of experience in pitching, obviously, because I've been doing it so long and most of my movies or a good proportion of my movies are based on original ideas, which is somewhat unique. When Rachel and I pitched, I generally I took the lead on the actual pitching of the material, and we had kind of scripted the material. Because of my feature experience, I don't know how to write the beginning of something unless I know the end, so we knew the whole story before we went in. We came in with a staggering amount of detail. We cut it down, so we weren't boring people to death, but we had all four chapters, and they roughly correlate to seasons. We had a bit of an act. And it was fluid. It wasn't locked in. But the funny thing that we discovered, like as humans and based on our background, when I saw it was going south in a pitch, or they didn't like it, I would start wrapping it up because I knew, like, this is never selling here. But she's a standup, and she is never say die. The more they resisted something, the more she would triple down. Like, they were going to drag her out, you know, with a hat and a cane in hand. The worst pitch, it was really interesting, we had this one terrible meeting, and I

8   Aline Brosh Mckenna

just started wrapping up my Ginsu knives and putting them back in my vest. And she just was not going to leave there until she made them laugh. It really was moving. That's the difference between a writer and a performer. She's a writer also, but as someone who has been pitching for 20 years, I could tell it was not going to happen.

We had nine pitches. One of the places, it was really funny, we sold it in the room, and they said it so casually. They said, "OK, let's do this." We walked out, and then Rachel was like, "Wait a second. What happened?" Because she thought that they would be jumping up and down and screaming. And they were very calmly saying, "Yes, let's do this." One of the things I love about working with Rachel is that I think I was a little bit, the word's not jaded, but I think I was a little bit like, cigarette in hand, "This is what it's like, baby." And she just had this dewy optimism always about the whole thing. And I love that, and I love being around that and it really reinvigorated me.

When somebody says, "Oh, you discovered her," I say that she had a YouTube following, and she was doing just fine. But in some ways, even though I mentored her, the reason that I became a showrunner, I was trying very hard to hire someone else to be the showrunner of *Crazy Ex-Girlfriend* at the beginning, but I wanted to protect her. I wanted to protect the show, but I also personally really wanted to protect her because I just have seen too many people get eaten up and spit out by the business. It's interesting to me that I had always resisted becoming the boss. I had not stepped forward to direct or to be a showrunner, any of that. And then the thing that made me become a boss, that made me step into that role, was frankly a maternal instinct. After becoming a mom, I just felt like I'm going to protect this woman, and this show, and that's what my mission is. That's why I often say, even though I discovered her, I feel like she discovered me right back. It was our shared vision and our desire to work together that made me step into this role which I feel so comfortable in.

ANGELA KANG
Permission to Go After What I Love

Figure 2.1 Angela Kang
Source: photo by Eric Fisher

Angela Kang got her BA from Occidental College and a Masters in Screenwriting from USC. She has written for *The Walking Dead* since Season Two and became its showrunner in Season Nine, credited with revitalizing the show by fans. Angela is an executive producer of the spinoff *The Walking Dead: Daryl Dixon* and is the 2021 recipient of the Etheria Inspiration Award.

I feel like part of why *The Walking Dead* hit with the public at the time it did is there's been this kind of underlying fear – and it's not unique to America,

DOI: 10.4324/9781003298229-3

10 *Angela Kang*

because my show is popular around the world – that things are out of balance and perhaps coming to some sort of a head. There's these issues of social justice that have been brewing, there's issues of class and equity and economic disparity. The world and its challenges have caused us all anxiety. There is environmental ruin and a global pandemic, and an underlying feeling that everything is falling apart. I think that's something that people have connected to in the story, but even more, the idea that you can survive something like that, although you might have to go through dark times to do it.

During COVID, a lot of people went through a journey like, "we're locked down, I'm going to learn how to knit and bake bread every day and read Shakespeare's library," and all these kinds of big goals. I do think as Americans, we tend to be very goal oriented, and I am guilty of this myself. I couldn't do the job I have if I wasn't this way. And yet, I think we're all going through a generational trauma that is unlike anything else. What's important isn't reading Shakespeare or making the bread every day – it's something else that's more fundamental. You start to think: do you make your choices only for yourself? Do you make them on behalf of the people you love? Do you take an easy way out? Do you do the hard grind? How much more can you bear when you're already under so much stress? These are questions that are very human. In various ways, we've been dealing with that on the show.

At the start of 2020, we were in the middle of working on a story that's about class. We were talking a lot about 1968 and the civil rights movement and how class and race intersect, and how when frustrations are really pent up, you're eventually going to have civil unrest. That was all before the start of the pandemic in the U.S. and then everything hit. And we started to see certain things in real life happen in the ways that we were predicting in the story we were working on. So that was surreal. But it tells you something about how you can't really predict what anyone is going to do at any given moment, but there are patterns to the way that humanity responds to crisis, for better and for worse. In my writers' room, everybody is deeply interested in history, so we spend a lot of time talking about what happens during times of turmoil historically. What happens during war? What happens when things don't feel right? What happens as a result of trauma to an entire generation? We write a zombie horror narrative, but zombie stories are actually always about social issues because the monsters are *us*.

The Walking Dead also deals so much with processing grief and loss and figuring out how to find meaning in the world. Those themes really speak to me. I lived in a multi-generational household growing up and in the course of one year when I was a teenager, my grandfather died of a heart attack, my mother died of cancer, and then my grandmother was hospitalized and almost died. So I think a lot about what is meaningful in life. What are the relationships that sustain you? What are the choices you make that ultimately define you? A lot of the art that I'm drawn to deals with that. In terms of *The Walking Dead* specifically, something fundamental to the show is that we're constantly exploring different characters from very different walks of life who are crashing into each other. Everybody's in an apocalypse and everybody has these monsters to deal with. Certain constructs in the world have fallen away, although not entirely. You see different forms of small governments forming. It's been interesting to explore very different people who have very different philosophies about what is the right way to govern, about the right way to deal with other people. It leads to a lot of deep conversation that's very intellectually stimulating because yes, we love doing the zombies and the horror and the action, but that's like fun make believe. I think what deeply appeals to me is you get to peek into the souls of different people, and sometimes peek into very dark ways of looking at the world and try to understand it so our heroes can fight back.

The idea of fighting back against unfair systems is part of the DNA of the series, both in front of and behind the camera. I'm Gen X and I have some skepticism about posturing on social media, but I'm feeling more like there's a responsibility to use your platform to highlight issues of invisibility. With AAPI folks, for example, there is this "model minority" myth, a "white-adjacent" myth that is very damaging because it erases the very real existence of anti-Asian racism. The first time I stepped foot in Georgia to work on an episode of my show, I saw Confederate flags and I felt deeply unsettled and scared. I went for days without seeing another person who was an Asian-American other than the actor on my show, Steven Yeun. But for the most part, I found a friendly atmosphere there, so I gradually became less scared. But one of the things I talked to my studio about was that it is really hard for my Black writers and actors to step foot in a state of the Confederacy and see the symbols of the Confederacy around. We're scouting locations that still have four bathrooms because of the history of segregation. We're looking at places where there was a history of horrific violence and that has a psychological effect. I had a Black writer who was scared for her life. A Black actor whose Uber driver wouldn't pick him up. The studio actually said, "We've never thought about that." To those executives' credit, after that conversation, they said, "We have to look harder at the places we film and what are ways to make the talent feel safer in these places?" The news that came out of Georgia (of the Atlanta spa shootings in May 2021) really affected me because you can kind of think, "I don't know, maybe the world is good. Maybe everything's fine. Maybe it's getting better." And then there are these really stark reminders that everything is *not* fine. On the other hand, Steven Yeun being nominated for an Oscar for *Minari* was just wonderful. But there's this bittersweetness to thinking about how many years it took for this kind of acknowledgement to happen, because a lot of times, roles for Asian-Americans are not fully fleshed out. *Minari* is the most like my family that I've ever seen onscreen in the United States. It took me into my forties to see that.

For *The Walking Dead*, I'm pretty proud of the diversity of our series regular cast. A majority of the characters are from historically underrepresented groups. In addition to race, ethnicity, gender, and sexual orientation, we've also been looking at neurodiversity and disability. We've often had important characters that are older. We're trying to look at it from all angles. It's not perfect, but we're trying. We have self ID programs with the studio to diversify

12 Angela Kang

our crews, and we brought in interns from a variety of educational backgrounds so people who couldn't afford to go to film school don't have that barrier. And what gives me hope is that I'm seeing more and more series where people are trying. When I was on staff while Steven was there, there was a year when there was another Korean American writer on staff with me and it was so unusual at the time. Like, there's two of us! That sounds so horrible, but it's very common to be "the only one." And it becomes your job to represent every underrepresented group somehow. But we were able to have really frank conversations early on about stereotypes that Asian American men are not virile, they're cowardly, not strong, not hot. And we were like, "We have to write this character in a different way than that." It's so much weight that any one minority character carries in a show, you know? But when Steven was ready to leave and his character died, one of the beautiful things was that the fans had fully accepted he is one of the heroes of the show. They accepted his humanity. It should be a given and it's not.

I'm grateful that we've got such a dedicated fanbase who support what we're doing in terms of representation. We have viewers from many different communities. We have fans across the political spectrum. We have people who are from different countries who don't relate at all to the ideas of American politics. They might be from a socialist country, or communist country, or from Middle Eastern countries that don't fall into either of those categories. I'm so grateful to fans who say that they feel like I've reinvigorated the show or that are responding positively to it. Because there's also plenty of people who are like, "eh, it hasn't been good since the first season." And everybody's entitled to their opinion. I only know how to tell the story from the perspective of the characters and what they want, and what feels like real obstacles to them in that world. But there is also a part of me that is like the kid with the dimmer switch. That's like, "more fun here, more action here." The craft of this show is very specific. You have to be a person who likes character stories, and then you also have to be able to do the zombies. That's its own skill set that you have to come in with or develop, which a lot of people on the staff have done. I've learned a lot in my time on the show. I appreciate that I've been given the opportunity to come into my own. There are times that I think, "Oh my god, this show is so massive." Our budget is so massive. The reach is so massive, and it seems surreal that I get to call the shots on this series.

I feel like I've grown up so much and changed in the ten years that I've been on the show. I became a mother and I feel like I've gone through a process where I found my voice and my strength in ways that I don't think I had fifteen years ago. We also live in a different time. As with many women who came up in the TV industry around the same time as me, or before that, there were times as a woman and a person of color where I felt dismissed and not heard by certain people. One of my co-workers talked to me many years ago about the anxiety of speaking up in a writers' room and how especially as a woman, you just feel like you're not listened to. And she really admired this particular female showrunner and asked her, "How do you

Angela Kang 13

have such confidence when you're pitching? How do you just own it?" And the showrunner said after she gave birth, she felt like she wasn't afraid of anything anymore. I respect that not every person who has those reproductive organs is going to go on that same journey. Pregnancy was not magical for me. But there was something about the combination of the time in history, and how hard my pregnancy was and how difficult that birth was – my son was born three months premature – where I do feel like I kind of came into my own afterward and just started to feel like, "Why should I be afraid anymore? I went through something that was so difficult and scary, why am I scared of work? I shouldn't be." I finally feel like I've got my own permission to just go after what I love. And becoming the boss of the show has really been a wonderful journey. There was so much built-in support because I'd been with the show so many years. I felt like there was a trust there. For the most part, I've been lucky in the places I've worked. I was hired by people who really believed in me and trusted what I was trying to bring to the table over the years, but I had to get over many decades of feeling "less than."

I feel lucky that I've had people around me who are supportive, which makes such a difference. The showrunners I've worked with have all been really supportive and I've learned things from every single one of them. I feel like I've taken things from every job that are useful to this day. I also take a lot of comfort from my peers and my colleagues. That lateral connection of a peer who is not competing in any way is so crucial. I'm definitely of the school of thought of, "There's enough pie for everyone." I don't think a scarcity mentality works for me. My pointing you to an opportunity does not take something away from me. I've tried to do that for others, but I've also benefited from these wonderful, generous women who have done that and advocated for me to other executives. I guess it's a little sideways from the traditional idea of mentorship, but peer mentoring is just as important.

In my time as Showrunner, the series has moved away a bit from guns and cars and more towards nature taking over and handmade tools. Norman Reedus, who plays Daryl on the show, has said it's less about "chest thumping." One of the things that the long termers on this show really seem to connect to is the idea of basic survival and the world being difficult. In some ways, cars and guns make things easy – makes it easy to kill, easy to get from place to place. When you have to fight hand to hand, whether it's the zombies or another human, it's more brutal. So it just takes on a different quality. I think a lot about the state of the environment. While it's not overtly an environmental narrative, we have a community that was an ecologically friendly, sustainable community before the apocalypse, and they survived and thrived as a result. It's been fun to establish and explore that. I actually wish we could do more with the idea that nature rushes through everything and fully takes over, but it's very expensive. You can't find locations that look like that because everything is so settled in the real world.

We're also dedicated to having bad-ass women characters who are kicking ass and don't need to be damsels in distress. But at the same time, one of the things that's important to us on the show is *people* looking out for each other, and that can go in any direction, regardless of gender. For us, it's more about this family of people who come together and help each other. We talk about the male gaze, and what constitutes a strong woman on screen. For so long, women have been either invisible or a two-dimensional type who exists in video game terminology as a "non-playable character." They literally just exist for the male lead to go through, and they've got no inner life. I don't like that kind of story. Now you have men who are maybe feminists or position themselves as such. They write kickass women and that's better than nothing, but a lot of times those are still shaped around a male gaze, so there is a kind of unattainable perfection to them. They are still expected to conform to a certain visual aesthetic and the stories are sort of limited. I think for us, it's always been important that the women be complex, so not only do they kick ass, but they have full emotional lives. They can make mistakes. They can be awesome. They can be smart. They can have moments of weakness. Having fully formed people is what allows you to look at characters as humans and not just this sort of construct of what you want them to be. I do think that there's this kind of toxic perfectionism that can come with female characters. I don't want to lean into that, and it's not always popular when we have the women on our show make mistakes. But I would tell that kind of story for a male protagonist. That's how they get to have a better story. They've got to struggle. So, if you're going to have female characters who are heroic, they also have to struggle against themselves, and against external forces. Of course, we don't always know our own gaps in understanding, but we're always trying to evolve the conversation and be truer to who we think these characters might be if they were living, breathing human beings.

I do think for myself, there's this aspect of me that, I don't know…My mother died when she was young, she was forty, and her mother died in her fifties. And I have Lupus, an autoimmune disease. So, at times, I've really struggled to walk, and it affects a lot of my life in different ways. I have a kind of lack of patience sometimes, a feeling like the sand's about to run out of the hourglass. To put this in terms of story, we're doing a scene right now where the kids are playing and talking about their parents going out on missions all the time. On the surface, it's a scene about a card game, but it's really a scene about what it means to grow up in a world where you know you're not going to get enough time with the people you love. Scenes like that connect strongly to my own sense that time is short and the most valuable asset we have. I'm not somebody that needs to buy a lot of nice things. The thing that I value most is always time. I think that our characters are the same way. They are just trying to hang on to what they can, you know? That's the most human thing. It's like they're all terminal patients and what matters most now? It's trying to create safety for the people you love and having a little time with them. That is something that transcends language and cultural barriers and is universal in some way.

BARBARA HALL
We're All on the Side of the Show

Figure 3.1 Barbara Hall
Source: photo CBS

Barbara Hall was born in Chatham, Virginia and worked her way up on staffs as a writer on *I'll Fly Away, Northern Exposure* and *Chicago Hope* before creating and showrunning *Judging Amy, Joan of Arcadia* and *Madam Secretary* for CBS. In addition, Barbara has written eleven young adult novels and is a founding member of the band The Enablers, with whom she released the albums *The First Seven Songs* (2003) and *Come Back Soon* (2004). Barbara followed that with solo albums *Handsome* and *Bad Man*. She has won a Humanitas Award and has been nominated for many Emmys and WGA Awards, among many others.

DOI: 10.4324/9781003298229-4

16   Barbara Hall

When I started in television, it was all pre-Anita Hill. There was a lot of, "We need a woman on staff," for the woman's voice, not the whole script. And then you'd get in the room, and you could do it all, so they let you. The great thing about television is that it's so time-consuming. You're always in this time crunch so anybody who can do it, once you're in the trenches, you can do whatever. There's an opportunity for TV to be a meritocracy, because we make so much of it, and we have to make it so quickly.

Back in the day when network ruled, there was nothing complicated about why shows got left on. If the ratings were good, they got left on. If not, they were canceled. So, if you could deliver what people liked and would watch, you could rise to the top. You would have a lot of job security because this was a pretty quick way to test it. We make it. We put it out there. If people like it, we're on. If they don't, we're not, and that would override a lot of politics. That's one of the good things about television. Now there are different business models, it's a little more complicated than just people like it or don't like it, but still, there's a lot to be said for that aspect of TV.

My journey was that I started with – talk about the Golden Age of Television – some of the best writers in television. I started being a producer with Josh Brand and John Falsey, on one of their shows called *I'll Fly Away*, and the person running that show was David Chase (who created and ran *The Sopranos*). So, I worked with these great people who taught me how to do it. This has a little bit to do with being a woman: I knew I should not take my shot until I knew exactly what I was doing. I really understood on a cellular level that we don't get to make as many mistakes. And I still believe that. You need to really know the job. I didn't skip any steps because when I finally got a shot to make a pilot, I knew it had to really work. I couldn't fail. Nope.

The beginning of female showrunners, of letting women do that, it was a test. We had to prove that we could do that. Because that's where the glass ceiling is of television. Women can write up to a point because that's okay, but if you want to run the show and hire everybody and make it your show, then you really had to be able to do it. So, I was conscious of really putting all of my time and learning everything I could from these guys because they did it the way I wanted to do it. Even to this day, a lot of my habits came from them. For example, Josh Brand, John Falsey, and David Chase, they didn't want to micromanage everything. They wanted to teach you to do it. They were visionaries and they knew exactly what they wanted, and you had to do it exactly the way they wanted it. They were not very lenient in that regard. But, if you could do it, they would shoot your words. They didn't need to shoot their own. And that's incredibly motivating.

I had to learn how to raise my game to what theirs was because if I did, then I could see my words produced and shot. That's a greater way to motivate people than out of fear and intimidation. But it's not about being easy on anyone. You can be incredibly demanding in terms of where the bar is and demanding that people hit it. But, if they do, then you just let them do it. Josh and John threw me in the deep end and said, "You need to swim if you want to stay here." They knew what they were doing and what they expected and who they were. I saw the great results. I saw the shows doing well because of how we all contributed.

One of the best things David Chase did for me was he taught fearlessness in writing for sure, but fearlessness in tone and mixing tones. That's how I found what I really wanted to do. Where it's incredibly dramatic one minute and the next scene can be funny, and the next scene can be absurd, and the next scene can be action. You can mix all these tones together if everything is of a piece. All of my heroes – from Mark Twain on – did that, change gears, the emotional whiplash. If somebody at the top knows what they want to say and they have a clear vision, then you can do anything within that. All of them taught me – which has become my rule – that we're all on the side of the show. It's not about the promotion or the aggrandizement of any one person or aspect of the show. It's about the show and so, that becomes its own entity, and its own thing.

You just have to decide, create the rules (of the world), then have a template for other people to follow. You have to know it before you start. Before the pilot. You really have to understand what you are setting the template for. For example, with Josh and John, with *Northern Exposure*, they understood what they were going to do before they ever started. Things can emerge, but everything is in service to that vision and that tone and that world. Also, it's why everybody's job is the most important job. That's the other rule I have. There's not an element of the show that isn't serving the show, and every element of it is important and then everyone gets to have pride of ownership, which has a great effect on how good a show is. And mainly, the attitude matters, the work ethic matters.

I stayed on with them – I did all of their shows – *A Year in the Life, I'll Fly Away, Northern Exposure*. I ran the writers' room on *Chicago Hope*. And then, I did three pilots before I got one on the air – *Judging Amy*.

There was a time in the '90s when people – especially focus groups – had a lot of trouble with women in positions of power. You know, it wasn't just the powers-that-be in Hollywood. We would test them and people weren't ready or willing to see. But as those examples change in the world, then it opens up a pathway for us to do it on TV. Because one of the things when I created *Judging Amy* that was driving me was getting so tired of seeing women on TV and in films who couldn't cope. That's all women do. Women are the copers. And it's the notion of the way I live, and the people I'm around, and seeing women holding their worlds together. And then when you tune in for some entertainment, they're falling apart over every difficult decision. That's not my experience. And one of the ways that women cope obviously like most people, is with humor.

For *Judging Amy*, honestly it was a little window of time where there was a need for a female-driven story for CBS. But at the time it was one of the

18 *Barbara Hall*

very few, maybe only, dramas ever about a single mother. Candice Bergen was doing *Murphy Brown*. Comedies were doing it. But the one-hour drama, which had typically been the legal world and the cop world, a much more male-populated world, didn't have that. The women (characters) either weren't married, which is fine. Having a career and you're not married that was fine (for a character). Or, if you are married and have kids, then that's a different kind of thing. But the divorced single mother with a career that was a little bit new at the time. I know it seems crazy, but it was. My women characters weren't falling apart. They weren't victims of anything. She wasn't a victim. She was a woman who was doing very well in her life.

Honestly, the other thing with *Judging Amy,* we had a little pushback in the beginning because she was a single mother and what I wanted to do with that show was show just really what that looks like – to raise a kid as a single mother and have this high-profile job and she didn't do everything perfectly. So, there were a lot of concerns with, "Oh, does this make her look like a bad mother?" Parenting is not a perfectible job. And in the '90s it was treated as if it were. And it's just not true.

Later, what I wanted to do with *Madam Secretary* was show the full spectrum of a woman's life, because I don't think it was anyone's idea of feminism or women's rights for women just to act like men. And I think we went down that path for a while. With the shoulder pads and the short haircuts. If you look at a picture of me in the '80s, it's like, "Really?" And then I think we sort of went, "Well, that doesn't entirely work. Women want to own their femininity and all that." So, the second round doesn't undermine your strength. Because of that sort of trend, I was able to create this character and do the whole context and let her be as soft as she needs to be at home – because I think that is the dilemma for women. If all you had to do was be hard and tough, it's not that difficult to be just the one thing. The problem is you have to be hard when you need to be and soft when you need to be. Being able to take the audience home with her and see her in that world and see all the sides of her character gave a more rounded idea of what a woman in a position of power is and can be.

In *Madam Secretary*, when one person serves, the family serves. I have military in my family and I know that with my own family. It's kind of a contract the whole family has. You might be worried about it, or complain about it, but the fact is there's kind of an understanding about what my parents do, and this is what my life is and there's just a commitment to that way of life. There are a lot of religious (scholars) and advisers in The Pentagon, so I made her husband a religious scholar. It was very important for whoever she's married to be her equal. But it's a tricky thing, and it obviously has to do with the way it's written, but also the actor. And Téa certainly brings all that. And the humor is important. The tagline was, *You're meeting with the President of the United States in the morning and the president of the PTA in the evening*, because that is really what happens. I want to write about that. I wanted to give these characters the full landscape.

The magic bullet is that people responded to it. Audiences respond to it and then you can be on the air. Like I said about TV, when it's a meritocracy, it is. Once people go, "Oh, yes I want to see this," then your world really opens up in terms of what you're allowed to do. But it's also really painful to write something you love and not get it made. It's twice as painful to get it made and not get it on the air. The one consolation I always had when I got a pilot made was, "Well, film is forever. I'm going to make this little movie and I'll have it."

It's just this weird profession where you're asked to have your heart crushed every season and asked to get right back in it. You have your weekend with the Kleenex and go all the way into, "You know what? I'm done. I'm going to just grow lilies in Montauk." But the business doesn't wait for you to do that. I roll my sleeves up, like any other profession. And I just say that because, oftentimes, people treat women's jobs like they're hobbies. This is my profession and I keep doing it because this is what I do. I understand people wanting to take their (toys) and go home. It's something that women go through because you feel like it's stacked up against you. But then you don't get to play. And that's just the reality. And so, you just hang in there. I mean, we're in the circus. We ran away and joined the circus. If you're lucky, you're consoled by the work itself.

But it's a crazy business and it's going to be feast and famine. It takes a while to get to the place where you can feel pretty sure you're going to get a job offer. If you're not there yet – if you quit, you can't play the game. Really, you get to play if you stay. One of the things that's good now is that there's so much being made. It might not always be an ideal situation, or even something financially that makes sense, but a lot of times there's something that you can do. And I know it's a cliché but it's because it's true – it's cyclical. TV has died about seven times since I've been in it. It's like, comedy was dead and then drama was dead and then TV was dead and then movies were dead. You learn to just sort of roll with it.

My rule for people regardless, especially when they're starting out, is that you have a job to do, and your job is to perfect your craft. People feel powerless, like they have no control. But that, you can control. You can control how hard you work at your craft, not at getting people to like your script, or meeting the right person or whatever, but really, actually, developing your skill like a muscle and believing that that's what it is instead of some magical, unpredictable thing that people either respond to or not. Do your work and always work a little bit harder than everybody else, and just stay focused on the work because the rest of it is completely unmanageable.

I think people get confused about what our jobs are. Is it about meeting people? Networking? No, your job is to keep making it better, keep raising the bar for yourself and executing. There are two things that never really change. Whether or not you can hold an audience will always matter, no matter what your business model is. And the basic rules of storytelling aren't going to change. You have to engage people, in order to keep them coming

20 Barbara Hall

back, and there are a lot of ways to do that. Because if you lose your audience, it's over.

The thing about TV is that it's its own medium. It isn't movies on a smaller screen. It's not the place where we just don't know how to add sixty pages to our scripts. And if you want to work in it, I think it's worth your time to figure out what makes it work and why. Whether episodes are self-contained or not, it's serialized storytelling. But mainly, there's a big difference between who you want to spend two hours with and who you want to spend ten years with, every week, and let them into your home, or let them into your space. It's a different experience to go to the movies. You understand what your commitment is. You don't expect them to ever write or call when you leave. It's like, "We're done. We had a beautiful time."

But in TV, your expectation is, "Is this going to be a relationship? Am I going to want to see you again?" The rules for establishing that relationship are just different. You have to put something in the formula that makes people want to stay engaged with not just the person, but the world. Then, the serialized element of it is just something that draws you, since Dickens and before. You look forward to the next installment because you're engaged in it. The first question you ask yourself when you develop something is, "How many seasons does this have? What are the elements that are going to let this have a long life?" That has to do with everything, but it mainly has to do with the world. Is it a big enough world? Because if you can see three or four seasons, then you don't worry about five or six seasons because that's going to take care of itself.

When *Judging Amy* came out, it was a real Cinderella Story because it broke out. And that was all anybody cared about. The show did well, and then we were off and running. You know what happens in TV is that that creates a path for people to make more shows like that because there's an audience for it. We've proven there's an audience for it and then, you know, more female voices, more female-driven shows, and more female showrunners. The wall gets chipped away at. But the thing about TV – it's just reflective of the rest of the nation. There isn't a reason to think we are doing any better in TV than we are in corporate America or the world. The numbers are the numbers. And the parity issue is real everywhere, as it is here. So, the problem with the fact that there is fanfare about, "Look, we're letting women do this" – it shouldn't be. Why is that a story? And real equality is when there is obviously no need to make a distinction. Showrunners are just showrunners. And that's just true of (all) women in positions of power everywhere.

I feel like that's what everybody wants; to not have to be called a woman showrunner – just be called a showrunner. But until things are a little more equal, we have to make those distinctions. And I think, obviously, there are many high-profile women and female-run shows now that are helping that cause. Because what you need to do to make a change is give people a visual, give them an understanding like, when you do *Madam Secretary* and you give people a visual of a woman in this position of power, everybody can see what it looks like and feels like and then things are going to change. It's a great thing that we have these high-profile women running shows because then we know what it looks like. It's been my experience that women have to re-prove their stripes and men don't. That is the biggest difference for me, because, honestly, I've had the opportunity to be able to do this more than once. And it's not that anyone or anything has stopped me or blocked me, but I can tell you I've had to prove it again and again. I feel like women have to prove it more than men do. There's not a bank.

CHARLOTTE BROWN
The First Woman in The Room Who Wasn't There to Take Lunch Orders

Figure 4.1 Charlotte Brown
Source: photo courtesy of Charlotte Brown

In 1976, Charlotte Brown was the first woman showrunner to run a multi-camera sitcom filmed in front of a live audience with *Rhoda*. Charlotte worked her way up, writing episodes of *The Mary Tyler Moore Show, The Bob Newhart Show, Rhoda* and many others before taking over *Rhoda*, which was one of the most popular shows of its time.

DOI: 10.4324/9781003298229-5

Charlotte Brown   23

Here's how I got my break: I gave my dentist, who was my brother's best friend, a spec script that I had written for *The Mary Tyler Moore Show* to give Jim Brooks, who was a patient and friend of his. Although I had said in high school, "I want to be a comedy writer for television," I wasn't sure how to make that happen back then. After teaching high school English for two years, I had landed in an advertising agency as a copywriter and had become the go-to comedy person. I gave an envelope with every commercial I'd ever written and the spec script to my dentist. I wrote the spec in a weekend. I didn't know any of the rules. But not longer after, Jim called me and said with much enthusiasm, "I just read your script and it's got so many problems! But what you do have is an ear for dialogue and a wonderful sense of comedy. You just have no idea about plot construction or story. But that's a skill you can learn. You have talent, though, and that can't be learned." He very kindly invited me to come to run-throughs of the show on Fridays, before they shot the show that night.

I started sneaking out of the agency and going to the run-throughs of the first year of *The Mary Tyler Moore Show*. It was shot in Hollywood at a place called General Service Studios. The first day I showed up there, looking for the soundstage, the first person I met was Valerie Harper, who was unknown to me and most everyone else at the time because she hadn't done anything in TV. Jim and Allan (Burns) encouraged me to pitch stories to them and gave me piles of scripts to read – first drafts, second drafts, etc. – to learn the evolution of plot construction. I would come in with maybe 12 story ideas and pitch to them, and they would say, yes, no, no, no, no, yes. And then I'd go home, and I'd develop the yeses and go back again. This went on for several months until one time I went in there, and they bought one of the ideas and gave me my first break. But they never filmed that script because the show moved to the studio in the Valley, and I got caught in the chaos of that move and my script didn't make the cut. Needless to say, that was disappointing. I had quit the agency, eventually went on Unemployment and after a year of starving, I wrote another spec script for *Mary* because I hated thinking that I had failed. Miraculously, they bought that spec script and it was filmed and aired. That first script was a false start. This one was the real beginning of my real career.

My first successful year, I wrote something like 13 different shows from *All in the Family* to *Mary Tyler Moore* to *The Partridge Family*. I can't even remember them all. I freelanced for a couple of years and started writing for *The Bob Newhart Show* when that began. And for the first three years, I wrote about a quarter of those shows. Then they came to me when *Rhoda* started and asked if I wanted to come on staff. It was different in the mid-seventies. Now you write an episode, and you go on staff of the show. That wasn't the way it worked then. I hesitated because I liked the freedom of freelancing, but it was *Rhoda*. And I loved that character and identified as most young women did with that character. So, I went on staff on *Rhoda*, midway through the first season, although I had already written a couple of the early episodes. The first year I was called executive script consultant and then Season Two, I became a producer. Then I became an executive

24 *Charlotte Brown*

producer. During or after the third year, Jim and David Davis and Ed Weinberger and Stan Daniels left to do *Taxi*. And so that's when I became the – we didn't have the term showrunner yet in those days – executive producer of the show. At that time, I was told that I was the first woman writer-producer of a multi-camera comedy ever.

Cleo Smith, who was Lucy's (Lucille Ball) first cousin, had a producer title on *Here's Lucy, Lucy in London*, and some of Lucy's TV specials; she was not a writer, but I think she predated me. When I started as a writer, it was really Jim Brooks and Allan Burns who gave women the start in comedy on TV. Up until then, it was a man's world in comedy. Women got their foot in the door in one-hour dramas earlier, but that's a different animal. And multi-camera comedies back in the day were all staffed by men, and the thinking was, "Well, it can get rough in that writers' room. They swear," as if women don't. I've been paid, I guess you could say, "compliments," like, "Boy, you really write like a guy," as if that's a compliment. And I never quite knew what they meant. Part of it perhaps was because I happen to be a big sports fan, but I think a lot of women are. I'm knowledgeable about baseball, football and basketball. I have a big brother. He was a big athlete and sports fan. That always impressed the guys because they didn't think women knew anything about sports. For my first one or two years when I was freelancing, virtually every show that I did, I was the first woman writer that producer had ever hired.

Treva Silverman and Gail Parent were my mentors too the year that I was struggling between those first two scripts on *Mary*. Gail Parent wrote with her partner Kenny Solms on *The Carol Burnett Show*. Treva was really the first woman to really do well in sitcom writing. She had done *The Monkees* and a few other shows with a male partner. It was often said that the precursor to *The Mary Tyler Moore Show* was *That Girl* with Marlo Thomas, and in many ways it was, but (Bill) Persky and (Sam) Denoff, two older men, were the producers. And I don't think there were ever any women writing that, though Marlo herself was always very much a feminist and an incredibly smart and successful woman. But it wasn't the same. She as the character wasn't *The Mary Tyler Moore* character, certainly not the *Rhoda* character. And those men – Jim and Allan – were really responsible for my becoming a producer.

When *Mary* ended and *Newhart* ended and then *Rhoda* ended, we all sort of went out into the world. That period at MTM – 1970 to 1978 – was really a golden age. It was like going to the Harvard of comedy. It was also just a magical time. When one of us was doing a pilot, everyone came to the run-throughs, and we'd come to the rewrites and help one another. We were a family. And we're all still very close.

When I left MTM and went out on my own, the only role model I had as a showrunner were Jim and Allan. And so, when I was going to a network meeting or studio, in my head, I would say, "When in doubt, what would Jim or Allan do?" What I didn't put into the equation was, but they're men.

Charlotte Brown 25

And so, I remember, once at a network meeting about a pilot that I was executive producing and directing actually, I was disagreeing with them about a story point or a casting thing. And I really sort of dug my heels in because I knew I was right, and they weren't. And what I was emulating was Jim and Allan, what they would do. And nobody stood on tables and threw things, but the reaction to me was not the reaction that Jim or Allan would have gotten from the network executives, who were all men, of course. A man who they didn't agree with on something but stuck to his principles, they'd say, "My God, I may not agree with him, but he really is a principled guy." When a woman did it, they'd say, "Boy she's a bitch. She's so difficult." Sadly, those perceptions exist to this day. I wasn't part of a team, and the women who were part of a man and woman team fared much better because it could be like a good cop/bad cop kind of thing. In most of those cases, the woman was really the creative force in the team, but the man could soften the edges and talk in those meetings and make it more palatable to deal with them. Where I was able to get around that was where the work was valued, what I had to bring to it was valued. It was just finding the right people to work with.

I remember many years later, around the first year of *Friends,* the women on staff at *Friends* organized a Saturday get-together. They looked through every show that was on at the time, comedies and drama, and invited every woman with the title producer or executive producer, just to get together. I was reluctant to go. There were probably a hundred people, mostly very young women. I knew a few of them, but they were mostly much younger. I just remember sort of mentally stepping back and looking at these women and thinking, "Look at you. You just take it for granted. You think 'Oh sure, I'm a show producer. Oh, that's not unusual.'" And I was thinking, "You have no idea." To some extent, I think we've come a long way because when I started out, the image of a comedy writer was a man with a cigar and a star sapphire pinky ring, wearing one of those cardigan golfing sweaters. I remember the staff of *Laugh-In* where Ann Elder was the only woman. The writers used to work at a motel across the street from NBC, where they shot the show. The thinking was, "We can't have a woman in this room. We're going to swear. We're going to smoke cigars!" Look at Joan Rivers. Joan worked in the worst, raunchiest strip clubs and dive bars, wherever she could get on stage and try out her material. The image of a woman standup comic was Phyllis Diller. You weren't supposed to be attractive, you had to be like the guys, instead of just a woman talking about whatever she wanted to talk about. We have come a long way, but there's still a long way to go.

I was the first woman in the room who wasn't there to take lunch orders or dictation. When I started, most women who came onto a show wanting to be writers, started out as – before it was not politically correct to say – secretaries. And I refused to do that. I worked my way through college as a typist. I knew that I could get my foot in the door on a show if I wanted to be a secretary, but I always felt that that might be a trap, and I was afraid to do it. But several women who became successful did start that way. We all

26 *Charlotte Brown*

came from so many different backgrounds to get to the same place. The only similarity was we all wanted to write.

I haven't seen *Rhoda* in years, but it's still embedded in my brain. When I would be with Valerie in New York, cab drivers would honk the horn and yell, "Hey, Rhoda!" On *Rhoda*, we got a letter from the women who worked in the West Wing of the Gerald Ford White House. The line that I always remember was they said they loved *Mary Tyler Moore* and *Rhoda*. And they said, "We watch *Mary*, and we see the woman we could be. We watch *Rhoda* and we see the woman we are." *Rhoda* and *Mary* were on Saturday nights. It became OK as a single woman to stay home on Saturday night because you were watching *Rhoda*. When Rhoda got married, all across the country, people had parties. Black tie parties. The night of Rhoda's wedding, during Monday Night Football on ABC, Howard Cosell apparently said on the air, "Let's get this game over so I can watch Rhoda's wedding." I cannot tell you how many hundreds of wedding gifts we got for her.

The main reason we finally decided to get them divorced (Rhoda and Joe) is that sometime in Season Two, we were on at eight o'clock on Monday nights. And there was something insidious that had been instituted called the Family Hour. There were a lot of conservative groups that were very unhappy with the content of TV. They put pressure on the advertisers who in turn put pressure on the networks to "clean it all up." Before *Rhoda* and *Mary*, half-hour comedies on TV were mainly rural stuff like *Beverly Hillbillies, Green Acres, Petticoat Junction*. Then *Mary* and *Rhoda* and *Newhart* changed the profile of CBS. We were sophisticated comedy. But there was enough lobbying done that between eight and nine o'clock Monday through Friday became called the "Family Hour." And those had to be shows that the whole family could watch together. We really were not an eight o'clock show, but they put us at eight o'clock, and it really hamstrung us. We put Rhoda and Joe in one bed, and we got a lot of push back for that.

It became harder and harder. What we wanted to write was a sophisticated marriage, what we would then refer to as a modern marriage. Rhoda got married in her thirties, which was still kind of revolutionary then. They brought a whole lot of baggage to the marriage, and we kept getting a lot of, "No, you can't do that," from the network. Even though they were really supportive of us, they kept getting pushback. And that's why we finally decided, with the network's approval, to separate Joe and Rhoda and then divorce them. And we got so much blowback from our fans because women so identified with Rhoda. When we did that, they felt that their marriages were threatened, that if she can do that, then that could happen to me. Her getting married and getting married to this great, good-looking guy was such a dream come true. To have it fall apart, it's just more than they could bear. We faced a lot of opposition, and I think the show saw the ratings suffer as a result. And so that was year three. If Rhoda was a single woman in New York, you have more writing possibilities.

During and even the first few years after, I can't tell you the number of ERA fundraising events that I went to with Valerie. And she spoke all over the country wherever they asked her to go. Feminism was still a fairly new

Charlotte Brown 27

thing when the show started. And we weren't a political show. Norman Lear did political shows and did them brilliantly. That's not what MTM did, but the character really became a symbol for the feminist movement, and Valerie herself was a feminist, as was I. There was a lot riding on our success and her successes as a character.

It was a dream job to get to write for *Mary* and then for *Rhoda*. Mary was 30 years old and had not gotten married yet. That was major. The guys originally wanted her to be divorced. And that's why she was moving to Minneapolis, and the networks said no. The compromise was that she hadn't gotten married yet, but to be 30 and not married and to actually say that's how old you are, what a big thing. And *Mary* went on the air in 1970. Women didn't talk about their age then. Once we got to know Mary, as a character, we knew she was not perfect. And her life was not perfect.

You couldn't ask for a better head of studio than Grant Tinker. Grant was the father figure. He so respected the writers and he always had our back. But that was more the exception than the rule. There was a novel in the seventies about Hollywood called *Blue Pages*, written by screenwriters Eleanor Perry and her then-husband, Frank Perry and before Chapter One there was a quote: "Writers are the women of the industry – Overheard at The Polo Lounge, Beverly Hills Hotel." Writers have always been – both men and women writers – taken for granted and not respected. The Writers Guild has battled to change that. When fans would come up to Valerie and say, "How do you come up with what you say," she'd point to me and say, "This is the person who puts those words in my mouth." Back in the day when I was already doing *Rhoda,* the manager at the little market near the studio, if he was checking me out on a Tuesday, invariably I would get his critique of the prior night's show. And finally, this particular Tuesday I had had a particularly bad day, and he started giving me his criticism of the show and I gave it to him. I critiqued the location of the produce department, that I would have put it on the other side of the store. And he stared at me, and I looked at him and I said, "You're just amazed, aren't you? That I, who knows absolutely nothing about grocery stores, I'm telling you what to do." He finally got it, and never critiqued the show ever again. Nobody tells a painter what color to use or tells a musician, "You know if you had done that in B sharp, I think it would have been better." But because everyone uses words, everyone thinks they can write. Everyone gives you criticism. Everyone thinks they know what you should have done. Everyone thinks that they can do it. And that's partly attributed to good writing. If it's written well, it looks easy, but it's far from that. TV, much more than films, is a writer's medium and that's one of the great things about writing for television; if you reach a certain level, you have more control over your work.

I think we have come a long way. More than ever, it's not unusual for a woman to be a showrunner. But we don't say a man writer. The day we can designate a woman writer as merely a writer, that's when we'll know we've arrived.

CHRIS NEE
The World as I Hope it Will Be

Figure 5.1 Chris Nee
Source: photo courtesy of Chris Nee

Peabody, Humanitas, NAACP and Emmy Award-winner Chris Nee started on *Sesame Street* International and wrote for dozens of hit children's shows including *Little Bill, Maya and Miguel, Wonder Pets!, The Backyardigans, Ni Hao, Kai-Lan* and *Angela Anaconda*, before she created the hits *Doc McStuffins* and *Vampirina* for Disney. Chris then signed a landmark deal with Netflix, where she continued to create new shows, partnering with Kenya Barris and the Obamas on *We the People*, and creating and running *Ada Twist, Scientist* based on the book, and *Ridley Jones*.

DOI: 10.4324/9781003298229-6

I'm trying to create a version of the world as I hope it will be, and if that is activism, so be it. I think it's really easy to take a paycheck in this business and not look at the entertainment value of what you're doing. But I for sure am also looking at how I go to work every day and how I feel I've made a difference. Especially in kids TV. You could just put on the pratfalls and have kids laughing, and have parents know this is a safe show that they can sit their kid in front of while they go take a shower. But that would not be fulfilling enough for me personally. I believe in trying to move people towards a better version of society.

Social justice is definitely important for me. But it wasn't necessarily a piece of my family's upbringing. I remember in high school saying that I wanted to go into the arts and a teacher who knew me well, a mentor, said, "I just don't see that happening for you." And I said, "Why?" I was a little hurt. Because this was a person who'd always said I can do anything I want. She said, "Because you want to change the world too much." Her point was exactly how I ended up feeling today. I have to feel like I'm making a difference, and not just in the current climate. So many writers come from some background of feeling like the other or feeling invisible or feeling lost, and frankly all the best people at some point in their life felt that sense of not fitting into the norm. And for me that was a very strong feeling. And to be honest, it was true.

I grew up in the '70s and '80s as a gay kid. I spent a huge amount of time in my head, fantasizing and telling my own stories. I was definitely the stereotype of the distracted scientist, but for me it was with storytelling. I got to be the hero of my own stories. I want all kids to feel that they can be the hero in their self-narratives.

There's no question that, for me, especially with kids TV, I'm trying to get kids to see a world in which, whatever they define as their community is people who they take care of, and they accept in whatever form they come.

My pitch for *Doc McStuffins* was very cheeky. I said I was pitching "*Cheers* for preschoolers without the beer," and it was that sense of a place where everybody knows your name, where whatever backstory you come from is irrelevant to the person you present yourself to be. Or for us, the toy you present yourself to be at that moment.

Vampirina is a show about a kid who is different. She moved from Transylvania to Pennsylvania. And what I love about her is she actually is hard to be friends with. I love that. It's hard for her two best friends who know that she's a vampire and know about her life, but they love her anyway. Instead of saying, "We're all the same and there is no difference," I'm saying there's a difference, and that's okay, good even. Half of the problem in this world is that we flip back and forth with our message and I get why, but maybe we've done ourselves no great service in saying there's no difference between us. Maybe the more powerful message is, "Yeah, we come with all kinds of different variations of human being. But they can all work together."

I went to NYU, but I was an acting major actually at Boston University in the conservatory until my junior year. BU has a conservatory where they cut

30   *Chris Nee*

three quarters of the students at the end of sophomore year. I made the cut. And then I was like, "Oh, I don't want to do this." Which I couldn't have said until they, you know, made the cut. And I really apologize to my parents for deciding my junior year. It was a really expensive program. Then I went to NYU and went into the Gallatin division and read the great books, got a degree in Arts Management and Literature or whatever the hell it was. So, no I never studied writing per se.

I think I'm always writing about communities. I love to write big cast character things, which sucks for an animation company. Someone I work with said, "Well everyone knows what it is to work on a Chris Nee show, it's going to be huge by thousands." Because for me it is so much about that interaction between disparate characters. A lot of classic kids shows are the one lead character and the two sidekicks. Which doesn't give me enough play for what I find fascinating about a world which is a much bigger universe.

First of all, I love specificity of character which, for a long time, especially kids TV, had gotten away from. We had watered down characters in a way, and watered down our storytelling in a preschool way. I started at *Sesame Street*, and I think one of the absolute most beautiful things about *Sesame* is that you can completely do a personality test based on those characters. They're so extreme. I'm a Prairie Dawn and a Grover. Which is like the weirdest combination. And the fact that they had a character like Prairie Dawn who is so extreme and frankly not necessarily likable, but there as her own character and still fitting into the mix. That was something that I really took away when we started working on *Doc*, wanting these characters to really stand on their own and be incredibly specific. I love bringing in new noise into a group and having everyone really stand in their own space in their own ground.

We had educational consultants on *Doc*. Everyone does. But we definitely worked with them in a different way. When I sold the show, we were still in the world of everything with "To camera" questions, so that there was this breaking the fourth wall, the asking of the questions. We know kids love that stuff. They love *Dora*. They love *Blue's Clues*. To me it was sort of a classic everybody chased the same tail. That became the only kind of programming that anyone wanted. We were testing these episodes to make sure that these little moments on questionnaires were answered correctly and asked in the right way. Back then nobody was asking the larger question, What's the heart, what's the storytelling? Or asking about the importance of pure wonder, of what it is to laugh at something you don't understand, of what it is for kids to feel something that they're watching. To me, there's the beauty of not understanding every moment of an episode. One thing *Blue's Clues* taught us is that we know the kids are probably going to watch any given episode five times. Which was absolutely groundbreaking for them and for us. It informs me I don't need kids to understand every bit of an episode the first time they watch it.

The classic answer when you're talking to somebody who writes for kids is to say, "Who do you write for?" Most people say I'm writing for the kids. I'm

Chris Nee   31

not writing for kids. I'm writing for myself. I'm trying to work out feelings I had as a kid. Feelings I still have today. I seem to have a really strong memory for the emotions that I felt as a kid about what those really real moments were. Those are the things I'm writing to. I'm writing almost always to larger moments and tonally I'm all over the place, which I think was a shift for Disney executives when I got there. But also true to life.

With composers, for example, it's always a steep learning curve when they're working with me because in one scene I will have a pratfall, a silly joke, and a character on the verge of tears, because I think that's how kids really are. One of the things I remember as those last few years prior to pitching *Doc* was hearing educational consultants saying, "You know each episode should just really have one clear emotion." Like have you ever met a kid? They're like opera to me. They're high, low, all over the place. A kid is crying one second, laughing hysterically the next. And I love playing all those notes. It took us a little while to actually get it to work so that the animators were understanding the sense of a scene. There was a period in the beginning where for length they would often cut out the jokes. And I was like, "No. Now the entire feeling of that scene is off." You could have a character who's scared and in the clinic and on the verge of tears, but then someone makes the joke and then you're back to the emotion. It releases all this tension as you're playing what I hope feels like weirdly true emotion in the middle of this stuffed world. Ultimately, storytelling for kids is the same thing as storytelling for adults, which is the place where we can test out our humanity. And the place where we can find out we're not the only one who feels fear.

Finding great writers for kids TV is a very hard path and there are a lot of reasons for it. There are a lot of people who are in kids TV who are the educationalists. The teacher versus the people who are just pure writers. Look, for all reasons – financial, the sexiness of what you do, the things you don't have to deal with, it's easier to focus on TV for adults if you're a writer. If you're just a pure writer, you could take those skills and go make more money, and have more respect. So, finding the people who want to be down here in this end of things and also not see the box – there are a lot of writers who just see the box of what you can't do in young kids storytelling. I find that box liberating. I love that game of finding out how much I can write without going over those edges. I think of it like comedians who choose to not work blue. That's part of the challenge they give themselves. "Can I make you laugh from your gut without using swears and telling sex jokes?" – To be clear, I work very blue in real life, just not on the screen – Disney let us do a show which was not the norm at the time that we came out. They let us do things like the Wicked King and these characters who have edge, like our hypochondriac. I wrote the hypochondriac snowman, Chilly, as a test in the pilot. I wanted to see what they thought of this. They never gave me a note on it and then I just kept writing to the same character. He's the only character who won his way into the main cast. He was a four-line one-off in the pilot. He became a phenomenon and Jess Harnell took the role. But I

32   Chris Nee

was just testing out to see if they were going to let me push the envelope of preschool storytelling.

Animation is for the patient. A single episode takes nine to ten months from start to finish. I don't understand people who do not break the story with their staff, which I know, in the kids TV business, definitely happens. If I take the hour or two hours to sit down with my staff and break out the stories, we figure out what the beats are and agree before anyone goes any further. We think in acts, even though it's eleven minutes. There's an inherent storytelling that's really nice in three acts. But there are such variances in how writers get to the gold at the end. It's a channeling. Something that I've learned over years of doing it, once you know you have a career and you are going to keep writing, there's a beauty in the volume of what happens in TV because you no longer obsess about each episode. Not that I don't want every episode to be amazing. But I don't have to tell a certain joke in this episode if it doesn't fit here. I'll find another episode where I will get to what I just found that seems like gold.

There are several big moments in my life that really started long before I sold *Doc*. One of the great gifts I got was being on a show at Nickelodeon when there still was enough budget to do this kind of thing, but the entire show would shut down for every episode for two days and we all went into a room and put up all the storyboards and every department talked about every frame of everything in the story. It was the education to really learn everything that went into making an episode. The producer, Mary Harrington, who started the Nickelodeon Studios and is responsible for a ton of the huge shows that you know from the glory days of Nick, came to me at one point and said, "You're going to be doing this someday. So, I want you to start to come to all of these things. Every meeting is open to you." She saw something in me. And she said, "Don't miss this opportunity." That did several things. First of all, seeing how it was all put together made me a much better writer, especially for animation. There's the classic thing in TV where you're writing the script versus the show. And there's a moment where you stop writing your script and you start writing the show that's going to be on TV, the episode that's going to be on TV, and you start to connect it in your mind. It's deciding that you're a part of the continuum of the production that goes through to the end. Not writing the masturbatory stuff that is never going to make it onto the screen. If you write a long script and you're handing it off, you're not being respectful, but you're also not in control. You're literally telling someone else that they're going to decide what gets to stay and what doesn't and how they're going to cut it out. Never give up that control.

Most animation is not covered by the Writers Guild. We have a separate union, TAG. But we do not get residuals. If I had residuals for the amount of work I've done over the past 20 years, I would not be talking to you right now, I'd be sailing on my sailboat. And the rates are very low. I am in the Writers Guild because I've written a good amount of live action as well. But the voiceover actors get residuals. The composers get ASCAP. All of those guys are tied to the success of the show in the way that the people who spend way more time and are the genesis of the stories are not tied. I would love to see that change. The second somebody gets a live action gig, even if they say, "I love this show and I feel like I'm doing good things in the world, but I just got a better deal," they take it. And I understand that completely.

Self-advocacy around deals is extremely tricky. For a certain period of time, I had the best deal at Disney in my side of the business. And I am a woman so yay for that. Look, I don't know exactly why I walk this earth with a huge amount of confidence. I do. I also grew up in a family of entrepreneurs. I was not the black sheep, but in theory I was the black sheep because I was in the arts, and they were all business people. And it took me years to realize that actually, I think all of us are entrepreneurs as well because ultimately the bottom line of being an entrepreneur is someone who doesn't take the job at the office. You're believing in yourself and you're calling out your own worth and you're bringing what you think someone should invest into. And I really wish that more writers would think of themselves as entrepreneurs. I had a really bad deal at the beginning of *Doc*. To be honest the anger that I had over that deal really motivated me to be not accidental about deciding what I wanted and charting the path towards it. I'm also a big advocate, especially for women because things don't accidentally come to us, but for anyone to take the reins of your own journey. It is up to you to decide where you want to be and to figure out the path to get there. Nobody else is looking out for your dreams or your best interest. This includes agents and lawyers. You have to be the one driving the ship. When we started on *Doc*, no one thought this show was going to be a hit. So here I am, a first-time showrunner, just somehow thinking there is going to be something here. I'm going to want to feel taken care of. And you should be tied to the success of the show. Again, the fact that writers don't get residuals, fueled a lot of this. I knew that if I had a show that was going to be a hit, that a lot of other people would participate in that financially, and I would not. And I could not stand that fact. And I very systematically went after something that actually didn't exist, which is about as far a goal as it can be to set for yourself. At the time, a participation deal did not exist for animation at Disney, period. I knew that other companies did. One of the things, and this would be advice that I would give to anyone else when you are in this position, I really pushed for control on my own show. All of it. I'm the 100% showrunner. I oversee the writing. I oversee records and mixes and everything else comes through me. But when I started my title was co-EP. And there was a budget line for the other co-EP, who was probably going to end up being the controlling EP and really being the showrunner. I called the head of Disney Junior and I said, "I want you to know that by the time we're done with development, you're going to make me the showrunner of the show and you're never going to hire another co-EP." It's always harder to have those conversations at the moment. I tell people to say what they want ahead of time, "I'm going for that, over there." Hard to say no to someone's

34   *Chris Nee*

aspirations. On *Doc* that conversation was a year and a half in advance of the need to declare it. To their credit, when the time came, the head of Disney Junior said, "You're now the showrunner and the EP, and we will not have another person in that role."

When I asked for a participation deal at Disney, I said, "Someday you're going to give me what you've never given anyone." She literally said, "Chris we would never. We don't give it." And I said, "But someday you're gonna give it to me. Because it's the right thing to do." And that someday came. Partially because they ended up giving it to someone else first and that person told me. That shared information was vital. Information is power.

Early in my career, I found somebody who was on a similar career path. We made a deal out on the basketball court at Nickelodeon, that for the rest of our careers we would tell each other the complete details of our contracts from that point forward. Hard or not hard, because it would only help us to know where the other one was at. And we have been doing that now for 15 years.

Doc McStuffins, by year five, on the record, had made like a billion dollars, with a hundred million viewers per quarter. There aren't a lot of people in this town who make a company that kind of money and still not a lot of people know their name. I'm certainly not treated the way the people who have made billion-dollar films are. But that's kids TV business. I'll go into a Producers Guild Awards and sometimes I look around and we're so clearly at the kids' table. We're always the kids' table. But there are a lot of people who are getting their asses kissed all over this place who I've brought more money to the table than, which ultimately is what our business is. Honestly, the math on kids TV is no more complicated. We just pretend it is, but it isn't. With a proper participation deal, if it isn't a hit, you don't pay anyone anything, but if it is a hit, that creator, those creatives, also participate in the success. That's the point of it. We're all in this together.

I very much take a mentorship role with the people on my staff, and I probably would have been a teacher if I hadn't been doing this. I'm always just trying to teach them to stand up and advocate for themselves and learn how to be not afraid being a writer. We are all so afraid. There can be a real weakness in writers. And then you see the ones who do well. Yes, there's a writing talent but then there's the flip side of that which is the people who have incredible chutzpah, who seem to not actually be great writers, but they sell stuff all the time. But in TV, if you're going to get to the point where you're showrunning, you are running a multi-million dollar business. And that's a different skill than writing. And they want someone who feels like they can do that job.

DAILYN RODRIGUEZ
Be An Advocate for Yourself

Figure 6.1 Dailyn Rodriguez
Source: photo by Alie Ward

Dailyn Rodriguez was born in Washington Heights in New York City, later moving to New Jersey, where she won early statewide competitions for her plays. After completing her BFA at NYU, she was accepted into the Disney Fellowship and launched her TV writing career. Dailyn has written for shows including *George Lopez, Ugly Betty, 90210, In Plain Sight*, *The Glades* and *Queen of the South*, where she was promoted to showrunner. Dailyn is co-showrunner for Season Two of Netflix's *The Lincoln Lawyer*. Dailyn is part of the Untitled Latinx Project, which works to bring more Latinx stories and creators to television.

It's taken me a long time to become a showrunner – seventeen years. I got into the Disney Fellowship Program in 2001, and then at the end of that program I

DOI: 10.4324/9781003298229-7

36   *Dailyn Rodriguez*

was staffed on the *George Lopez* show. I repeated staff and story editor a couple of times each. So, I was a staff writer on *George Lopez*, and then story editor, went back to the same production company for their new show *Freddie*, and they demoted me. Because the only way they could get a free writer is if they hire a staff writer who's a "diversity hire." I then transitioned to one-hours through the first season of *Ugly Betty*, and they actually did promote me to story editor, which was great. And then there was a regime change after the first season. And more than half of the staff was fired. You know, this is the business. And then my next show, I was not promoted. I was asked to stay as a story editor. It's just like that frustrating pain where you just can't get a leg up. It happens to a lot of minority writers in the business. It's a problem in the (diversity) programs. And sometimes it gets abused by showrunners who use it to get a free staff writer to fill a quota. Then after the first season, they don't bring them back so they can get another free writer next year. That person then doesn't get promoted. So, I got stuck in what I like to call the "Diversity Ghetto." And some of it has to do with the representation (agents) I had at the time. I think I filled the quota for my agency. I basically worked on all the Latin shows as the one or two of us on a show that had Latin themes. Then I fired my representation right before the 2007/2008 strike after the third time of me saying, "Please stop doing this." I went to a smaller, more boutique agency who took more interest in my career as a whole. That's when I said, "Put me on the whitest show on television." That was the reboot for *90210*, which was great. There were only two minority writers on that show, and I was one of them, which has been mostly my experience. I would say the most diverse staff I was ever on was *The Night Shift* and then *Queen of the South*. Being purposeful about changing what types of shows I was on was a good move for me because it got me out of tokenization a little bit. There are two types of tokenization. You're either a person of color that only works on shows that are about people of color, or you're the only person of color on a show, or one of two, as you filled the quota. And it's difficult for me to even say that I'm a person of color because outwardly, I'm Caucasian. I don't present as a person of color, but it's like a catch-all phrase. I am ethnically Latinx or Latine, which are the new terms these days.

I grew up in Washington Heights in New York. Because I grew up in a Latino and Black community, I never really understood that I was "something else." When I was nine, I moved to New Jersey, and I went to private school for sixth grade, and I was the only Latina in the entire grade. It was really weird. My graduating class in high school was about a hundred people, and there were I think five Latinos in the graduating class. I got picked on in junior high. Somebody put horrible notes in my locker telling me to go back to my country, stuff like that. My own background is very odd. My dad actually was a criminal, and he was in prison. My dad was in the Cuban mafia. He was a banker in an illegal numbers racket in New York City. If I'm ever telling another crime story, I'm telling that story. I mean, it was a very strange upbringing. I like to say that I

Dailyn Rodriguez 37

grew up a lot like Meadow Soprano. I couldn't tell people what my dad did for a living. I have a sense of humor about it because when you look at it through a kid's eyes, in retrospect, it's very like, "Oh, I didn't know I had a bodyguard. What do you mean that guy across the street is there to take me to school?" Stuff like that. And I just laugh my ass off now about it. At the time it was not funny. My mom had a horrible existence. My dad was a gambler, and it was just a really messed-up childhood. And it's a bit of a stereotype. My dad was an immigrant that came to America. He didn't speak English, didn't have much of an education, and because my dad liked fast money, he gravitated towards it. The Numbers was really big in the '80s and '90s. It's called Bolita, the Cuban Numbers racket and the Cuban organized crime.

People in LA look at you a little differently because your last name has a vowel or a "Z." It was very confusing. And there's a very specific idea of what a Latino looks like. I remember when I had my first meeting, in 1997 for a feature I wrote at NYU, I can't remember even the production company. I'm sitting there talking to this woman, and she's like, "I'm just going to ask. What's your last name? Is that your married name?" And I was like, "I'm not married. I'm Latina. My parents are Cuban," because I guess I didn't look Latina. Well, I didn't look like Jennifer Lopez or Salma Hayek, who were the only two big name Latinas that were working at the time in movies. I'm used to it now. It's a weird tokenization that I didn't really understand. This is what it did that was bad: it made me decide that I didn't want to write about the Latino community anymore, and I didn't want to write Latino stories. The sample pilots that I would write, I would put a Latino character in it because I couldn't help myself, because it's characters I like to write. But I found myself steering away from the subject matter, not wanting to go there. Then I had a realization when I finally became a co-executive producer, that I felt like I finally had an obligation to write about my community because it wasn't being represented, and the majority of the stuff at the time that was being put on television and stuff was like *Narcos*. I just basically said, "I want to start meeting the Latino producers." I was lucky enough to sell a couple of pilots. Neither one got made. It just doesn't seem to me that, at least network television, is making huge strides in that. Some of it has to do with the ratings. But I worry sometimes that there's a lot of lip service versus actually wanting TV series about Latinos. But I also think that the community needs to show up more for the Latino content. And I also think there needs to be more variety of that content.

I started moving around from different genres and writing on cop shows and then procedurals. I really think that there was a little bit of just chasing the next job because I liked to work. Because of the way that I grew up. I always was scared that the jobs were going to run out. I didn't realize that (being pigeonholed) was a problem until I started going up the ranks and realizing that other people that have been staff writers, primarily white men, had only been staff writers once. But you have to realize also that my parents are immigrants. My sister was born in Cuba. I grew up with an immigrant

38 *Dailyn Rodriguez*

mentality. Even though my dad was not traditional, I still grew up with, "You got to work hard, and it's difficult, and you just got to push forward." And my dad and my mom were always saying, "You're going to go to the best school, go to college, work really hard, and you're gonna make it."

I lived in a studio apartment for as long as I possibly could. I really had this mentality of like, "I just have to save, and then eventually I'll move up the ranks." I was also working on network shows, so actually I was making very good money as a staff writer. The business has changed quite a bit since I started. It's harder to make a living as a staff writer. Anyway, I didn't complain in that respect. In retrospect, I realized that the good thing that came out of it is when you're under the radar for so long, and you've spent five years or six years in the lower rung of the ladder really getting your chops, by the time I was a co-EP, I was like, "I can run this room." I get it. That's the positive of that. The shitty thing was seeing other people zoom up ahead of you and also people selling pilots. I think there was a shift in my career where I finally said, "Why am I just staffing and staffing and not developing? I have a voice, and I want to develop," and I really had to be an advocate for myself. You have to be an advocate for yourself. I have a different voice and a different story.

My dream is that in five, ten years, there is no diversity hire. I don't want to hear that anymore. I want rooms to look like America, and they should look like that because we want representation from everybody because everybody has a different story. I think it's going to change. As more and more people of color and women of color become showrunners and bosses and executives and agents, it will change. One of the main reasons why there are so many white male writers in Hollywood is because most of the agents are white males. When you're an agent, who do you want to talk to every day? The guy that you feel comfortable talking to. So, it makes sense, but that's why white advocates and allies are so important.

As far as showrunning, the most difficult thing about being promoted to showrunner is that now you're the boss of friends. It was weird because they weren't friends that I had before the show. They were friends I made on the show. So, it was a very weird transition. But I really do like managing people. I think I have a knack for it. I think the one good thing about show-running a show I did not create, was that that afforded me the ability to be a little bit more hands off in that respect and to delegate more because it's not my baby. I'm just there to get the baby through grammar school. I just got to make sure the baby's alive and fed and gets out the door. That's what I tried to do, as opposed to birthing it. I just had to be a super creative, responsible babysitter. Because of that, I think I was able to let go of a lot of things. Oddly enough – my husband even agreed – I found showrunning a lot less stressful than being number two. I think it's because the buck stops with me. If I make a mistake, I can apologize. I can course correct. I can figure out how to fix it. And the only people that I am responsible to are the studio and the network and myself. When you're number two, you still have another writer that's above you, that you are constantly trying to please, and you are constantly trying to manage the other group of writers so that they work efficiently, so that you're able to present material to the showrunner. It's a very stressful job where you're constantly trying to figure out what the showrunner wants.

Being a showrunner is just a different kind of stress. And to me it was a much more manageable stress. I make my own rules. I know what it takes to please me.

DAYNA LYNNE NORTH
Be Your Own Hype Girl

Figure 7.1 Dayna Lynne North
Source: photo by Dalvin Adams

After graduating from USC's School of Cinematic Arts, Dayna Lynne North started as a writer on the Lifetime series *Any Day Now* and moved up through many shows such as *Veronica Mars* and the ABC Family series *Switched at Birth,* before becoming the head writer on VH1's *Single Ladies*. Dayna Lynne North was a writer and executive producer on the HBO series *Insecure* and has signed an overall deal with Sony Pictures Television. She is the showrunner of *The Best Man: The Final Chapters*, which she also co-developed for television.

DOI: 10.4324/9781003298229-8

My journey took the path of writer's assistant, staff writer, story editor, executive story editor, producer, co-executive producer, to showrunner. I worked up the ladder, often spending time on certain rungs, and was able to gain the experience and understanding of how TV works. My first real showrunning experience was being a head writer on *Single Ladies* on VH1 in 2013. What I'm most grateful for about those years was building the skills that are required to actually get a show from start to finish. Nothing makes up for the time in the trenches.

Writing and making art that moves people is a way to be an agent of change. When I realized that, I saw that what I do matters a lot. I came from a family of PhDs. One of my sisters is a doctor, another is an attorney, my dad was a civil rights lawyer, and my mom was a teacher. Growing up, I thought, "Am I doing enough?" My family has always been so supportive, but it took my becoming more confident in my ability as an artist that gave me, not just full permission, but the full encouragement to do this. Because if there's a great purpose to it for me, it excites me.

There has never been a more important time to be an artist than right now because art has the power to transform our minds. It might take generations, but it's effective. Look at everything that's happened with the LGBTQ community. It might have taken decades, but there's no question that you can directly trace the impact that art, television, film, and theater have played in the transformative laws that are now on the books in our country. So, it excites me to take whatever skills I have as an artist and have fun and actually have an impact. When you're making people laugh, you are opening them up to more possibilities, to seeing things differently. Putting the message ahead of the art is often a tricky balance, but when you can hide a beautifully wrapped message in art that's both entertaining and powerful, I think it travels further. You may be planting seeds for trees that someone else will sit under, as they say, but it's still planting seeds in a really important way.

Speaking as a plus-sized Black woman, I have grown up in a world where I have been othered and marginalized all the time. I'm used to that idea of, "We're interested in something, but not quite what you are, not quite what you're bringing, not quite your story." And what's exciting about the moment we've been in for a while is that I don't know anybody who is discouraged by that idea of a "No" right now. I know that there are many other places I can go. Part of what has shifted is that there is a confidence among women, among artists of color, where we know we have options. We're not knocking or begging at just one door. I think all the knocking and begging and asking for permission, that's all kind of dated at this point, which is exciting. I recognize now that there's a benefit to having lived most of my life being perceived as being on the margin. You get to observe in a different way than if you're at the center of things. As an artist, I really started to come to appreciate growing up "on the margin." Whether as a Black plus-size

42 Dayna Lynne North

woman growing up on the "margins of society," of pop culture, or of what is considered popular. It just allows me a really interesting point of view that I value. So, my work and my writing being informed by that point of view, I think is a powerful thing, and it serves me well. And I'm grateful for it.

I also think another movement that's been happening slowly but surely is the recognition of the beauty and the relatability that is to be found in imperfection. All we all are is imperfection, running around being self-conscious about our imperfection, but there's so much great stuff in all of the mess and the mud and the contradiction and the mistakes and, for me, the frayed edges both physically and emotionally. There's so much rich, great material to write from and live from and play with, artistically. There's been, fortunately, a movement toward recognizing the beauty that lives in the frayed edges of all of us. And that's the place in which I love to tell stories. I think there's more of an appreciation lately for that beauty. Legitimate change is happening, but we have to really keep chipping away at it, keep calling it out, keep calling people in and encouraging action. I think it's important to make people aware of how they can be doing better in a way that invites them to do better. I'm a big believer in calling people in, in a way that invites them to make change.

Community is just naturally important to me. Community means when my spirit is low, and when I'm feeling run down from life and the business, and you feel like you've been hitting a lot of walls, having that community that is there for you and sees you for everything that you are, because it's not always easy for us to remember all of our gifts and all of our abilities. Having people around that can reflect you to yourself at all times, and that you can do that for them, has been tremendous.

My USC clique started building a wonderful community for me. All of the theater nerds and the film school kids, pulling people into our movies and plays. I love them. They're beautiful. And community is something that I've naturally continued to build and expand on in my business, in my life and career. I think it matters to really have a foundation of friends – people who may have similar goals, but you can support each other, whether you're up, whether you're down, whether they're up, whether they're down. They can be a spiritual and creative resource for you, as much as maybe a networking and job resource. Networking across is so much more important than networking up, so start building *your* circle. For me, that's really the spirit of Blackbird – which is a coworking space created around the idea of centering and empowering the community of women of color. It's been so beautiful to be a part of the founding advisory with my wonderful cousin and friend Bridgid Coulter. Wherever you are, whether you're in grad school, just out of college, on your first job, trying to break into the industry, who is your merry band? Just genuinely spotting people that you enjoy, that you admire, how they move through the world, and that enjoy and respect who you are. Consciously band together. It does require effort, but it does make a difference. Build it for yourself.

Speaking to the very first show I ever worked on, *Any Day Now*, I'm still very close with most of the writers on that show who were mentors to me, who read my material and helped me grow and learn as a writer, like Nancy Miller and Dee Johnson. I have also been fortunate working on shows where it is much more of a feel of a community than just a job. That means a lot to me. I've gotten even more aware of listening to that intuition. It is kind of a reflection of my personality.

It was such a blessing to work with Issa Rae on *Insecure* because we got to inspire and learn from each other in different ways. It was a difficult decision to leave *Insecure* in Season Three. I was so inspired by Issa. She is the living embodiment of that quote about how when you let your own light shine, you inadvertently give others permission to do the same. So, after three seasons there and everything that I learned, I was ready to take the leap and really bet on myself and start my own company, Loud Sis, fully investing in myself. The question is, how do we build our own tables versus trying to get a seat at someone else's table? I'm not really interested in a seat at the old boys' club table. It doesn't feel like it would be a true seat. It's being one, among many people who don't share my background or POV. It's often a draining experience that I don't want, to spend a bunch of time on, trying to educate somebody on why your mind should be broader if it's not already. It's about creating our own tables more and more. Like Ava DuVernay and Issa Rae's companies, creating our own financial stake in what we're doing and having an ability to do that, versus having to always look for a green light and permission and validation that is again, in this sort of very narrow club. It takes a level of having your own sense of agency and self-empowerment. Being willing to say, "I'd rather not make this show and not make this money, than make it in a way that is just chipping away at my spirit and that doesn't allow me to have any ownership." There are so many outlets available for distribution now. I think it's helping to chip away at these age-old models that don't necessarily benefit the artist.

My mission is to elevate and amplify voices of women of color and those who have been side-lined and the voices that are typically left out of the conversation, whether they're left out accidentally or whether they're actively ignored. I wanted to create a company that focuses on those voices. That's what excites me. That's the mission statement of Loud Sis. "Loud Sis" is a phrase I've been using going back to college, and it still pretty much captures the essence of Dayna Lynne North.

It's been fun to create clarity around my mission because it makes it easier to discern my yesses from my nos. When people are inviting me to be a part of projects, one of my consultants at Inspire Justice, which is a social impact company whose coaches I work with, will love to say, "If it's not a 'Hell yes,' it's a 'No.'" So, I'm trying to live from a place of leaning into my "Hell yes." What is my "Hell yes?" When projects come in or when artists reach out, is it a "Hell yes" for me to work with you? Asking myself that question, it's not as easy as it may sound because there are times when something might feel

44 *Dayna Lynne North*

like there are a lot of yeses. You might take a job because it's a smart decision or practical, but that's not the same as a "Hell yes." So, for me, being at a place in my career now where I am fortunate enough to have incoming calls and have requests for me to staff or to develop projects, it's a way for me to stay clear on what my path is and, "Does this fit into my artistic goals in a 'Hell yes' way?" It's a philosophy that is beyond just career and my artistic pursuit. Just in life, is this a "Hell yes"? Whatever it may be, because it can be easy, and women suffer from this more, to justify our way into a yes. "Well, this makes sense for this reason," "That's a really respected person," whatever it may be, versus do I get that immediate, visceral, "Hell yes" at the thought of being a part of whatever the thing is. That has been my true north.

That helps me feel like, "I'm just going to go for it. I'm going to be a little bit reckless. I'm going to be a little bit fearless. And I'm going to really go." For me, it's not even so much going really fast as much as going with purpose. It's the energy of, "I'm going to go for it for as long as I can. Until they catch me." One of my taglines about myself is that I'm a delightful disrupter. In the past few years, I've really been coming into the understanding of how much fun and joy and laughter and comedy you can bring into the space of transformative justice and change. I know for me growing up, Martin Luther King, the Panthers, and John Lewis all had amazing senses of humor, but when I think of the images of them, they were all very heavy. You've got to march, and you've got to risk real life. That is one way to disrupt and call for change. But you can also do it through art. You can also do it while making people laugh. *Insecure* is a form of social impact and social justice because it just shows Black and Brown women being themselves and laughing – the beauty of it. Centering on women that are not usually centered is a form of social justice and social impact, but you can have so much fun while you're doing it. Writing from the place of what's important to you, what's meaningful to you as a writer, is just the best place to start. I'm excited right now about a show I'm incubating that focuses on that idea of how we have to have our own sense of confidence. That before you can get to the space of hyping up others, you have to be a map for yourself. How to be your own hype girl, essentially, and finding that energy within yourself. So that you're not as affected by all of the waves of highs and lows and BS that's being spewed around on social media.

You've got to be your own hype girl. And be loud. My tagline for my company is *Be Loud Sis*. And it's not that it's always easy to do that, but I think getting there is so key. Getting yourself to that place of, "Yes, I'm going to do it myself. I am going to bless myself. I am going to give myself a 'Hell yes' if I'm not finding it somewhere else." Getting to that place can take some practice, but is so key to any kind of success that you find. If you are the first one to believe and recognize what you have to offer, then it makes it so much easier for others to invest in that and invest in you. It's another way of saying that you've got to invest in yourself first. Especially in this business, it's so much about people circling around energy. "What energy am I drawn to and whose energy do I want to be a part of?" People are very influenced by not only how you see yourself, but also the work that you create from that position.

All writers are not necessarily wired to be showrunners. They're two very different skill sets. Especially as a producer, as a showrunner, as a director, having that energy so that everyone understands, "We can safely fall in line with this person and we're going to get across the finish line together." There's an energy that's required for that. That's an extension of what I'm talking about, which is, I've got to believe in myself and my ability to get across first. Then I've got to call everybody into that with me. So, if I'm going to convince you to invest in me, whether that means hiring me for something, investing in my company, recognizing what I have to bring, I have to be the center of that. I've got to be able to do that for myself first in the most powerful way.

DEE JOHNSON
I Climbed Every Rung of the Ladder

Figure 8.1 Dee Johnson
Source: photo by courtesy of Dee Johnson

Dee Johnson worked her way up from writer's assistant to writer on *I'll Fly Away* and then wrote for *Melrose Place, Profiler, Any Day Now*, among others, before rising to executive producer/showrunner on *ER, The Good Wife, Boss, Nashville*, and *Mars*.

DOI: 10.4324/9781003298229-9

I was a military brat, born in the Philippines. We moved a lot, but the one place I found continuity was in television. I remember seeing all those names flying by the screen and thinking, "Wow, those lucky people." I watched a lot of stuff as a kid. Not only in primetime, but a lot of afternoon stuff back in the day when there was a lot in repeats and in syndication. What really made me think I could write for television was *Cagney & Lacey*, which I loved. Thank God for the hubris of youth because if my kids suddenly decided they were going to do that and move to some other city to pursue it, I would think they were bananas. But it really was that show. I just loved the relationship that I saw between these two strong women. There was nothing else like it in those days, in terms of how women were portrayed. I loved it. And I wrote a spec, and said, "I'm going to write for television." I still kind of marvel at the fact that I'm here. Because if you had met me at any point in my youth or my teenage years, there was absolutely nothing about who I was then that would have suggested I would be here now. No Ivy League education – I'm a college dropout. There's really nothing about me that makes it make sense. But here I am. So, everybody comes to it in a different way.

I've climbed every rung of the ladder. I started out as a PA and did all the assistant positions, writer's assistant, script coordinator, the whole shebang, which is invaluable. I was so lucky. I worked for so many talented people. But there's two big canyons. The first big one is getting an episode of anything. The second big thing is – can you turn that into a career and get staffed? For every one of my friends I came up through the ranks with, there's a dozen who spent twenty years doing it and never made that transition. And who knows why? It's not just talent that makes it; it's a recipe. It's just a combination. It's timing. It's being the right personality at the right place at the right time. I know a lot of really talented people who aren't in the business anymore, and it isn't because of a lack of talent. Nothing about this business as a writer in television is set up to make you feel good about yourself. Almost everything as a showrunner is receiving criticism of one sort or another. This could be network notes or writer notes or actor notes or department head notes. It's all about getting noted. And some people may not have a great social game. I know so many talented people that just didn't check that particular box. For every good job you have, there's probably about five that are really stinkers, that really kick your ass and make you want to quit, or make you question yourself. Any one of those things can send you packing. Sometimes you handle it better than others. But if you're lucky, you get the kind of notes that you think, "Wow, that's great. I didn't think of that." Good notes are fantastic. Notes that are just sort of picky, "I'm-justify-ing-my-job" notes or "I'm-trying-to-make-you-feel-like-shit" notes, which we've all gotten – what purpose does that serve?

I got my first episode of television on *I'll Fly Away*. It was such a beautiful show and I was lucky enough to have worked under David Chase, Barbara Hall, and Henry Bromell. This is way before Final Draft or anything and there was a horrible system called Scripter that we all used. It was this very small office, just me and another assistant. So, I was also David Chase's

48   *Dee Johnson*

assistant, Barbara Hall's assistant, and the script coordinator. But the beauty of it was all of the changes were handwritten. And so putting through every revision was like an education in how to write for television – it was a blessing. At the time though, the poor, broke writer's assistant that I was, I almost didn't take the job. I had two other offers. One was to go to script coordinate for this half-hour show called *Eerie, Indiana,* which was a good show, and paid $200 more a week. The other was to take the *I'll Fly Away* gig which paid $200 less a week. But I read the pilot of *I'll Fly Away* and I just thought, "This is the kind of thing I want to write." Luckily, I could live off of ramen at the time. And David Chase, who is a very interesting, brilliant character, ended up giving me an episode. That was my first script for network television.

Then I went to *Melrose Place,* which was a completely different kind of show. But you're not going to say no to your first staff job. I didn't know anything about it and didn't ever really want to do soaps. Because as a woman, I didn't want to be pigeonholed. But it was a staff job, and I thought, "How am I going to say no to this?" And it ended up being the most fantastic training ground ever because we did 34 hours a year. I think one of the hardest things to do is to do relationship shows because you don't have the engine of the murder plot or a medical case. It's purely relationship. And it's hard to manufacture stakes week after week with just relationships. And so that's where I was, the original *Melrose Place.* And it was a blast.

One thing I love about TV is that it's a team sport. I love having a writing staff. If I wanted to do it all by myself, I'd be a feature writer. I love having a team, love having everybody firing on all cylinders and being engaged and involved. What you don't want is to shut somebody down and make them feel like they're not a part of the team. I've seen it happen, and I hate it. And I've been on the receiving end of it.

My theory is anybody can run a show. But… if you don't take the mantle too soon. If you don't know what you're doing, every department will suffer. And you will suffer. You may still end up winning an Emmy, but it's going to be hard on all concerned. And it's unnecessary. I think for a lot of women, particularly of a certain generation, there's a need to feel qualified. It's the whole notion that women are judged on their experience and men are judged on their promise. I didn't want my qualifications questioned. I think that's less true now because I think more young women are like, "Fuck it. You can do it; I can do it." And that's great. However, it really helps to know what you're doing.

I was really lucky to come up through the ranks when I did, not only because I was blessed to work with some incredibly talented people, but on some really terrific shows and in the golden era of network television. I was on *ER* for five seasons, that was amazing, and we reached so many households. And you're so involved in every aspect of production. John Wells is a terrific manager. You come up through that camp and you learn how to do it. It's such a blessing, you know, and he made you earn it. Like I said, every rung, and sometimes going backwards. To go on *ER,* I was a Co-EP at the time and I had to step down to supervising producer to go on *ER.* That was the deal. Take it or leave it.

Dee Johnson 49

It was a huge hit, but I loved it. You know how, every once in a while, there's one of those, "God, I'd kill to write for that show" moments? That was one of those shows. So, it was worth it. The beauty of network television, or the horror of it, is that you're doing 22 plus episodes a year. If you're on the right show, you're actually producing. You become a better writer that way – when you walk the sets, when you're in editorial, when you're in all of the production meetings. It's invaluable training. And now more and more and more, there's such a loss there of experience. And I feel for the younger people coming in because they're not getting that. And it's even worse when you're thrusted into a position of showrunner – when you haven't had the benefit of all that experience. You can learn without it, but it's a baptism by fire. And I always think it's nicer to be baptized in a nice, warm water.

The other thing that's great about television is that, as opposed to features, you get to write more of the life of a character. A character can evolve, right? So, you can take somebody who's an asshole in Season One, put them through a bunch of stuff, and you can love that person by Season Three and think he's the best thing since sliced bread. It's just sort of looking at humans and then putting them through the meat grinder of life.

I never wanted any show I worked on to become my entire life. My family means a lot to me. And this was true of the John Wells camp and also with David Chase on *I'll Fly Away* – there were only four writers on staff on that show! They left to go home every night by 6 or 7pm, and it was a network show doing 22 episodes a year. If you are disciplined and if you know what you're doing, you don't have to be working until 3 in the morning. You're not doing your best work then. It's diminishing returns. I don't care what anybody says. But sometimes, you have no choice, circumstances being what they are.

If I did nothing else in my career, I probably was proudest of the Weaver storyline on *ER* where we used the word "wife." [*ER*, Season 10, Episode 18 "Where There's Smoke."] Everything is so different now, but it was scarier then. My partner at the time (and now wife) and I were embarking on having kids, and she had a strained relationship with her biological mother. And I had to jump through a bunch of different hoops to kind of ensure that there was some legal standing for me. And our fear was, "Oh my gosh, if anything ever happened to me or her, what would happen to our child?" I just sort of channeled that fear into that episode and had Weaver go through a similar thing with her firefighting partner. When she had come from a fire and was being worked on in the trauma room, it was important to me for her to say that "She was my wife." It doesn't feel very controversial now, but it was at the time. Not everybody on the show wanted that to be said. It got into 25 million living rooms though. That show was such a behemoth. The beautiful thing about *ER* is that the network gave us very little pushback on anything. There are moments that do shift the culture and that show helped do this. Someone who's watching TV now, someone who's 16 years old, has no idea how different the culture was then. I don't know that I entered into writing as

50 *Dee Johnson*

a career with making change at the forefront of my mind. Maybe it was because of what was going on in my life at that time but it became super important, and it was a blessing that I was able to do that.

It's said that when you're gay, you come out a thousand times a day because every little circumstance is fighting a set of assumptions. It seems silly now, but I was interviewing for a job, and I used to wear a wedding ring on my ring finger because I was in a long-term relationship. And there was a moment in this interview where somebody said, "Oh, you're married. What does your husband do?" And I'm in an interview for a staff job and I'm like, "Oh, what do I do? What do I do?" The panic, you know? And I was honest about it, which is hard. There are times when it was less about just putting forth a character who was LGBTQ, it was more about how it was pushing the limits in terms of what that character could do or was allowed to do. My experience has never been, "Oh, we don't want that character to be gay." It was more like, "They can be gay, but…" You had to really ease into things. You couldn't just be out there. And I think that's so different now, which I love.

When I was on *Melrose Place* and we had Doug Savant's character kiss his boyfriend, it was a huge fucking deal. It was just the most chaste kiss, sandwiched by bed-hopping galore with all of the heterosexual characters. It was very much, "He can be gay, but we just don't want to see that much of it." I think it's very different now. And that's a really lucky thing.

Having my own show on the air has been a very elusive brass ring for me, and it's something I've wanted from the beginning. I don't know why I'm not more discouraged, but probably because there's nothing about who I was born to be that would suggest that I even would have gotten this far. There are things I still want to achieve, but I've done pretty okay. So I don't beat myself up about it too much. I still want what I want though. And it's annoying of course, that it has been so elusive. I have a story about my mom being a guerilla in the Philippines during World War 2. I came here with that story in mind, a personal story that I was committed to telling at some point. When I tried to sell people on the idea, I just kept hearing, "Who's the audience for this? No one's going to watch it." Also, I've always felt that if I had been a guy, I would have been much further down the road than I am. You still have a majority of showrunners who are male. Not to bang on the guys, but people go where it's familiar. They go to their comfort zones, and for some, it's just hard to sort of make the extra effort to expand the deck a bit and look elsewhere.

I've been fortunate to have worked for a lot of great guys, but a lot of people still don't like having women bosses. The whole mentality is, "Let's just check a box." It isn't, "Let's cultivate this person's talent and make them shine." It's just, "Let's check a box." There is so much that women bring to the table. It's different now, I think, but still there is this automatic respect, a built-in confidence that's given to the guys, while women have to earn respect. This sounds really jaded, but if *Game of Thrones* had been pitched by a female team and they had to reshoot the entire pilot, first of all, they wouldn't have gotten a gig. And secondly, if they did get the gig, those mistakes wouldn't be tolerated. Men are still Teflon. They can have a big flop and still get another crack at it. But if you, as a woman, really have a massive flop, it will be hard to climb back from that.

I was at a WGA event maybe a year or so ago; it was an Asian American event. And I realized, I hadn't even thought about it that much to be honest, but I had only been on a writing staff where there was another Asian person one time. I was on *ER* with Yahlin Chang. The only other time it was when I hired Monica Macer on *Nashville*. I was just really lucky because I know people who tried and not that many made it over the other side of the canyon.

ELIZABETH BERGER
We Loved the Way Television Made Us Feel

Figure 9.1 Elizabeth Berger
Source: photo by Joseph Cultice

Elizabeth Berger and her writing partner, Isaac Aptaker, were the showrunners of NBC's critically acclaimed *This is Us*, a multigenerational family drama that spanned six seasons, from 2016 to 2022. Elizabeth and her writing partner worked their way up on shows including *Zach Stone Is Gonna Be Famous*, *The Neighbors*, *About a Boy,* and *Grandfathered*. They are the creators and showrunners of *How I Met Your Father* and the Hulu series *Love, Victor*, about a high school student coming to terms with his sexual identity.

DOI: 10.4324/9781003298229-10

When I was young, my dad (Lou Berger) was the head writer of *Sesame Street*. I could hear the voices of *Sesame Street* characters coming out from behind his door. Occasionally, he'd let me in on the process. He'd show me his script, and he'd read it aloud. Probably just to make me feel important, he'd ask me for notes and feedback and thoughts. From a very young age, I saw that writing was this real job that you could have. I loved going to work with him, and I loved being around the other writers and puppeteers. I loved the experience of being with this family that was coming together to put on this show. When I applied to Dramatic Writing at NYU, my long-term goal was to be more of a dramatic writer. But then when you finally get to LA, obviously you'll get in any way you can. I did also love writing comedy. Isaac Aptaker, my writing partner, and I were both so excited to leap in and take any job we were offered, and that included comedy for a few years. But the transition to *This is Us* felt like a natural one because it's exactly the kind of writing that I had always wanted to be doing.

Luckily, I don't think I made any catastrophic mistakes that truly derailed us, but we did make some beginner's mistakes when we were starting out. We look back and regret how much time that we spent saying yes to everything, just because it's such a natural instinct. I think when you are starting out, you want to take whatever's offered to you and hope that it's going to be a life-changing opportunity. That meant a lot of hours of free labor, putting your heart and soul into these projects. I'm totally for it, if someone comes across the dream idea, even if there's no money behind it, you should do that at the beginning of your career. But that did not prove worthwhile for us. We still have a wonderful manager named Eryn Brown who kept trying to tell us, even from the very beginning, "Guys, take the projects that are really speaking to your hearts. Those are going to be the ones that stick. Those are going to be the ones that make a difference." It took us a while to really absorb that lesson. But when we finally slowed down and started listening to that advice, things went much better for us.

My partner wanted to announce who we are in a really clear way. For us, that meant being a comedy writing team who wrote with emotion and heart. We decided to be very clear about that. Even though we are very different people, there is a shared sensibility there that makes the partnership very natural, which I think is very hard to find. I think it's really rare when you can find a collaborator who sees the world at least generally the way you do. Our mission is to create content where people feel something, and they laugh, and they feel emotional at the end. They walk away feeling hopefully better about humanity than when they sat down to watch the program. A mentor of ours, my partner Isaac's first boss, this wonderful movie producer named Robert Cort, who produced films including the *Bill and Ted* movies, *Jumanji*, and *Cocktail*, was like, "Guys, you're young. You're just starting out. Write something that feels really personal that you can really sink your teeth

54   *Elizabeth Berger*

into and makes sense for you two to be the writers of." That was really great advice early on. That doesn't mean that it has to be exactly our experience, but it has to have that kernel that we really relate to deeply. That's at least what really gets us excited, and where I think we do our best work.

I don't know that there was a conscious decision or even a conversation about how what we were doing was a little different tonally than what was maybe the mainstream, or than prestige shows with anti-heroes. I think we really bonded over the television that we'd grown up with and loved. Isaac and I both watched hours and hours of *Nick at Nite* with our parents as kids. We had these kinds of old references of *I Love Lucy* and *Mary Tyler Moore*, and we wanted to do content that felt fresh and modern and of the moment, but we also kept coming back to the idea that we loved the way that television made us feel. That we remembered sitting down with our families, that we remembered laughing and feeling and caring about the characters. I think that we really trusted that love that we both shared, also because neither of us was naturally saying, "Oh, but shouldn't we do something darker? Shouldn't we do something edgier?" It was very easy to kind of land on the kind of content we were going to create together.

Our voice really matched nicely with the kind of work that Jason Katims and Dan Fogelman create. Dan writes from such a place of emotion and heart and feeling, and he's always been very steadfast about the idea that he's not going to bend his vision to cynics out there that think he's too sweet or too this or too that. He's just going to tell stories that he loves, that he believes will make people feel good. I think it's been really formative for us to see him stick to that vision so resolutely and to see it have such an unbelievable result with *This Is Us*, where a lot of people would have said, "Oh, it's too emotional." And then people responded to it in such a tremendous way. We did one season of *About a Boy* with Jason Katims, and Jason similarly just leads from his heart, and he doesn't care if other people would find it too soft. When he would hear a pitch that moved him, he would instinctively hold his heart and say over and over, "Oh, that's very moving, that's very moving." You could see him feeling it in his body truly on a visceral level. I think getting to work with two people like that has been inspiring, and it has really shaped the way we approach our work and the work we want to do.

I think that these kinds of shows are still really hard to execute. Dan had a very specific vision for *This Is Us*, which you can feel, and he wanted it to be such a human and emotional show. But he also did want it to be filled with surprises and twists and things that sort of make you lean in and talk to your friends by the water cooler and say, "How do you think Jack died?" He wanted it to have that mixture. Dan had assembled this group of writers, a lot of younger writers, a really fascinating and diverse group of people. And we just spent those first couple of weeks telling our life stories to each other in a much deeper way than I ever had on any other show, which makes sense because I worked on comedies. But I think even for a drama, this was unusual. People were just saying out loud the most difficult, tragic, brutal experiences that they'd gone through in life. They talked about losing family members, and they were talking about dealing with sick parents, and it was the fastest I've ever bonded with a group of people because everyone just kind of laid it out there. We all come home from work just completely drained and exhausted from sharing and crying. But it became really clear very early on, this is the show. Everyone has these things. Everyone's life looks different, but everyone in their daily lives is facing these unbelievably difficult, over-the-top emotional situations at different points. We really leaned into that heavily. We just kind of trusted that we all had stories to tell and that that was going to shine through in our season. We were off to the races from there. That was the origin for Season One of *This Is Us*.

If you watch the show, I think it becomes very clear that our message is, yes, we are all different and unique, and we never want to gloss over that. But there's also so much that unites us and so much that is shared in terms of our humanity and our overall hopes and dreams and goals and the fact that we're all looking to find people to love and to move through life with grace and dignity. For the most part, that became our guiding light. While we wish this wasn't the case, we're very aware that many of our viewers, when they watch Randall Pearson's family, that's the only interaction that they're going to be having with Black people for sustained periods of time. Those are the Black people that they'll be closest to. And that gives us the responsibility to showcase a Black family authentically. That always seems to be our sweet spot, to just present people living their lives and hoping that the message sinks in that this is who's out there. This is what they're doing. This is what they care about. I think, very organically, we delved deeper and deeper into the Black experience with the help of the brilliant writers on our show.

You can have a big notion of what your show is about, but it's not until you're in the weeds, and you're hearing from the team you've assembled, and you're hearing people's stories that you kind of step back and go, "Wow, we have an opportunity here to tell a story in a very specific way." It doesn't stop at your writers' room. It also goes into who are your people up top across the board? Who are your people in every department that are weighing in and making your show richer and more diverse? And that includes, obviously, who's on your set, who's in your costume department, who are your non-writing executive producers, all of these things shape the world of the show. We've watched that continuously evolve, and we've watched the rewards be really great in terms of diversifying in those areas. It's really to the benefit of any creator or showrunner to have a diverse writers' room, because it's the way you're going to have the most interesting conversations and think of things that otherwise wouldn't be thought of. Hopefully people have also been able to feel that. We want our show to be a place where people emerge and flourish because tremendously exciting things happen when you get out of the way sometimes.

I'm very aware that my experience has been different than a lot of women's because Isaac has been my partner from the very beginning. I can count on one hand in the last 13 years the number of meetings I've gone to without Isaac sitting next to me. I think that has greatly influenced my experience. I can't speak for what it would have been like to go to those meetings alone, and I can't speak to what it would've been like to move through a writers' room as a young female writer alone, because that was just never my experience. I can say that, in my opinion, behavior in writers' rooms has changed drastically since I started in the business. When Isaac and I started in comedy rooms, you could really feel that the women in the room, especially the older women in the room, had had to sort of force their way into a boys' club. That manifested itself in different ways. It often manifested itself in feeling the pressure to tell very dirty jokes, feeling pressure to laugh at jokes that men made at their expense. I remember being a young 24-year-old writer and not really being able to understand why people were behaving this way because I had no context for the journeys that they had been through. I found it really shocking. That behavior has dissipated over the years, as women have realized that they don't have to play that game anymore, that they don't have to be the butt of the joke, that they don't have to desperately try to fit in with the guys.

I now have such great respect and such great empathy for all the women that came before me who had to do all of that in order to just have a seat at the table, and in a really lovely way that has changed through the years. That being said, there are still things that I'd love to see improved. I don't know exactly how many executive producers there are on *This Is Us*, I think about ten, and I remained the only female executive producer on the show until Season Six when we promoted two female writers, K.J. Steinberg and Kay Oyegun, to Executive Producer. When you're the only woman at the table in those meetings that sort of puts the onus on you to be speaking on behalf of all women, and that's never the position you want to be in. I say that as someone on a show with men that I love and respect and who treat me extremely well, but it's still just not the way that it should be. I think I've experienced great progress, but I've also experienced the ways where we're still falling short.

ERICA KODISH

You Girlfriend, Are Going into Battle, You Have to Get Ready for That

Figure 10.1 Erica Kodish
Source: photo by Shoots and Giggles Photography Inc.

Erica Kodish has written for *CSI: New York, FBI, Cold Case,* and *The Good Wife* among others. A graduate of Northwestern University and USC School of Cinematic Arts, Kodish was the showrunner on Season Four and Five of *Being Mary Jane* and is currently a consulting producer on *The Equalizer* with Queen Latifah.

As a teenager, I loved *Thirtysomething*. I was not the demographic at all for that show. And yet, because it was a show that was about these small moments and these yuppies who were just trying to make their way and raise children, and because my own personal family background was kind of chaotic, it was wish fulfillment for me. It was dramatizing normal life and relationships. That was appealing to me. The writing was so impressive. It was the first time that I thought, "I want to do that. I want to write for

DOI: 10.4324/9781003298229-11

58 *Erica Kodish*

television." Looking back on it, it was an exceedingly white show, but that was a given in the late eighties and nineties. That was not a deterrent for me. It was aspirational for my life and then for writing as well. It made me ask, "How do I write like that? How do I get to a place where my problems are about whether or not to have another kid or when this renovation will be done?"

It's so interesting that *Thirtysomething* was my inspiration, and then my first show was *CSI: New York*. I got my job on *CSI: New York* off of a *Shield* spec that is still one of my favorite things that I've written. That speaks to my eclectic taste but also, when I started pursuing a job, television had changed. These gritty, dark shows were getting a lot of attention. It made sense that I liked *The Shield*, a show where I felt the writing was impressive. That spec led me to *CSI: New York*. Once you get your credit, get your foot in the door, and gain that procedural muscle, naturally your agents push you to stay in that lane because it's easier to take the path of least resistance. You don't go from *CSI: New York* and then write on a show like *Parenthood*. Cop shows were where the opportunities were. At that time, in the late nineties, network television was very segregated. There were no Black writers on any one-hour long dramas, or maybe one. Shows about Black people on network television then were sitcoms, and I didn't want to get pigeonholed in that genre. The Writer-Producer Felicia Henderson paved the way on Showtime's *Soul Food*. She and other writers made some noise about the segregation that was going on. They opened up the door so that there were opportunities for me. But again, I was very much aware of being pigeonholed into that limited space, and because *Thirtysomething* had been an inspiration, I wanted to do different types of stories. That's another reason why I chose to go and work in procedurals and cop dramas.

As I moved up, it became a goal for me not just to run a successful show, but to also create a work environment that was not toxic. Only now are we really starting to see a reckoning with that. There was this accepted view that it didn't matter what the work environment was like as long as the product was good. I didn't believe it. I felt like, although this is a creative profession, it's still a profession, and people should be treated professionally and with respect. I also felt that most of us don't respond well to abuse and toxic environments, and that we are much more productive and creative if we are in healthier environments. I learned from some of my painful experiences that made me more determined not to make those mistakes, but I also learned from those showrunners who I felt like set a very good example, like on *Cold Case* with Meredith Stiehm and Veena Sud, which was very professionally run. They provided the training ground for the next generation of showrunners. It felt like I was going from basic math to calculus, but I recognized how valuable that experience had been because of how much I had learned. That's the experience that I brought to my position as a showrunner when I became one. Meredith and Veena were also very mindful of having diversity in the room. There were a number of women writers and women of color and people of color. It was a great experience that really laid the foundation and where I learned that even as you're putting your head down, you can have some fun and get good work out of writers without having to be awful and toxic.

I saw what happened to friends who tried to stick it out in those toxic environments where they felt marginalized and disrespected. It can be really damaging and sometimes it would set their careers back three or four years, because of the PTSD. They were just so bruised and broken that it took them a while to shake it off and start moving forward. They all did eventually, but it could be a very hard way to proceed through your career. I think my nature would have been to stick it out in some of those environments. In some instances, other writers stepped in and said, "We love you, but you need to thrive. You need to leave." And they were absolutely right. In other instances, the universe spoke and removed that opportunity. When I did turn back to writing shows that weren't as procedural, in some ways it was kind of scary because character dramas are a much different animal. I hadn't had practice in that, though I definitely always had an interest in doing other types of shows and later in my career, I was fortunate in doing shows like *The Good Wife,* that had a bit of that balance.

I got the job running the reboot of *Being Mary Jane* because of my work on *The Good Wife.* Gabrielle Union was a fan of the show and sought me out. At the time, I was not interested in running a show. I just didn't feel like I was ready professionally and because of where my life was personally. I'd just had my first child, a newborn, and I did not want to take that job on. That's when I learned the power of the word no. I kept saying no and meaning it. And then at one point my husband was like, "I think you're taking this job." Because they just kept asking. They just didn't go away, you know? So, I thought, "Yes, I guess I'm doing this."

I inherited a huge hit. Gabrielle Union and the network wanted a reboot of the show, to come back from an extended hiatus with something very fresh. It needed to be different, but also, they didn't want to alienate the loyal following that the show had. It was one of my first opportunities to write for a diverse cast, plus the character is an African American woman, a professional woman, so it was the first time I had the experience of being able to draw on my own experiences. It was a real opportunity, but it was also fraught, in that rebooting was like writing a pilot on the fly, with much less time than writing a pilot. I had to come up with something new and different, but not too new. Fortunately, I had a fantastic, collaborative team and that really helped. There was a lot of pressure from the fans. It was my first experience with Black Twitter, which is a formidable force. I'm sort of introverted and shy away from social media, so it put me in a space that I was not at all familiar with or comfortable with. I had never experienced that sort of fan engagement. I've been at shows that have a huge following. *The Good Wife* fans were very passionate about the show. Occasionally, you'll receive an email or a letter. Whereas with *Being Mary Jane*, it was instantaneous feedback when a show would air. You cannot allow the fans to direct

60 Erica Kodish

the storytelling, but there is some value in letting some of it in. It's a very tricky balance not letting that completely erode your vision, but then also being flexible. If you start letting too much of the noise come in, then your vision is lost. That's where you're really flailing. It is hard to decipher whether these are just the noisy ones, or is this a huge groundswell of what people are feeling? You have to brace yourself going into those shows knowing that you're going to get a lot of feedback. I feel like in general with shows with huge Black audiences, you're in a call and response position because they will let you know how they feel.

I was just going on what I felt, because I did have the privilege of being a viewer of the show before I worked on it. I had grown frustrated with the character. Because I was feeling frustrated, I felt like other people must be feeling frustrated. I think part of why the character was beloved is because she was flawed, but I felt like there needed to be some growth as well. I really felt like it was time for some maturing. That was purely guided by my own personal reaction to where the direction of the show had been going. It needed, in order to keep the character relatable, to be steered back to a place where we could understand her mistakes and where they were coming from. That was my goal.

I've been fortunate to have support from other Black women in the industry. I credit my success to my informal group of writer friends. We were supportive of one another while trying to get our careers off the ground, getting that first credit. They were the ones that I looked to for advice, guidance, and a shoulder to cry on, as well as to vent. I think that's really important. So now, when my former assistant got her first staff writing job, I submitted her name to Black Women Who Brunch (an informal social and professional networking group started in 2014) and she became part of the group. One of the assistants that I had promoted to staff writer on *Being Mary Jane* is now part of the group and has gone on to great success. I'm a bit jealous that it didn't exist when I was starting out in my career because I feel like it is fantastic for those that are just getting their careers off the ground. I didn't have that access. The advice that I was given when I was trying to break into the industry was that you've got to get a showrunner to read your work. Well, how do I do that? It was like saying you need to bump into Princess Diana. Showrunners were like these mythical figures. In the last ten years, barriers have broken down a little bit, whereas before there wasn't a lot of embracing the younger generation. In part because of social media and where collectively we've gone as a society, it's much easier to have real access and relationships with writers who are in the upper-level ranks, to reach out or get a response from a showrunner. And there are many more showrunners, and many more shows.

Still, grit is the most important quality if you want to be in this industry. You have to have this view that you are going into battle. Even though you're maybe a nice, sweet girl from the South or the Midwest or whatever, you girlfriend, you are going into battle, and you have to get ready for that.

You have to have that level of determination, and that does not mean you won't get knocked down because you absolutely will. That's part of battle, that you get knocked down. But you get back up, and you keep moving forward. You have to just keep your eye on the prize. I think from the time that I graduated from USC, it took me eight years. And during that time, I saw people starting families, getting promotions, buying fancy cars, buying homes, and you feel like you are stuck in this endless loop. You're not moving forward at all. And it starts to feel helpless. I'm happy that I stayed on. I just stuck with it because the thing is, although eight years sounds like a lot, and I was embarrassed that it took me so long, but then no one has ever looked at me and said, "It took you eight years." It's only when you're going through it that it feels like it's a scarlet letter, like everyone else can see it. And that's not the truth. Those who I was struggling right alongside with, who just stuck with it, those who it took even longer for, now they are doing fantastic. You have to view it as the long game. It's a marathon. You have to summon whatever sort of grit and determination you have to persevere.

I started practicing Buddhism, and some people think of Buddhism as tranquility and that sort of thing. But it's not just about peace and tranquility and that sort of stereotype, it is about writing your own story. And you have to be very determined about that, and direct your actions toward that, and towards believing that that is possible. You are Buddha, and you can create the story that you want to create with your life. You are the storyteller. You have the pen and the paper. So, what story do you want to tell?

FELICIA D. HENDERSON
Sometimes, You've Got to Put on Your Sasha Fierce

Figure 11.1 Felicia Henderson
Source: photo by Matthew Jordan Smith

Felicia D. Henderson began her career as an apprentice on *Family Matters* and *The Fresh Prince of Bel-Air* and went on to write and produce *Moesha, Sister, Sister,* and *Everybody Hates Chris,* before turning her attention to television dramas *Gossip Girl, Fringe, The Punisher, Empire,* and others. She developed, executive produced, and directed the TV series *Soul Food* for Showtime, the first successful, Black-themed drama in television history. It was nominated for an Emmy for its music and won five NAACP Image Awards, including three for Best Drama Series. Felicia co-created and was the showrunner of *The Quad* for BET and was the showrunner and head writer of *First Kill* for Netflix. Felicia has an MBA in corporate finance, an MFA in screenwriting, and a Ph.D. in Media Studies. She is an Associate Professor in Northwestern University's Department of Radio/Television/Film.

DOI: 10.4324/9781003298229-12

Felicia D. Henderson 63

In my twenty-plus years working in this industry, I have been given a lot of advice about how I should behave or carry myself. I tried everything before I settled into being comfortable with who I am. I've been told, "You're a strong personality. You make people uncomfortable." Or "You have to remember you walk in as a big Black woman, and you have to remember your physical presence can be intimidating." Or "Make sure you smile more." I don't think men are being told to smile more. I've gone through periods where I've tried to be less intimidating. And at the end of the day, it took me too long to just be true to who I am. I never want anyone to feel stupid or dumb. That's never my goal. I never want anyone to be intimidated, but I'm no longer willing to take responsibility for how someone else responds to my confidence, talent, or intelligence.

When I give advice to young people, or anyone new to writing, because there are some people in their forties deciding to write, and I think that's great, I tell them to go for it. Get in where you fit in. Take whatever job you can get. You have to get in the door so you can meet people. When I got my very first job, I was just out of the Warner Bros. Writers' Workshop. I was placed on a family sitcom, *Family Matters*, as a writer trainee. Family sitcoms were what I grew up watching on TV, so I was over the moon. I loved laughing. I was always told I was funny. I wasn't disappointed to go on *Family Matters* even though I was hoping for *Friends*. I believe in making the absolute most of wherever you find yourself. I had a wonderful opportunity to start my writing career pitching Steve Urkel jokes, and those jokes still make me laugh.

My career in Hollywood began as a Broadcast Associate at NBC. One of the shows I was assigned to as a junior executive was *The Fresh Prince of Bel-Air*. To come back to the show as a writer a few years later was heaven. I was a huge Will Smith fan. Luckily, I have worked steadily ever since. I've been blessed. I've been on the writing staff of amazing shows. Everything I've done, I wanted to do at that time. When I was starting out, I wanted to write family comedies. We were big TV watchers in my house. As a kid, I watched every single comedy on television with my family. After writing family comedies for several years, however, I wanted to do something else. But I had a challenging time when attempting to transition to adult comedy. That was very frustrating.

It wasn't until my agent pursued other opportunities that never materialized that I realized I'd been pigeonholed as a Black family sitcom writer. I wanted to do so much more. I had great sample scripts – your calling card if you're a writer – but we had no luck. I consider this moment in my career, the first time I actively decided on a career pivot. To this day, I'm a big believer in reading the tea leaves of your career, or your life for that matter, and knowing when it's time for a new direction, time to make some tough decisions.

I went back to school, and got an MFA in screenwriting at UCLA. I hadn't been trained as a writer. I got my start doing what I did naturally, from my gut,

64   *Felicia D. Henderson*

from studying people. I wanted to learn more about story structure, theory, and philosophies of writing. I've always been a person who seeks knowledge, yearns to learn, and desires to understand. I wanted to be able to speak the language of film. I wanted to become a better writer and a better communicator about my vision for writing compelling characters, fulfilling stories, and wonderful surprises. This pivot was the key to my transition from sitcom writer to drama writer. While at UCLA, I wrote my first feature-length screenplay. It was a family drama loosely based on my own family. That screenplay won the UCLA screenwriting contest, and became my new calling card, a calling card that eventually led to me being hired to adapt the feature film *Soul Food,* for television on Showtime. I consider *Soul Food* a legacy TV show. And I'm proud of that. It was the first television drama series featuring a Black family to become a multiple-season critical and popular hit. The series proved that there was an audience for Black-themed dramas. Black families didn't have to be confined to half-hour comedies. It brings me so much joy to see more dramas about the Black experience on television now.

I mentor young writers and they often ask what it's like to be a woman in Hollywood. My students ask the same question. Or more specifically, they ask what's it like to be a Black woman. I always steer them away from such questions because I never want young writers, particular writers of color, to focus on those things, quite frankly. This doesn't mean I don't know racism and gender inequality exists. I know it firsthand. But I'm not a victim and I don't want to encourage my students and mentees to behave like victims either. So, I encourage them to focus on their goals. Be Michael Jordan. Keep your eye on the basket, not on the defenders trying to keep you away from the basket. If I focused on how hard the world is for a Black woman, I couldn't also focus on my goals as a Black woman who is a kick-ass writer-producer-director. To be clear, I think it's very important for people of color to be well-represented in every facet of this business. Not just for other people of color to see us and know they, too, can do anything. Our presence normalizes our existence for mainstream folks, too. It's just as important for them to see us navigate the waters of Hollywood, and realize we're capable of swimming in the same waters they're swimming in.

I approach my creative work the same way. When I'm pitching new show ideas and/or writing, my goal is to demonstrate that we are all three-dimensional people. I don't feel a need to combat negative stereotypes. I do have a responsibility to create interesting, complex characters and then to show you why those characters make the decisions they make. Whether I'm creating a supreme court justice or a neighborhood drug dealer, they both deserve to be depicted, and to have their layers pulled back and investigated. Certainly, when I was growing up, I was taught not to share our family's business in the streets. It was wrong to air our dirty laundry in public. But that didn't stick for me, I guess. I once told my sister, "You need therapy." She said, "I'm not telling some stranger my business." It made me think about the way Black characters, specifically Black women, are often treated in the media. Black women characters aren't always allowed to be fully realized. Don't we deserve to be investigated on a creative level as widely and deeply as anybody in mainstream America? I have a brother who spent twenty years of his life as a criminal who was in and out of prison. I believe a character like him deserves to be represented on television and written with an empathetic pen. Doing so doesn't mean I'm glorifying the life he once lived. Hopefully, we will learn how he became who he is, why he's the way he is, and why he thinks the way he does. If that character isn't written in this way, all we'd have is the stereotypical portrayal of such a person. I'm often asked if this kind of writing is a challenge. I don't find it a challenge at all. Because I hope I'm depicting all my characters this way. Whether Black, white, green, or orange, all characters should be complex.

On the academic side of my life, I'm interested in issues of race, class, and gender in the television writers' workspace. I think about the fact that I've been called difficult, and how I wish there were more people in the business like Charles D. Holland. Charles has been my partner-in-crime for many years. I co-created *The Quad* with him. We first met on *Soul Food*. He was one of the writers we hired. We became good friends and comrades. If you're going to the mattresses, he's the kind of friend you want to take with you. We read each other's projects and give each other notes. We pull each other up when the other is down. *The Quad* was the first time we created a show together. He once told me about a phone call he got from someone seeking a reference for me. "I hear she's difficult," the person commented. Charles asked this person if they wanted to be more specific. Among the examples shared were: She never takes no for an answer. She'll fight to the end to get her creative vision on the screen. She'll call up executives directly to fight for something. She expects you to share her work ethic, even if it sometimes means working long hours. Charles' response: "That sounds like every showrunner I've ever worked with who's trying to do something special. It certainly sounds like every male showrunner I've ever worked with."

My point in sharing that story is that we don't have enough Charles Hollands in the world – people who are willing to call out those who ascribe negative language to women for the same professional behavior that is acceptable for men. Too often, men in positions of power with strong opinions are described as visionaries, while women in similar positions are described as difficult, or worse. However, if being "difficult" means caring about the work I do and the people I do it with, I'll take it. Of course, the downside is that there aren't enough people willing to interrogate such comments when they're used to describe women in the workplace. So, women get the reputation of being "difficult," and it affects the number of opportunities that come your way.

I'm very family oriented. When being assigned office space for my writing staff, I'm always angling for an extra office, for instance, because I'm looking to turn that office into a family room. A place where a writer/parent can bring a kid who maybe didn't feel well enough to go to school that day. Or

66   *Felicia D. Henderson*

some place a nursing mother can have her baby's caregiver come so she can nurse or simply see her baby for a few minutes. I'm a natural nurturer. As much as I can, I want to help my writers not feel like they're constantly choosing work over family. When I'm hiring writers, I tell them, "You are always welcome to bring your family here. Because you're going to see my kids." I have nieces and nephews whose lives I'm very involved in. I have a brother who is the primary caregiver for his four children. And they're with me half of every summer. So, the more the merrier.

In my volunteer/non-profit work, I'm dedicated to serving underserved children, kids who might not otherwise go to college at all. For every show I work on, I have new ideas about how to serve this community. When we were producing *The Quad* I thought that if one kid who didn't want to go to college changes his/her/their mind because they watched an episode of a show that took place at a fictional HBCU, all of the hell of making that specific show will have been worth it. And there was plenty of hell. I also started a college internship program on *The Quad*. We shot on the campuses of Morehouse College, Clark Atlanta University, and Spelman College. We had to give students at those schools a chance to learn about the business through the production of a show on their campuses.

I have a different manner of serving this mission, depending on the show I'm staffed on. If I'm working on a show like *Fringe*, I go out and speak to students more. I want kids of color to see that a woman of color is writing a sci-fi series. In case sci-fi is what they're interested in, I want them to see that people who look like them are doing it. And I want them to know that any part of the process of developing, writing, and producing a television show is within their grasp.

As far as my process for creating shows, I enjoy doing research. Even if the subject is one in which I'm well-versed. I have an idea I'm circling around now. A family drama idea. I'm from a very big family, so I know crazy family drama. But I'm doing research and reading about big families and families where a sibling had to raise or take one of another sibling's children. Although I know this role experientially, research is where it starts with me – research and determining from whose point of view I will tell the story. Read as much as you can because there's always something you didn't think of. After I'm done with my research, I start handwriting general ideas, bullet points, etc. I first write ideas long-hand because, for me, the deep, creative thinking still goes from my head to my fingers, to a legal pad. At some point, I'll have enough to know where I want to be, and then I start typing up the document I've been writing down. I always think of bigger, philosophical, or thematic issues first. What is it that I want to say? What are my themes? What my rules of engagement are going to be? Who is my protagonist/main character at his/her/their core? Character is everything. Will my protagonist's POV be the only one I pursue? Usually not, for me. Part of defining a character is knowing what other characters believe about that character. What will the character's frailties be? Every character, big or small, had better have faults that will compromise them in some way. The bottom line, how do I create a character with whom viewers will want to spend 100 episodes? Or in today's world, dominated by streamers, with whom they will want to spend a miniscule 40 episodes? And then, in terms of the mechanics of pitching, I have my fifteen-page document, double-spaced, font size 14 so I can see it. And yes, I have memorized every word of it.

Pitching is only partially about the creative idea you're attempting to sell. It is equally about the performance of that idea for an audience of executives, and to perform I have to be uber-prepared. My pages are my security blanket. I may never physically touch my pitch document in the middle of a pitch, but I have to have it with me. I happen to be very good at verbally pitching my ideas to an audience of studios and buyers I hope will buy my project before the meeting ends. However, I have a complicated relationship with the fact that writers have to be good performers in order to get a chance to do what we do – write. And if you're not a good performer, that can lead to your perfectly amazing project not being bought.

If you come in and look a little too weird, or you're a nervous wreck, or stumble over your words, it could be the difference between a buy or ending a meeting with the words we never like to hear, "Great job. Well told. Let us talk internally and get back to you." Even in the classroom, I have a special responsibility, as a working artist who happens to love teaching, to help my students get ready for the real world, that first job. I am always studying my students, watching for those who don't give me much eye contact, speak quietly, or never speak up at all. At the end of a class meeting, I will point to those quiet students and say, "You, you, and you, come to the next class having created an alter ego who is bold and confident and tell me everything I need to know about this character." I do this because I was a shy person, as well. And even though I'm not so shy anymore, I'm still an introvert who has learned to put on an extroverted version of myself when necessary. If I'm pitching, for example, I have to leave introverted Felicia at the door because it's time to perform. Sometimes, you've got to put on your Sasha Fierce – Beyoncé's alter ego – the part of yourself you conjure up, bring out to play, when you need a bit of extra help. I've seen some really fun characters come out of this exercise, and some great performances. Ultimately it is a confidence-building exercise.

As a woman, when I enter a room for a meeting, I am casing the joint, looking for other women. I am intentional about giving other women a lot of eye contact. It's my way of validating them and letting them know I see them, and I'm happy they're there. Actually, I do the same thing with people of color, especially Black people. Additionally, in a meeting where you're pitching to other women, it can be tricky. Often, because women are accustomed to being slighted, or having our ideas stolen or dismissed, we're looking for the slight, almost waiting for it. It may be natural to make the most eye contact with the most senior person in meetings. But it's necessary to make sure the women in the room feel respected, as well, because women expect

68   Felicia D. Henderson

men to give other men more deference. But they don't so readily accept it from other women. Therefore, if, as a woman, you suddenly find yourself in a position where the women you pitched to weren't as excited by your idea, it just may be attributable to her feeling disregarded by you in that meeting. And of course, sometimes, because all creative endeavors are subjective, she may simply not have responded favorably to your idea.

Also, I tell my students that they need to have social and political intelligence. They need to be smart enough to know that if you do the job you're hired to do well, even if it's your job to get coffee every day, someone will eventually ask, "What is it you want to do?" Because you've impressed them with your ability to commit to the job you were hired to do, they become interested in your future. I've been in situations where the PA is asking if I'd mind looking at his script on his third day on the job! And I'm thinking: You haven't gotten my tea right once, and you're already asking me to read your script? Focus on impressing all those around you with how well you can do your job, and always offer to do more. Always look around and see what additional work you can do. That's how you make yourself indispensable and it's why someone will eventually ask what you're working on and then you can tell them about your script.

This is what it means to "read the room," or being able to walk into a space and understand your place in it. Being present where you are, and less focused on where you want to be. Whether or not you understand the politics of successfully being present in the writers' room will determine if you will be welcomed there. If you're really talented, and you're not working yet, you might have to look within, but don't give up. Great writing always finds its way into the right hands. Skillful writing will always win. And again, I would say to students of color, don't focus on being a writer of color. Focus on being a writer, being the most superior writer, period. You know you have to be better because you're a writer/director/producer of color. Focus on being better. Focus on being the best.

I help facilitate this kind of thinking when I can because it's important for me to give back. My philosophy is that someone should get an opportunity they may not have otherwise gotten, simply because I was there first. I was a sickly kid, so I missed a lot of school. But a teacher took special interest in me, put in the extra effort, and helped me to excel despite my circumstances. If that had never happened, I don't know where I would be. I have a responsibility to be that hope and inspiration for underserved and at-risk kids. And "at-risk" doesn't necessarily mean socio-economically disadvantaged. For example, one of my mentees is a girl from a middle-class family who didn't know she had any value because she suffered so much childhood trauma. She's at-risk, too. To help her see her value, to help her separate herself from the facts of her past, and take ownership of her story. This is the work of my heart. I want to help people see their future reflected in my eyes. I want them to believe that only they are the keeper of their dreams. They are the only ones who have the privilege of determining their future.

GILLIAN HORVATH
I'm a Lot of Things and Only One of Them is a Woman

Figure 12.1 Gillian Horvath
Source: photo by Wendy D. Photography

Gillian graduated from Yale University and started in Los Angeles, working as a writer's assistant and selling spec episodes. Gillian came up on shows as diverse as *Baywatch*, and on some cult favorite sci-fi shows such as *Highlander, MythQuest* and the reboot of *Beauty and the Beast*. Working out of Vancouver, she created and ran *Primeval: New World*. Recently Gillian was the head writer on *Supernatural Academy*.

70   Gillian Horvath

Growing up, it didn't seem unusual to me that people could grow up to work on the other side of the television screen. My dad worked at CBS News and so did my stepmother. My mom was a freelance copy editor. I was surrounded by liberal, female politicians. I worked with my mom on Ruth Messinger's run for City Council in New York City when I was a little kid. I wasn't plagued with doubt as to whether I could become a TV writer. When I see new writers regardless of their age, or new female writers doubting whether it's worth trying because they've heard that it's harder for women to break into TV writing, I realize it was a big advantage that it never occurred to me that it was a problem. It didn't cross my mind until later. And that kept me from self-sabotaging early on. I have made it a bit of a project on Twitter to let people know that yeah, it's hard to break in regardless of your demographics. It's just difficult to break in in general, but it has been done many times. Look at me, Amy Berg, Jane Espenson, Lisa Klink, Sera Gamble. What worked for me was just to be unaware of the barrier and just assume that everything would be fine. It's not that those obstacles aren't there. I'm not suggesting that there is no such thing as sexism or that there isn't a problem with the numbers of women getting hired. But I managed to establish myself with my first two credits before I realized that there was a sexism problem. So, the privilege of being oblivious worked out for me.

Genre and sci-fi is a good place for women. Many of the writers' rooms that I have been in, in sci-fi, tend to be more balanced than the statistics for the industry as a whole. I don't know if it's because the showrunners and executives in sci-fi are more enlightened. Sci-fi writers really think about social issues. Were there better men at the top opening the door for women, or is it because women are really good at writing sci-fi? I'm not sure what the reason behind it is. But when I think back about the rooms I've been in, they're usually smaller than big network procedural rooms. A lower budget show, it's a smaller writing room. I've been in rooms where there were only three writers and one's a woman, so that's 33 percent right there. I've been in rooms with five writers and two women, so that's a 40 percent room. And I hear that the numbers across the industry are more like 15 percent[1], but I've never been in a room with a balance that bad. When I was in a room with twelve people, it had five women in it.

Maybe the underlying secret is that there are a lot more women who love science fiction than people think. You get to work with characters who aren't saddled with the problems of our world in the same way. It's really hard to write police procedurals that are not focused on sexual violence. It's hard to find a cop show or legal show to watch that doesn't have a lot of sexual violence in it, but there's a lot of science fiction shows in which it just doesn't come up as an issue. It's not part of the storyline. And that's a nice space to work in. I have all the respect in the world for the fact that (Gene) Roddenberry actually set out on purpose to create *Star Trek* because he wanted to address social issues. He wasn't allowed to address issues of race in a cop show set in the real world, but once he had *Star Trek*, it was a place where he could use metaphor to address issues that the network

Gillian Horvath 71

didn't want to put into a realistic show. I respect that choice that he made and I think it's exciting when TV does those things, but I think in science fiction, those things happen organically. You don't necessarily have to set out to create a show with the purpose of, "This will be a social commentary," for it to be able to create role models or give people hope for another way of structuring their lives.

People should chase the kind of writing that they like and are good at. I think people should write the kind of shows that they enjoy watching as opposed to approaching a career through the lens of, "I hear there's more open doors in science fiction so I'm going to force myself to try and write science fiction, even though I actually would rather be writing police procedurals." I don't think that's going to work out.

I met Dorothy Fontana through my friendship with David Gerrold back in about 1993. I can't remember a time when I didn't know that D.C. stood for "Dorothy," but it was not something that was necessarily publicly known. She was a real trailblazer, and she was an amazing writer. I had the benefit of just assuming that women were everywhere because they were everywhere in my own life succeeding. *Remington Steele* was one of my first favorite series. I noticed the writers' names on it, and I thought, "Oh, I want to grow up and do that. People write these shows." And the great producer Abby Singer was the producer of *Remington Steele*. So at the end of every episode, it would say "Produced by Abby Singer." Well, Abby Singer was a guy, but I assumed it was a woman. It was "Abby." So, I always assumed that that producer was a woman and that might be someone I would someday meet or work with.

My first internship in LA was between my sophomore and junior years of college with the TV Academy. I spent the summer at Universal Studios and my intern coach was a woman named Charmaine Balian, a development executive at Universal at the time. Although the other executives in her department were men, it was again a situation where if I looked around me, I saw a mix of genders. I was not surrounded by only men. And Charmaine made a point of asking people on the lot to let me follow them around for a day so I could get exposed to lots of aspects of production. So, my first summer in Los Angeles, I met Karen Harris, who was running a show called *Island Sons*. She was supervising the ADR stage that I was visiting. Again, everywhere I turned, there were women doing the job. Everybody was white for sure, including me, so I did notice that. But there did seem to be a good mix of men and women.

A couple of years ago, a Lego ad from the seventies went viral that showed a little girl in pigtails and overalls building with Legos. And I was a little girl in the seventies and I wore overalls and I built with Legos, the same ones that my brother had. But nowadays Legos are gendered, and Legos are for boys and there are special pink Legos for girls. And I'm like, "What happened? We were so close back in 1975 and it just somehow all fell apart." So, I think, without knowing the numbers, I would absolutely believe that there was some kind of moment there in the late eighties, in the early nineties, when I started, when things were sweet. It was a golden age of earning.

72 Gillian Horvath

There was severe profitability for the networks and the studios. When people are comfortable, they can be generous and magnanimous. When there's plenty of money to go around, you can take a chance on things. Do that noblesse oblige thing that some men like to do where they're like, "Oh, let me help out the less fortunate."

I started young. I came out to LA for my internships while I was still in my second year of college. And I caught the tail end of the previous generation of TV, pre-cable TV when Universal Studios and NBC network were high on the hog. Bill Hamm was an executive at Universal, who I knew from when I was interning at Universal. Bill Hamm and I had a good rapport, so we kept in touch and he was always kind of on my side to support me in my goal of becoming a writer. I gave my spec to Bill and he wasn't blown away and my ego took a blow. I just crawled back in my shell saying, "Oh, it's hard to be told it wasn't great." When I did finally come back to it after a year to do another pass and gave it to him again, he then liked it. He passed it on to Tommy Thompson, who worked on *Quantum Leap*, who then suggested me as a freelancer to his bosses. It's a long time ago now that I was selling my very first two scripts, which I sold almost simultaneously: a *Quantum Leap* and a *Beverly Hills 90210*. They both came through almost at the same time. I kind of went from, "maybe someday I'll write a script," to having written two scripts just by coincidence of the timing.

It was when there was still a culture of freelancing. It was genuinely the way that people auditioned writers. They would give freelances to young people, new people who hadn't had a script produced yet, and depending how that went, they might bring you on staff in the future. That was the process. Even at the time, women trying to break in did have this other track which mirrored how D.C. Fontana did it, which was working as an assistant, which gave you access to the material. It was a great learning experience. You get to read all the drafts of all the scripts. And of course, you got to meet all the writers and producers. And then you had people who would read your material and consider you for writing assignments because you had met them in this context of being a really good writer's assistant or producer's assistant. At that time, that really was a way that women were getting in the back door while men were doing it through freelance scripts or through meeting producers over basketball games. A lot of assistants are aspiring writers and a lot of assistants become writers. And that's partly because being a writer's assistant is probably the best film school you could ever go to because you're right there on the ground, seeing how it all gets done. So it makes sense that assistants move up into writing jobs. Hopefully, they're going to be a better writer after a year being an assistant than they were when they came in the door.

I'm actually a big believer that everybody's entire career depends on the first room that they are on staff in, because you will meet terrible showrunners and realize if you trace back their career, it's because their first showrunner was terrible, and they just learned a way of being that's toxic and then they replicate it. Whereas I was lucky, my first boss was really a

Gillian Horvath 73

mensch and really generous and diplomatic and democratic about creativity and had no interest in keeping other people in their place or anything like that. And so that's how I learned to write. How I learned how to be in a writers' room was that we're all here together and we're not stabbing each other in the back for credit or money.

I thought about what the skills are that made shows run smoothly and I realized that a lot of it boils down to a great piece of advice I got from Damian Kindler, who was one of the showrunners on *Sanctuary,* which is: the last thing you want to do as the head writer is write all the scripts. It's technically your job to deliver all the scripts in producible form, that are good and can be filmed (or animated if you are a head writer in animation). And so, you're the backstop. And if the other writers don't turn in good scripts, you have to write all the scripts yourself because it's your job to make sure they're all good. But that's not a successful outcome. Really, the less work you're doing, that means the better you are doing at your job, the more someone else is writing a good script while you go, "Good job, great script," and the more successful you've been at the role of head writer. You really want to empower yourself to be as lazy as possible. Who can I hire? Who's going to do a good job? And then how can I create a scenario in which they are enabled to do the job. And then if they turn in something that doesn't meet what I need, how can I communicate what I need, as opposed to just telling them, "Never mind, I'll do it." You wind up with happy writers who do their best work. You wind up with good scripts and you wind up not burning yourself out at both ends. That's the ideal scenario where you get the other people to do good work and don't have to try and do it all yourself. I think it all translates back to showrunning in the same way. Being the showrunner shouldn't mean that you're picking out every prop or sitting in on every casting session. And if it does mean that, then you're doing too much and you will burn out. That level of micromanaging means something has actually gone wrong somewhere. If you can manage to set it up so that as the showrunner you actually get a good night's sleep because someone else is on set overnight, I would call that successful.

It's a really challenging scenario because writers are not trained to be managers, and showrunning is a lot of managing. You might be disappointed in a draft and need to say, "This didn't come out well enough and you're going to have to do more work on it," but to say it in a way where they feel empowered and not belittled. Those are all skill sets that nobody trained showrunners in. So either it comes naturally to you, and to some people it does, or you're going to mess it up and learn from the mess ups and do better the next time. Or you're going to be bad at it and muddle through and just somehow get it on screen. And that happens too. There's plenty of shows that are not being well run, but the show is still good. That happens all the time. As long as the output is good, there's no mechanism for caring whether a show is well run or not. It only matters if the show is successful.

I'm not saying I'm necessarily a fabulous showrunner. I think I have the good fortune of having had my early jobs be with people who were good at

74   Gillian Horvath

their jobs, so I could see what modeled a healthy way to get a show made and a healthy way to interact with the people you're working with. I know for a fact that there are mistakes I made the first time I ran a show that I didn't make this year. That's where I will toot my own horn to say, "I definitely made mistakes that I learned from and did a better job after."

On *Primeval: New World* we had a very balanced cast and crew and producers. Everywhere you look, there was a 50–50 split of department heads, behind the scenes, male and female, the directors. It was co-showrun by me and Martin Wood. So, right up to the top, balanced gender. And it was when we were wrapping that show up that I looked at it and said, "We got through a whole season, and no character was ever treated a particular way on the basis of their gender." No character ever said, "Oh, you're a girl, this isn't your place to be." And there was never any sexual violence in it. And we thought, "This is great." And we didn't even do it on purpose as some kind of social statement. It's just that our characters were all treated as humans, as opposed to some of them being reduced to body types. And I remain proud of that all these years later. And if we'd kept going on the show, I hope we would have stuck to that choice.

As I've moved through my career, I have seen how prevalent sexual violence was in TV. I started coming up with different ways to write. There can be an alien that's trying to murder everyone. It's not that there can't be any violence or threat. But I've noticed that every female character seems to get threatened with rape. And it's like, "Can't they just all be threatened with getting eaten by a dinosaur?" It's preferable to me as a viewer and I've started to feel like that's preferable to me as a writer as well. There's plenty of people still making the other type of show. We're not going to run out of them anytime soon.

When I was breaking in, I was working with good guys – they were guys, but they always treated me as a writer, not as a woman who happened to write. But the one thing that I have found frustrating and still have to work within the confines of, is that people have certain expectations of what kinds of shows a woman showrunner is expected to bring to market to sell. It's been said explicitly many times that people are interested in meeting me and hearing my pitches because they're looking for shows with female leads. Which is just an assumption that I would only pitch shows with female leads, or that I would only be considered as the showrunner for a show with a female lead, that the reason I would connect with any material is because I'm perceived as a woman and the lead is a woman and that's what the connection would be between me and the material. I can't fight that perception and so I pitch shows with female leads because that's what people are looking for from me. I certainly have stories in my quiver that meet that brief, but I broke into the business writing *Highlander* and *Forever Knight*, two shows with male leads, who I was really good at writing for. And the notion that I could never bring forward a story like those, that if I went into pitch a show about an immortal warrior man and his adventures in his inner life, people wouldn't be excited to hear that pitch from me, they would expect that pitch from a man. And for me, they want me to pitch about a warrior princess. Men have created many great female characters, and right now, there's a good interest in women creating female characters, but I'm still waiting for women to be in the position to create male characters and nobody find it odd or surprising.

When I did a season on *Baywatch,* they brought me in to have a young woman to guide the voices of the new young female characters. But I was far more interested in writing scenes for the guys, and the rest of the writers were far more interested in writing things for the women. People look at you and they decide who you are, and they want to see stories that are about that. I'm a lot of things and only one of them is a woman. I understand when I go into meetings that people are looking to me for a certain type of show with a strong woman in the lead, and right now I guess I'd rather do a great show about young women actually written by women and not someone else's fantasy of how women are, than to keep fighting for the fact that I actually have a great idea for a show about a macho guy and that I should be given that opportunity.

TV also has an advantage because it is team written. So if your show has a cast that has different backgrounds, you can have a writing team with various backgrounds in order to not have somebody crossing a line that makes someone uncomfortable with trying to understand something they're not familiar with, but then you run the risk of a different situation which is in the room winding up with this unintentional sort of cubbyholing where each writer is expected to primarily write for the characters that match their visible identity. That's not a great outcome either.

We have so much power as writers because we can generate material without anyone's permission. We can write scripts. We don't have to wait for someone else to put us in a role. We can just write scripts any time. We are constantly creating new calling cards. We do have a certain amount of control over our own destinies, because if things are looking bleak and the phone isn't ringing, you can type and write your way out.

Note

1 The numbers are always changing, but rarely moving substantially. As of 2022, the WGA's latest study found women to be 44 percent of the writers on series. However, the percentage of women showrunners is substantially less, stuck around 27 percent for close to two decades. The percentage of women showrunners of color, and women writers of color is substantially less, and in the single digits. So too, the number of women directors has remained in the low single digits for decades, though there has been a recent small bump. It remains to be seen whether numbers will continue to increase or stay essentially stagnant.

GLORIA CALDERÓN KELLETT
They Don't Know I'm Superman

Figure 13.1 Gloria Calderón Kellett
Source: photo by Abby Guerra

Gloria Calderón Kellett is an award-winning writer, producer, and actress dedicated to uplifting marginalized voices in the entertainment industry. She has worked on many shows including: *Jane the Virgin* as an actress and *How I Met Your Mother* as a writer and producer. Gloria created and ran the Emmy-nominated revival of *One Day at A Time*, for which she received the American Latino Media Arts Award. Her company GloNation has an overall deal with Amazon where she created and showruns *With Love* and executive produces *The Horror of Dolores Roach*.

DOI: 10.4324/9781003298229-14

I love multi-cam, that's my favorite thing and that's proscenium writing. After college at Loyola here in L.A., I didn't know anyone in Hollywood and wanted to live somewhere else. I loved London, so I went to Goldsmiths' College for graduate school. There I earned a playwriting degree, not for the writing of plays but the analysis of them. I worked at the Royal Court Theatre and won the International Student Playscript Competition, awarded by Alan Ayckbourn. That and my other writing awards really helped me feel like I was on the right path, like I was being seen as a writer. Then when I came back to the US nobody cared about those awards. So, I worked at Houston's in Century City.

But I was trying to put myself out there, any sort of entry-level industry position, just to be close to it and start to understand it a little bit more. A friend of mine was working for Cruise/Wagner and Cameron Crowe needed a second assistant. They wanted a writer because it was a lot of sitting around, waiting for packages to arrive. I was with him during post-production for *Vanilla Sky* and when we wrapped, I worked out of his house. Cameron would leave me a list of things to do, and he didn't care what order it was done in, so I could audition, or I could go to meetings. I could do anything as long as everything on the list got done by the end of the day. At one point he said: "Well, you love plays, and you love short plays. You should write TV. You should write a spec script." I had no idea what a spec script was. I started going to the Paley Center, which at the time was the Museum of Television & Radio, in Beverly Hills and spent hours breaking down television and teaching myself TV. I was raised on multi-cam. Those were the shows that I watched when I was a kid. *Family Ties, The Cosby Show, Growing Pains, Who's the Boss?* Those were the shows of my youth. I find it comforting and nostalgic for one. I also love theater. It's my favorite thing. Theater is my church. The lights come down, and that's the calmest I ever feel. A story is about to unfold before my eyes. It's such a community event. In this time of social media and phones, there's just a lot of separation and isolation. But theater is all about the shared community experience. There are things that you will laugh out loud at with other people where you wouldn't laugh out loud at home by yourself. There's something simple about it and old school and low tech in a way that I feel like we need culturally, or at least I do. All of those things combined just make multi-camera sitcoms feel warm and fuzzy to me. I love the energy of the show night and doing what is, for us, a live play. It's not a laugh track. Those are real people laughing. We want that community back. We want to feel we can sit together and hold hands and watch something and laugh together. I think there's a need for it.

It makes sense to me that people want to come together. We want to laugh together, and we want to feel feelings because we're afraid and divided. What we can do is come together and see this beautiful family on *One Day at a Time* go through their struggles and feel less alone in the world, for

78 Gloria Calderón Kellett

sure. As a showrunner, it's just trying to really earn each of the moments. Mike Royce and I, this is our favorite type of writing because it's also how we live our life. We live, we have children, we have spouses, we have parents. There are real things that we deal with every day, and we find comfort in it. We cry a lot. He and I are both criers, but we're also big laughers. We don't put jokes in because there needs to be a joke on every page. We have jokes where we feel like the joke would organically go, where a character would feel uncomfortable and want to make somebody laugh, or a character would have a unique point of view on the situation that's funny. But it's never "three jokes a page." That's not how we do it.

It's been a lot of hustle for me to get here. It wasn't overnight. I've been heckled when I did stand-up, and I've put on my own plays and hoped people came. But I didn't have a choice. My parents sacrificed so hard for me to be here. I can't for one second sit back and put my feet up and watch TV when I get home. I can't do it. I know what they've done for me. I have a responsibility not only to them but to other people coming after me to make something of this. I just have to. It's not even something I really think about. It stems from the fact that my parents are really nice people. I kind of won the parent lottery. The resilience comes from knowing that there's no bad day I've had that they haven't had a gazillion times worse. Coming to this country with thick accents, not knowing the language, trying to work and hustle and raise a family. There's no comparison.

When I was starting out, I got into a "if I build it, they will come" sort of headspace. I'm just going to put a play on and invite anyone I know. Many of those people at the time were assistants who would tell their bosses to come. And their bosses came, and the rest is sort of history for me. At least twice a week I'll talk to a young writer. I honestly feel like half the time when they get me on the phone, they're like, "OK, Gloria what's the password? Just tell me, I won't tell anyone. Just tell me what the password is." I really feel like they think that's what it is. I say, "It's years of hustling and hard work. How many scripts do you have? One? Yeah, that's not going to do it. What else have you written?" You can't say, "I want to be a doctor," and just take out a knife and say, "Let's do some surgery." Have you been watching a ton of TV shows and teaching yourself the forms of the rhythms and what it sounds like? Are you comedy or drama? Are you multi-cam or single cam? That's all the work you have to do before you try to get an agent.

So much has changed from when I started out. The fact that these conversations about #MeToo, equity and inclusion are happening and that it's encouraging more people to come forward only makes things better. When I was coming through, I really felt like the only way to change it was to become the boss so that at least it wouldn't be that way in my writers' room. I always talk to women and say, "If there's ever anything, please talk to me," and they have, and we've put an end to it. We've had open conversations. It creates a safer environment with which to create. That's what's of interest to me. I had good experiences and bad experiences, mostly good. But there was certainly a lot of misogyny and a lot of things that were considered "acceptable" at the time. And you had to deal with those things or not get the work. I think that young women know that they don't have to put up with crap. We didn't know that and I'm glad things are slowly changing for the better.

I'm actively working to change the industry. I'm involved with the Untitled Latinx Project, an intersectional power movement in arts and entertainment to get the leadership in our industry to reflect the diversity that we see in the country. We hope to see more of this reality reflected in movies and television because when writers and actors are looking to be represented, if it's sixty-year-old white guys who are deciding they're the tastemakers, they say, "I read it, and it didn't really resonate with me." Well, it might not have resonated with you, but it might resonate with a lot of other people. If the leadership can be more inclusive, it means more of these stories will get to be told and more of these people will be represented. It will really change the landscape.

The shift that I have seen is that people really want to buy Latino content or content from people of color. I don't know that that has led to more content being made for us. How many of us will actually get to air? It's better in that there's interest. It's not better because I don't see it reflected on the screen. There's an unfair thing that happens where over the years maybe one Latino show would get picked up. And maybe it wasn't very good because the writing wasn't very good, or some of the actors weren't very good, or it wasn't directed well, things that have nothing to do with it being a Latino thing. But because it was a Latino thing people would say, "Oh, we tried the Latino thing. It doesn't work." No, *that* Latino thing didn't work. You try 55 family shows every year. How many of those work? It's deceiving. And Native actors, Asian American actors, Indian American actors – it's far worse for them than it is for Latinos. There's barely anything.

I really try to commit to a 50–50 room of men to women and people of color. I try to really practice what I preach with my hiring, which is what we did on *One Day at a Time*. I know how hard it is to be the one person that's twenty years younger than everyone, the only female, also the only person of color who is saying, "I don't know that you should make Rosa the maid be the one that wants to have the boob job." It's really rough to do that. You have nobody who has your back. You have a bunch of people who don't have that experience so they will say, "No, that's not a real thing." Whereas it's great to be able to pitch something in the *One Day at a Time* room and half the room says, "Oh my God, me too! Oh, that totally happened to me." And then the other writers are like, "Really?" And I would say, "Had I been with all of you, you would not have let me put that in the script." And you wouldn't have believed that was a real thing. And I have half of this room telling you that it is. So, it's very hard. How I survived before was just excusing myself to go to the bathroom: "Excuse me guys, I'll be right back. I've got to pee again." And then I would just weep my eyes out in there, splash my face a couple of times with some cold water, and go back in.

I decided I was going to be undeniable. Steve Martin had some great quote about like, basically get so good they can't ignore you anymore. That really resonated with me. If I just put my head down and do the work, and keep doing the work, the cream will rise to the top. That's what I'll do, and one day I'll have my own show.

This is where I credit my lovely parents who I think really brainwashed me into believing that being Cuban was my superpower. It was something I really never looked at as a negative. They made me feel as though that was the thing that made me special and cool. I see people be ashamed and kind of hide who they are because that's what they've been told. I never had to. I definitely credit my parents for making me believe that that was awesome. I am very grateful. I felt like I was Clark Kent. They don't know I'm Superman. They're just going to assume that I'm one of them. I'm a human with my glasses, and I'm just a nerdy reporter. But one day I'm going to rip open my shirt, and they're going to see that S.

ILANA PEÑA
Let's, Like, Do Big Things

Figure 14.1 Ilana Peña
Source: photo by Lio Mehiel

Ilana Peña grew up in a Cuban and Jewish family in Miami, graduated from Northwestern, and worked as an assistant on a variety of shows until she landed on *Crazy Ex-Girlfriend*, where she ultimately moved up to staff writer. Immediately after, Ilana created and sold *Diary of a Future President* as one of the first original shows for Disney+. Ilana was subsequently signed to an overall deal with CBS TV Studios. Ilana is continuing to develop television projects at CBS in addition to features for various studios.

DOI: 10.4324/9781003298229-15

82 *Ilana Peña*

I bring my background to my shows in a lot of ways. Sometimes it's specific, like how on *Diary* Gabi drinks Cafecito, Cuban coffee, or the Cuban food they eat. My grandmother has literally emailed me recipes like arroz con pollo that I've passed along to the props department. The theme song for *Diary* is by the brilliant Cuban royalty Emily Estefan, the daughter of Gloria and Emilio Estefan. I couldn't believe I got to work with her. I'm the daughter of somebody who came to this country looking for freedom and opportunities, so it was always instilled in me that I had the agency to dream really big, to try to make a difference, to not take my freedom for granted in any way. The entire concept of the show, of a young Cuban girl who grows up to lead the country, I like to think of it as a love letter to my background.

I recognize that I'm young and that I did get this promotion to showrunner before I thought I'd get it. There was someone I worked with who kept bringing up that I was younger than his daughter. I don't even think he meant it in a condescending way. I think he was more befuddled. We ended up working well together, but there was this initial wariness of like, "Who are you?" I was aware of having to prove myself. If someone came to me and said, "What do you think," I was afraid that I would flail, would not know the answer, would show my age. But there was this gut instinct that kicked in that I was very grateful for. I'd grown up making my own projects and collaborating with people, and this was obviously the big-league times a billion, but it felt like I was making a play with my friends. When I know what I want, I can access that. I think the other part of it is also admitting what I don't know and taking advantage of the brilliance around me in order to learn, to collaborate, to be able to say, "I don't know," and look to find the answer, and not expect that I'm going to know everything out of the gate as a first-time showrunner. I've never felt like my age was a detriment. I never felt like anybody didn't take me or the show seriously. Once I was able to stand in my power, I was able to prove to everybody, "It's okay. I know what I want this to be, and we're not going be flailing in that regard. The stuff that I'm still learning, we can all muddle through together and collaborate." I think it created a really lovely atmosphere.

To me, innocence is so complex and it's so exciting to me. Innocence feels a little more untapped. I remember when I was pitching *Diary of a Future President,* I had a potential producer say, "We love it. We're obsessed with the concept." They were so onboard. And then they said, "But can we make her older? Can we put her in high school?" And I asked why, and they said, "Well, people have a purity issue. Audiences have a purity issue with girls where they can kind of compute being young and wearing Mary Janes and being sort of pure, and then they can compute like *Riverdale*, older and being more of a woman. And then that middle space is a harder sell." And to me, it was a deal-breaker. I want her to be young. I want us to be in that sweet spot and that untapped little amazing nook. Hopefully, she can grow up on the show, but I wanted to start in that kind of tweenage bubble that we were all in once. I love seeing the world through Elena's eyes. There's so much hope there. I think we could all stand to look at the world as our younger selves every so often. And I think that the kids on *Diary* and the sweet spot of this age are complex because of their innocence. Because they're observers of the world, because they're not there yet, because they're taking it in and trying things on, figuring out what works for them and who they want to be. And that discovery, to me, there is infinite complexity in that.

Elena has this very hopeful view of the world. And I think that the show, much like in real life, is showing her that the world is not perfect. You know, your school mascot is sexist, your best friend can turn into somebody who is not your best friend anymore, and change is constantly happening. It's the growth of that, and the realization that the world is malleable and not exactly what you thought it was. And then, for Elena, like the clicking in of, "I can do something about this," whether it's activism or being a better friend or the things she's learning. That to me is so much fun. We approach every episode and think, "OK, what's a lesson Elena can learn that will make her a good leader one day?" And that is just a well of things because we have this character who's a piece of clay that's not totally formed yet. And we're taking her view of the world and her fierce love for her family, her desires, her perfectionist tendencies, and we're trying to turn things on its head. We're thinking about the moments that define you when you think, "Oh, this isn't how I thought it was, and what does that mean for the future?"

Working at *Crazy Ex-Girlfriend* was a dream. That was my fifth job out of college. And to even have the access to know about that job, I had to have been at so many other jobs before then. The access is so important. It's the only thing that separates being an emerging writer from being a writer writer. I've been a PA, an executive producer's assistant, a showrunner's assistant and a writers' assistant. And I was a theater major, so I've acted. I remember my friend and I were giving advice to a hopeful writer, and her advice was, "Find mentors that you can hitch your star to." And I nodded along, but I didn't have that at the time. I had amazing bosses who were lovely, but I didn't really have any mentors who had a vested interest in my voice and my future. And I found that with *Crazy Ex-Girlfriend*. I was already a huge fan of the show, and I'm a huge theater nerd. I love musicals, but on top of that, I was working for these two incredible, fearless women. And I soaked up absolutely everything from Aline and Rachel.

When I started, I was both of their assistants, and even just watching them would have been a masterclass, but I had the added privilege of the two of them really, truly wanting to be mentors. I would bring Aline something on set and she would say, "Come sit, hang out. Let me walk you through why we're shooting it this way." All the writers welcomed my opinion and my voice. They let me believe it mattered, which was huge for me. I remember pitching my first successful joke on my birthday, a joke that made it in the script but did not make it to air, and Aline took out her phone and took a picture of me and tweeted it and was like, "This girl just pitched her first successful joke." In that moment she gave me the agency to keep pitching.

84 Ilana Peña

And by the time I was a writer, I was still obviously a little intimidated, but I knew that I had a net. I knew that they would catch me.

Rachel is somebody who had her own show at a young age as well, and watching her go from acting to writing, to writing a song, to editing, she made me believe I could do this. They're both constant sources of advice and guidance, and when I have questions, they're always there. These women make it a goal to nurture everybody who comes in, which is special.

When I first got to LA, my friend Maddie and I were craving an intimate artistic community. We were hustling as assistants, working these super long days, but we wanted an environment for us and for our friends and our contemporaries to do our own stuff. Where we could take risks and be vulnerable and celebrate each other's work without the pressure of Hollywood. And that's what we've been doing for about five years with See What Sticks. Once a month, in a black box theater, people can put up anything. And we don't curate. Anyone can do it. It just has to be a work in progress. Afterwards we all hang out. It's been such a joy to watch our community grow. We would joke because we were assisting these bosses and these showrunners, and we were observing them and bringing the stuff we were learning to See What Sticks. It was like showrunning. And also, we were providing something for the community that really did feel like a need.

Diary is an origin story. We're seeing all the puzzle pieces that come together to make a great leader. And all of that is happening while I am learning how to be a great leader, and hopefully being a great leader. So, I'm very aware of that parallel. Showrunning is obviously different from being president thankfully, but I do feel a parallel in our journey as I try to be the best leader I can be, by utilizing the lessons I learned, whether from mentors, from See What Sticks, and from my family. I'm constantly going back and into the annals of my brain and thinking about the character in terms of standing in your power. Women are powerful. Everyone else in the world tries to have us believe that we are not worthy in any number of ways, tries to silence that power, step in the way of that power. I remember when I was little, I made a list of all the things I wanted to do. And then I got older, and I lived in the world. And I started thinking things like, "Well, I don't know anyone in Hollywood, so I'll never get anywhere," or "I'm going to be stuck as an assistant forever," or "Does anyone actually care what I have to say? Does anyone give a shit about my voice?"

But there was a moment, or a series of moments, where I realized that my secret weapon was my voice and that it was the thing that made me different. It didn't matter that I didn't have connections. I have no family in the industry. My point of view is the only thing that's mine. With the knowledge of that, I was able to tap back into that 12 year-old self who was like, "Hello, duh! I've been waiting for you. Let's, like, do big things." It's very meta to me that the first show that I made is about that voice and that self, because that is my purest self. I'm obviously aware of, and grateful for the privilege I've had that has allowed me to succeed in this industry, that I was able to use

Ilana Peña 85

my voice, and people listened. I think there's a reckoning happening right now, and I hope that Hollywood listens and gives opportunity to others with stories to tell, whose voices have been left out of the conversation for too long and who have their own 12 year-old selves who are like, "Hey, I'm ready to change the world." Because we're all here and we're all ready. We just need to be given the opportunity.

When I was five, my dad passed away suddenly. He was 37. He had no underlying conditions. He was healthy. His heart just kind of gave out and stopped. And that does something to a person. Growing up with that knowledge. Growing up with one day, your dad's going to drive you to school and the next day you are learning, you will never see him again. I think in the ways that it's affected me positively, if you want to use that word, it's made me not take any day for granted.

But people who know me will tell you that I'm a joy seeker. I very much seek joy, and being able to create something that not only is cathartic for you, but other people can connect with, brings me joy. Comedy is healing. Being able to laugh and look at the world and hold experiences up to kind of a stained-glass window and examine it from all angles, every experience is so nuanced and so rich. I just feel like I'm such an anthropologist of the human experience. I'm so fascinated by the human experience, by our resilience, by our pain, by our hope and joy. And that moment, that my mom told me that my dad passed away, and my extended family was kind of looking at me expectantly, there was so much at play. I was trying to comprehend the magnitude of the loss, but I was also trying to comprehend the expectations of the people around me in the role that I thought that they wanted me to play, that I knew would bring them relief in some way. To be able to see, "Look I'm going to comfort this five-year-old child now, because then that is the role that I will play."

And I used to talk about how that moment was my first performance, and the first time I was thinking from a writing perspective too, the first time I observed what was happening around me and made a choice of how to act. I wrote the script, you know? Then I started a few years later doing theater. I was doing children's theater, and I was eight-years-old, and I played a young girl who loses her dad. And I was sort of, not even that consciously because I was still, again, working it all out, but I was able to hold that experience up to the light, to examine it from all angles, to bring that to this girl and her own experiences. And to a certain extent, that's what I've been doing my whole life, dissecting these moments, exploring them, examining them. And I personally find a lot of catharsis and joy in that dissection. But I also think doing it with other people, having a writers' room, being able to collaborate, having things like See What Sticks, makes that process so much more joyous, and then it's like a twofold, fun thing, right? Because you're talking about human experience, then you get to talk about it with other human beings, and everyone is bringing their own experiences to the table, and you can create something that's universal and hopefully can bring something good to the world.

86 Ilana Peña

In our writers' room, we always try to hold space for how tough it is too, when things are happening in our country, when things are happening in our world. And you can't divorce what's happening from what we're doing. Because you know, we're human beings and we're feeling things deeply. I think our country has so much work to do. And you see so many young people are stepping up, becoming activists, donating their time, their money, using their platform for good, attempting to change the system. I think *Diary* for me, as our country hangs in the balance, I do feel like there are young Elena's out there, whether they're in middle school or college or, you know, looking to AOC (Alexandria Ocasio-Cortez), who are paying attention and using their voice and will make a difference. I am finding hope in writing this character who we are crafting, this leader. And we are crafting her not to be perfect, but to be good, to be truly, inherently good and believe in the good of people. Obviously, again, this is my own tiny, tiny way to plant that seed, hopefully, but I've got to believe. I hope that there are Elena's out there who will lead the way. I am hoping that young girls and boys, and nonbinary kids, and everybody can see a show like mine and see examples of what this country could look like.

The thing that allowed me to succeed was that people believed in my voice. I had the freedom to pitch. I had the freedom to share. They never made me feel too young or too inexperienced to have a point of view. I tried to do the same thing with the assistants on my show, to give them episodes to write, anybody can pitch. Anybody's voice is valuable. This is an opportunity that I want them to get as much out of as possible. And I know it can feel intimidating, but I try to cultivate that environment. And I would say my advice is your voice is the thing only you have. Your point of view is the thing that's the most valuable. If you're in that room, whether you're a young writer or an assistant, it's because we're excited about that point of view in that voice. We're excited about you. So, I want writers who are starting out to feel free to chime in. To not just pitch in the room, but to be proud of who they are. No matter the level or experience, I would tell a writer starting out, hold tight to that voice. To not try to be the Hollywood version of what you think your voice should be. I was feeling this way starting out. I was like, "OK, what is the niche I'm going to fill? Who am I in Hollywood, and what does this industry want me to be?" And I very quickly learned that what the industry needs, not just wants, but literally needs is you. It needs the sort of unfiltered version of yourself. The stories that only you could tell. And I would say, do the things in the room that you like. Pitch the story or the joke that you're excited about. And also make the thing that allows you to be you outside of work too. I was running a workshop. I was being an assistant. I was writing my stuff. I was doing the stuff that made sense for me. Make that short film, do stand-up, start a writers' group, but don't feel like you have to do all of those things necessarily. Do the thing that's you.

ILENE CHAIKEN
You Have to Believe that You Know Best

Figure 15.1 Ilene Chaiken
Source: photo by Ricky Middlesworth

Ilene Chaiken started in development then transitioned to writing features. She broke new ground when she created *The L Word* (Showtime), the first American series focused predominantly on the complex lives of a group of lesbian women. Chaiken was then pursued by the creators of the breakout hit *Empire*, a Shakespearean family drama set in the world of rap recording-industry moguls. Chaiken was the showrunner for the first four seasons, before stepping aside. *Empire*'s enormous ratings, from its very first episode, gave new hope to those working in network TV who were struggling with ever-diminishing audience share. Chaiken held the rights for *The Handmaid's Tale* and worked on its development for television and gave her blessing to the reboot of *The L Word,* on both of which she is credited as executive producer.

DOI: 10.4324/9781003298229-16

88 *Ilene Chaiken*

The L Word just kind of ruined me for anything else. I was doing exactly what I wanted, and I was doing something that wasn't just fun, it was loads of fun, and also felt meaningful. It felt like it changed the conversation, moved the culture in some way, and I just have a very hard time being interested in anything that doesn't. *The L Word* is part of a bigger cultural phenomenon. And the reason that it has meaning isn't because of me, it's because of where the culture is. *The L Word* will always be mine. I love it dearly and I created it and it means everything to me, but when it occurred to me in 2017 that it was finally the right time to reboot the show, I wasn't sure. The actresses who were my partners on the new show had been really keeping the conversation alive. And then there was this moment when I just instinctively knew that it was the right time. Not enough had changed. A long time had gone by, and nothing had taken its place. I had just assumed that there would be many other shows. And there really aren't. There's *Orange Is the New Black*, which is a fabulous show. But really, overall, gay women are not represented on television. A lot of the fans of the show were talking constantly about missing it. The actors who were my partners were missing it and it just seemed like it was a good time. And then there was this little matter of the 2016 election. I couldn't really do the reboot of *The L Word*, but I didn't think I should do it anyway. I proposed they find some new young lesbian who has something to say about the world and who would talk about what's happening now in the same way that we talked about it years ago. And that I would love to have some role in helping to choose that person but it's not going to be my show. It'll be her show. Those characters that I created, it would be a continuation of the story. I'll be like a rabbi.

Similarly, I had been involved with *The Handmaid's Tale* from its early development. Well, it will always be Margaret Atwood's, but I met with Margaret, and I developed my version of it. I spent years getting the rights, wrote the pilot, but when Hulu greenlit it, I was not available. I feel like I'm a spiritual godmother to the project, but I had nothing to do with it from then forward.

I find my projects in different ways. I'm always thinking about stories that I want to tell. Sometimes they're original stories. Sometimes people bring me ideas. Usually, they're my own stories. And it's always just kind of pulling from the ether until something clicks. *The Handmaid's Tale* was back when I was in production on *The L Word*. I was in Vancouver, speaking with (Showtime Entertainment President) Gary Levine, and I guess it must have been Season Three or Four. And we just started having a casual conversation about what I might do after *The L Word* and I just said completely, kind of whimsically, "I think I'd like to adapt *The Handmaid's Tale* if we can get the rights." And he said, "Oh that's a fabulous idea. Let's go." And we went and tried to get the rights, more than ten years ago, and spent a whole year trying

Ilene Chaiken 89

and couldn't get them. But it was just that. It was, "What do I want to talk about? What feels exciting? What feels potent? What feels meaningful?"

Though I appreciate small and more literary, introspective and beautifully rendered storytelling, it's definitely not what I'm drawn to. And I appreciate those shows too. It's not what I write. As a television maker I tend to like things that are big, loud, and juicy. "Delicious" is a word that I use a lot. Meaningful work, and delicious juicy storytelling together, it's the opposite of mutually exclusive. It's not a struggle. It's not a conflict. I find that, absent those underpinnings, nothing is interesting. And at the same time, life is juicy. Just find the story you want to tell. I have to be excited, have to be inspired by the themes that I'm writing about, but also excited by the story that I'm telling. It's not bringing two antithetical things together. They live together. I used to call television "stealth activism." I think I came up with that term when I was trying to woo an actress to a project some years ago. In my experience, the actors that I'm drawn to tend to also want the same thing I do, which is to make meaningful work. To do important, powerful work. And this is going back to before everybody was doing television. It was before all of the biggest stars in the world were not looking at television as a step down. It was at a time when it was still exciting to woo a movie star to television.

Writing for TV is about sifting many different points of view and understanding what's valuable, what you have to address and how to address each kind of thread, because they mean different things. They are coming at you for different reasons. But in terms of pushback, there's always this assumption of, "How do you get those political themes? How do you get those edgy things?" Never ever have I gotten pushback on any of that. I guess I'm lucky because I've gotten almost unequivocal support and enthusiasm. The network, the studio, and the storytellers all have the same goal, which is to make great television and to make it about something and to make it authentic. I think if a show is working, one of the reasons the show's working is because it's about something. It's speaking to the audience. If we were doing something that was purely polemical, it wouldn't be working, and the audience would be saying "no." But not because it's political, because it's not working.

Passion. That's the only other thing that's absolutely critical to me. I'm not interested in working with writers who look at it as a job or who just don't care deeply. I welcome the debate, and I really want to work with people who feel strongly, who are excited about the show, excited to be doing the work, and also really, really care about what it is they want to say and what we're all trying to say. There are so many characters in an ensemble drama and it's very hard sometimes to get everyone in. Sometimes the writers in the room aren't tracking everything and it's ultimately my responsibility to make sure, both for the actors and for the storytelling. So, in my pass, I'm sometimes just delivering on the promise and the responsibility that we have as writers to advance the character drama. As a showrunner, there are all kinds

90   Ilene Chaiken

of ways that I can create space for more writers' voices or help and support and offer mentorship. Sometimes that means stepping aside.

I think as a writer, as an artist, that we're always full of self-doubt. And you kind of have to be. Somewhere in that doubt is where the creative inspiration takes hold. But at a certain point I just simply believe in the story that I want to tell, and I will defend it. You know I think that that certainly is part of being a writer. It's especially part of being a showrunner. You have to believe that you know best. If you don't, you shouldn't be doing this job. Hopefully you can do that without being obnoxious, while still being able to hear from all quarters in a way that enables you to take the very best and make what you're doing better. But ultimately as the showrunner you have to know, you absolutely have to know, no matter how hard somebody is pushing back against you, if you haven't heard something that has changed your mind then you have to be confident that you are the one who knows the right answer.

But it's a process of enlightenment. Portraying rape on screen I think probably is something that I would not ever want to do again. And I think that I did in *The L Word* portray a rape. We spent a great deal of time thinking and considering all of the implications of it. At this point of time, I would say just simply "no." There is simply no way to do it that isn't a violation in some sense. Somebody is going to look at that and take from it the very opposite of what's intended by me as a filmmaker, and I won't be responsible for that.

I dislike formula, but really value conventions. And you learn conventions and you learn to adapt them and to disguise them, but you use them and use them well because that's craft. And so to some extent knowing your craft and knowing it is critical, but ultimately, especially with serialized drama, it's gut. I write a script or read a script or rework a script and it's very hard to articulate exactly what it is that makes me know that this is working. Or this is not working. If I found it, I found the moment. In broadcast television you're dealing with act breaks and they become a part of your craft. You have to know how to land them, or even if you're doing something subversive it still has to work. You have to find those moments.

There's no formula. It's alchemy. Sometimes I know it when I've written it, but then until you've cast it and shot it, you don't really know whether it's happening. And it's not just a character, it's the ensemble, it's the magic that comes when the show comes together. It's true in movies and in television. You just never know until everything has come together whether you've made magic again.

I don't think women have to be difficult, but I think we can be and should be, if that's who we are. There's a hunger for something that makes a difference, that thrills people and enlightens them and says something new, and we are the ones that have something new to say. Push on. Have faith. But also forget that old, dead and dying white male storytelling voice because, really, it is just out of juice. I'm talking to the studios, the networks, the financing companies. "Why isn't it working?" Because it's old and tired. Especially broadcast television, it's not dying if you give the people what they want, if you give them something new that's really exciting. And there's just still so far to go. So many stories that haven't been told and voices that haven't been heard that I do think that we're gonna own this bitch. We got this.

JANINE SHERMAN BARROIS
I'm Going for the American Dream Daily

Figure 16.1 Janine Sherman Barrois
Source: photo by Gloria Mesa Photography

Janine Sherman Barrois started her career as a writer in comedy before transitioning to drama and working her way up the producer ranks on *Third Watch*, eventually executive producing *Criminal Minds* and *ER* for multiple seasons. She was the executive producer and showrunner of *Claws* on TNT and *Self Made: Inspired by the Life of Madam C.J. Walker* on Netflix. She now showruns *The Big Cigar* for Apple and ran *The Kings of Napa*, which she created for OWN. Janine has an overall deal with Warner Bros. through her company, Folding Chair Productions, which she started to amplify diverse creatives.

DOI: 10.4324/9781003298229-17

Janine Sherman Barrois 93

Being a woman in TV is hard as hell. When you're first starting out, it's hard to even get a job and get into a writers' room. But I think, slowly, the boys' club of television is being dismantled by some very fierce women who are coming up. I've been in the business for 20 years, and there's definitely more opportunity now than there was at the beginning of my career. When you're climbing the ladder, it can be difficult navigating the patriarchy of a writers' room, because that's who's controlling it. You need to figure out how to speak up, how to get your points in, how to be yourself and not be a shrinking violet, and how to be aggressive but not offend. Men are dealing with just as many issues while they deal with you. You realize once you're in a writers' room that these guys are working out stuff with their wives or girlfriends or mothers or grandmothers, and you are the embodiment of that. Navigating that dynamic as you are rising through the ranks can be challenging because you don't want to squash your voice because your voice is what makes you who you are. The objective is to find people to collaborate with, to work for, who actually allow you to shine. That is the key for people of color, and for women of any color—to be in rooms where you can be a creative force and *be you*. And that's where it gets hard. Once you rise to the top, it's even harder to just get your stuff on the air. It's hard to get showrunning gigs. I think we're dealing with systems where people are so accustomed to trusting men with the money that we are still having to dismantle the belief that women aren't able to do the job. We're still having to prove that women can be creative beings and not be micromanaged by the people in charge because of their own fear and insecurities.

Right now, there's a lot of television being made, and so you're seeing more writer-producer-showrunners who are women and who are people of color. But the numbers are the numbers, and the majority of creatives getting a hundred million dollars to make shows are white males. That's what it is. It's a corporation. If every episode on average is four million, before you even get into what the marketing budget is, you're entrusting somebody with 50 million dollars for the season. Then you're giving them whatever the marketing budget is and trusting them with that. If the marketing budget is 25 million, you could be giving them 75 million in all. The question becomes, how do we continue to equalize the playing field so that women and people of color are trusted with the money to actually make art? I think we need some people to retire from the business. We need people to make room for the new generation of executives, managers, and people who see the world differently. I tell younger writers that someone they know will get a showrunning job in three years or get it in five years. But most of the people I know are getting it in 20 plus years. It takes longer being a woman. And even longer for women of color.

But it will happen eventually.

I've had to have resilience and stamina in my career. Much like the women in *Claws,* it's being a woman who doesn't count herself out. My resilience comes from my parents and them pushing me to go after whatever I wanted,

94 *Janine Sherman Barrois*

whatever I dreamed of. Both my parents felt like people died so that I could have a path in the world. They believed that if I wanted to be a writer, I should drive out to Hollywood and become a writer. My parents were proponents of the idea that this is part of civil rights and changing America—that you have to have Black kids see themselves as becoming anything they want to become. While a lot of kids that I grew up with were pushed to be lawyers or doctors, or go to business school, my parents were like, "You and your best friend from Howard, get in the car. Drive across the country. Here's some money. Good luck!" I think the confidence that came from knowing I had a support system to help me if I ever fell was huge, because in Hollywood you get rejected constantly, and it can either bury you or build you. For me, it has built me up. I challenged myself to ask, "What great things can happen tomorrow? OK. I got rejected today. Something good is going to happen. What's next?" I keep asking myself those questions and pushing myself. But if I'm being honest, the number of times I've driven down Cahuenga crying, thinking, "I'll never make it in Hollywood. I'm going to be sent home,"—well, let's just say it's a pretty high number.

But there was something in me that just said I have the right to tell stories, and I'm going to find the people and the alliances that let me do it. That's why now, creatively, I am attracted to stories where women, despite all the odds, are going for the American Dream. I feel that's the mirror being held up to me. I'm going for the American Dream daily. With *Claws*, when I read the pilot, I said, "This is for every woman who's been counted out." It didn't matter what color they were. Then, when I was brought in on *Self-Made*, I recognized Madam C.J. Walker as somebody who, in 1910, saw herself as bigger than the station in life she was allotted. She said, "I'm going to be bigger than this. I'm going to be an entrepreneur. I'm going to get a piece of the pie." I think those are the things that interest me. I also find myself inspired by and writing about relationships. Because one of the biggest relationships in my life is marriage, I write a lot about it, focusing on women who are strong, who are dealing with and unpacking complex issues with their partners, still trying to rise above in their careers, and in some sort of way trying to find happiness and peace. Those complexities have always been interesting to me. Even some of the stuff that I'm working on now is still about women who are not being seen, or whose voices are not being heard, but who are going to make you hear them by any means.

It's so funny, a year or two ago, I was yelling at a network about something. The studio was on the phone, and we got pissed off. I was very aggressive because I thought they were being very aggressive, but I was speaking my truth as a creative. I said my piece, got off the phone, and my assistant comes in, and she's bright red. She was like, "You can't say that. You're Black. You sound angry." And I'm like, "I am Black, and I am angry." I mean, I'm allowed to be both of those things. I cannot modulate myself every single day and put on an act for fear of a stereotype. That's their issue. I'm allowed, as an artist and as a person, to be pissed off. My assistant looked at me like, "Well, what if you lose your job?" And I asked, "What if I lose my job? Who cares?" And then she got it. There's a point where you must ask yourself, "Are you actually doing your job? Are they trying to squash your voice?"

When you work with people who try and suppress your voice, don't immediately buy a one-way ticket home. Stay. Tough it out. Call me. DM me. Truly, keep going. Try to find an ally, because there are a lot of allies out here who want you to win. There's no point, if someone doesn't see you or respect your voice, in going to work and having your talent suppressed. If you live in that state of holding it in all the time, that's not healthy either.

Learn to pitch with quality and the quantity will come. I pitch with quantity and quality, because the more you pitch, the more you get it. If you pitch a lot, even if you get rejected, you just keep pitching. You become very valuable because you know how to keep stories going. If, on top of that, you know how to be funny when you're in a drama room, you're like a Mercedes because you know how to find the humor in anything. If you're doing a cop show or a medical show or a family drama, you can punch it up and help with structure. That skill comes from being in comedy, because in comedy, your everyday survival depends on pitching. If you make the transition, like I did, from comedy to drama, you actually don't know how to be silent because you're like, "Oh my God, they're going to fire me today if I don't pitch." So, you just pitch, and you stay up late researching medical ideas and cop ideas, etc. because you know your value depends on being prepared. You also know, as a Black woman, you don't have the luxury of saying nothing. Picking up these skills along the way will make you invaluable. A lot of times I dealt with people who sometimes felt like, "Oh, she's pitching too much. Oh, she always has something to say." But I actually just didn't feel like I was allowed to do anything else because I am a woman, and I am Black. Some people could get away with saying nothing all week in a room, but that's just not the case if you're Black. We don't have that luxury.

I got on *Third Watch* in 2000. I was there for five years, and I was able to write drama and make the paramedics and the cops funny. My scripts immediately popped because I knew how to blend drama and humor together. And I got to be around people who had similar writing styles. While working on *Third Watch*, John Ridley became a mentor to me. He was somebody above me who I looked up to. Charles Murray and Ed Bernero were on the show as well, and they could write drama but knew how to cut it with humor. At the end of the day, if you look at the show's creator, John Wells, and you track all his other projects, whether it be *Shameless*, *ER*, or *West Wing*, you can see the mix of the two mediums.

After I did *Third Watch* for five years—I started as a co-producer and left as a co-executive producer—John and I had a conversation about how to keep me in the fold. There were upper-level slots open on *ER*. And again, that kind of writing, with drama and humor, was what *ER* was known for. I felt very much at home in that type of storytelling. To use *ER* and *Criminal*

96   *Janine Sherman Barrois*

Minds as examples, we did 24 episodes a season. You wrote four or five episodes. You went up to bat getting grilled, getting beat up, getting dissected, being on set with Forest Whitaker and John Leguizamo and Stanley Tucci, and having people be rigorous with your work. You'd go to set and learn to rewrite on the fly. One of my biggest learning experiences happened on *ER*. I was in my office, and Sally Field called me and said, "Come to the set now." I go to the set, and I'm like, "Oh my God, I'm walking towards Sally Field." I'm feeling so cocky. I'm thinking, "Sally Field's about to say that I'm a genius, that she cannot believe the amazing monologue I wrote for her. She can't believe it. This is amazing." When I get to set, everyone is there, and she comes up to me and hands me her sides (scenes for the day printed out) and a pen. Sally says, "I can say this with less." And I squeaked out, "Less?" I remember initially writing those scenes thinking, "This is brilliant!" But I cut a few lines for her, and I hand it back. She then hands me back the pen and says, "More!" I keep cutting. I hand it back. Now I can see people smirking. She hands it back to me, and I'm thinking, "Oh, shit." So, I keep cutting. It comes down to two words. I don't even remember the two words, but it comes down to two words. I had a monologue, she got it to two words. Then she says, "Watch this." I went back to video village (cluster of monitors for key crew) and watched, and she said my whole monologue with her face and two words. You don't get that training unless you're able to continuously write. You learn to go home and stay up all night and do a rewrite and turn it in to the proofer in the morning and edit your pages really quickly. Then those pages are taken to set. However, I know it's getting harder to hone that skill and rigor when it's only 10 episodes, but you have to write everything and learn everything from everyone to kind of finally define who you are. I am grateful for all of it. I think you just have to get yourself dirty in a lot of different waters.

I got lucky getting the opportunity to work in the John Wells camp and to have him as a mentor. Everyone was challenged to be at the top of their game. That was part of the culture and the bar that John Wells sets for his shows. I was on John Wells' shows for nine seasons. Right now, that consistency isn't as common and it's like the wild, wild west. Everyone's developing. Everyone has a pilot. But when I was coming up, nobody did. You didn't do that. You stayed on staff, and your allegiance was to the show you were on. Your summer break was you resting up so you could come back, and you better swing hard for the A-team because they didn't mess around. There was an understanding that you had to learn the craft. While you were there, you kind of buckled down and you learned. Same goes for people that got into the David Kelly camp or into the David Milch camp or the Yvette Lee Bowser or Mara Brock Akil or the Shonda Rhimes camps. There was a real pride that came from getting mentored by them. There still is. People were really committed to the shows they were on. You didn't have any free time because you were in the room all day, and then you had to go home and research, or you were writing all weekend. Saturdays and Sundays are

Janine Sherman Barrois 97

great days to write. But it's important to find your balance. Those are the stretches where you can actually work and write. When my friends were all going out to brunch, I was home writing and working all weekend. That's why I tell people if you don't have it burning in you to be a writer, just don't do it, because it'll be too hard.

The hardest thing about writing is finding your voice and writing from that voice. Then having the wherewithal to rewrite it to make it better. The best work in the business is something that strikes a chord in all of us. We're all challenging ourselves every single day to find work that sparkles. When you try to write what you think the industry wants, it will probably be good. But I think when you write what *you* want and what's in your heart, it'll be great. What you want to do is be rigorous so that you actually have the space for greatness. Greatness takes time and space. It takes you being able to not write what you've seen before. It's about rewriting and knowing that that first draft or even the fifth draft is not good enough. We're all striving for greatness, and it's hard, really hard. I think people are often not aware of how much story the average person has seen throughout their life. We've grown up on stories. We've seen so many stories. When we haven't seen something before, we're like, "Oh my gosh, look at that." It connects, or it makes someone go, "What the hell? I have never seen that, oh my God." You learn as the story unfolds.

I was attracted to *Claws* because of this sense of raw humanity. When I read the pilot, I thought it was brilliant. It sounded like the Tennessee Williams of today. I was moved by it. I loved the idea of collaborating with Eliot Laurence to get the show on the air. I knew that this show was special, that these ladies were special, and that their voices were special. They were people who were perceived as the wallpaper of the world. They're supposed to be the background players, not stars. They're women who are in a strip mall eating, you know, like fried shrimp, who you're not paying attention to every day, but they are the stars of their own movies. They just popped and felt visceral. It's funny. There was no indication of race for the women in *Claws*. A lot of people were fighting in town to play Desna, and they were of all different races. But when Niecy Nash walked out of the room, we were like, "Oh my gosh, she's Desna." And then Carrie Preston became available. We knew she was Polly. We started to fill the cast out, and it just became clear who was going to be who. I think if that show had been all white, it would not have been special. It would've missed a moment. We were very strategic in saying this was about a group of diverse women. They were friends, and they were sisters. They had each other's backs, and they came from all different backgrounds. I think that's why it *sparkled*. We were just so grateful that there was no pushback on our diversity and inclusion. We were able to have these women from all walks of life shine, and again, I think that's what made it a hit. You were like, yes, that's the world. That's it right there. I think inclusion is very important, not just for people watching television, but for history. You look at the Black Lives Matter marches, and you see how

98 Janine Sherman Barrois

around the world, people of all different races came together to support Black lives. That needs to be reflected on TV. To me, when I see things that are not inclusive, it doesn't look right anymore. It looks old and archaic. We need to make the small screen world look like the real world. But I also know we live in a world that doesn't always believe the same thing.

Handing off projects to other women coming up has become really important to me. To get more female showrunners a seat at the table is one of my major goals. I want to continue to help and highlight the women that are already there but still need a shot. I want to continue to cultivate an arsenal of fierce women that rise up and get their own shows and build their own empires. You have to make room for talent to rise.

One of my biggest idols is Ava DuVernay. She is so inspiring. I think she's changed the television game, but she's also changed the way women artists view themselves. I think for so long, we've been striving to just get a job and be validated. Ava has such an entrepreneurial spirit that she's telling women to not wait for permission. Make your own movie now. Just do it. Figure out how to do it independently while working within the system and rising up through it, but don't wait for the system to give us things because the system is messed up. A lot of people are trying to change the system and make it better. But in the meantime, women and people of color need to make art. Whether we shoot a short film on our phone, do a small show on YouTube, or raise a hundred and fifty thousand dollars and shoot a movie in one house—it's vital that women get to make art. I think Ava's inspired so many of us to say, "You know what, I'm just going to do my stuff and tell stories." That "Ava effect" and entrepreneurial drive is something you also see in Lena Waithe, Numa Perrier, and Issa Rae. I think we need to replicate that spirit. For the people who wind up on a CBS show, with all that money you're making with residuals, I say go shoot something. Keep writing. Be true to your voice and be open to your voice changing, developing and growing. We're going to write our way out of this. We have to.

JENNY BICKS

In a Good Room, It's Magic

Figure 17.1 Jenny Bicks
Source: photo by Peter Konerko

Jenny Bicks is an Emmy award-winning writer and producer in both film and TV. She wrote on *Sex and the City* for all six seasons and eventually rose to the rank of executive producer. Bicks was the creator and showrunner for *Leap of Faith, Men in Trees, Welcome to Flatch,* and the showrunner of *The Big C,* and HBO's *Divorce.* In the feature film world, she wrote *Never Been Kissed, What a Girl Wants, Rio 2,* and *The Greatest Showman.*

DOI: 10.4324/9781003298229-18

100 *Jenny Bicks*

I started in sitcoms. The world of sitcoms, back when I started in '93, '94, was all male. I was working until three or four in the morning, and it was a very different ethos. I was the only girl in the room most of the time. And there was this big divide between the actors and the showrunners. Mostly it was fear. I think the showrunners didn't understand actors, didn't want to understand actors, and so if they got called to talk to an actor, it'd be like, "Oh my God, here we go, what's gonna happen?" I think it was a language that they didn't want to talk and couldn't talk. For me it's changed because once you start to do single camera, you're dealing with actors. And then you learn that some of them are bizarre, like writers, and some of them are totally normal, like writers, and you learn to understand what their needs are. You're putting them in a position in front of the camera and that's very vulnerable for them. I think as showrunners we're all being trained better to work with actors and to understand that people need to go home at 7pm as opposed to staying until 4am.

Back then, there had been female showrunners with a male sidekick like, Carsey-Werner, Marta Kauffman and David Crane, Kauffman-Crane, which isn't to take anything away from her [Marta]. We just GENERALLY weren't allowed to be on our own. It was rare to be a female alone doing it, without a person who was a male, who was your partner, helping you not to be "crazy". So when I did *Leap of Faith,* which was 2001, there really weren't women running a show. When I think back on it, there wasn't a mentor I could turn to and say, "How do you go through this, and how do I have to approach it differently as a woman?"

I went to a girls' school from kindergarten through twelfth grade. We weren't told what women couldn't do. There wasn't that sense that the world was going to have an issue with you as a woman. It just didn't exist in our world. That allowed me to be who I needed to be, which was this kind of class clown writer. Nobody told me how to be a certain way, or to shut up, or…anything else. So, I think it's funny if a guy thinks that I can't do a job as well as he can. I don't take it seriously. But it was an adjustment when I came out in the real world. I didn't realize that "Oh… men don't think women are funny?" When I started in sitcoms, they told us, "We had to have a woman in the room, but we don't think women are funny." But women are funny. It was interesting to go into the real world and have showrunners who hired me to be funny, say, "Women aren't funny." I actually had a showrunner say that to me, but also tell me I was funny in the same sentence. His explanation was, "Yeah, but you're not a woman." They had to make peace with it somehow. I encountered that throughout my time in sitcom.

I was interviewed by a famous male showrunner to work on his show and one of the questions he asked was, "So are you going to wear short skirts in the room?" It was a test to see how I would respond, because it was a show about sports and he knew that he wanted a girl who wouldn't have trouble with shit that gets said. I was like, "Yeah, that's what I'm going to do."

Jenny Bicks 101

Something like that. "Of course I will." But whichever the response was going to be, it needed to be self-assured and that, "You didn't throw me by throwing that kind of stuff at me." There was definite a testing ground of, "Are you going to be OK if I make this comment about this girl's tits or something?" and/or "If I say something mean, are you going to cry?" And that's a very interesting question too about vulnerability and how much vulnerability you show as a female showrunner.

And I think there still is this kind of unspoken rule that you should not cry. And if you do, they'll be like, "Here they go. Told you, women can't do it." There's a lot of pressure on us as female showrunners to present this united front that we can't break. And I think over time, the more of us who do it, the more we'll be able to have our different styles. I think a lot about, "Boy, should I act more 'crazy'?... If I acted like an asshole, would things go better for me, or would they go worse?" Because you look at some of these guys and they sometimes do get what they want by acting like babies. They throw a tantrum and then people get scared of them. As a woman, if you did that it probably wouldn't go well unless you were someone like Shonda Rhimes. And I'm not saying Shonda Rhimes throws tantrums–If you've reached the point where you have more power than they do, that's one thing. But I think the guys I see don't have much power and often it works for them. We have to act contrary to what they expect.

I understood how to run a show by coming off of *Sex and the City*. When I got there on *Leap of Faith*, I actually knew more than I thought. But they did pair me. They put me with a producer, a guy, who was in the studio's pocket which I didn't realize. I think I did a good job of running that show. I was young, but I was ready. There was a lot of pressure, they put me on after *Friends*. It was a time when they thought anything they put on after *Friends* had to retain like 97% of the *Friends* audience. And we retained like 87% of the *Friends* audience. So, "You're off the air. You're done." But it was a great experience for me. I had a great cast. But there was a lot of pressure also to make it like *Sex and the City*. Everybody wanted *Sex and the City*. The networks were dying to imitate it. Knowing what I know now, I wouldn't have allowed them to push me as far as they did to make it similar. I still think it was its own thing, but I caved on things that now I wouldn't cave on. And perhaps that's smart, to not immediately go in and fight. But that's a very female thing, I think. Now I've learned if you want to say, hire someone, you've just got to say, "It's going to happen." Guys do it all the time. They say, "No, I got to have my buddy." You've got to push.

You have to trust your gut about things you don't want to give away. You learn that if something really matters to you, you'll know it. And then the rest of it, you have to be collaborative. This is a collaborative medium we're in; it's a business. This is not independent film. It's a mistake to walk in thinking you're so precious that you don't have to take notes from anybody. Listen to them. Because they may be right. And if you are easier to work with, even if your show's on the bubble, they'll be more inclined to want to work with

102   *Jenny Bicks*

you again. I do believe that in some ways biologically, women have a better ability to collaborate and multitask, and say "OK, what's happening over here?" And pay a little more attention emotionally to where people are at. And a lot of what we do is that. It's like being a shrink. We have lots of different jobs as showrunners, but one of them is to be able to know when a person is angry. So you can deal with it versus just ignoring it, because that never works.

In a good room, it's magic. A writers' room generally will become a dysfunctional family where someone will become the mommy, someone's the daddy, someone's the wayward kid. Are you the mean mommy? Are you the supportive shrink? Are you the fun-loving sister? And you have to take it all on. And that's hard, at the end of the day to let go of. It's important to hire people that you respect and trust to do their job well and let them do it. I think at first I was trying to hold on too tight. You can get so involved in the minutia that you're actually not running your show. I tend to be very maternal. I don't have kids, but I tend to be very maternal with my staff. I want people to have lives and make them feel heard. Whoever has the answer, that's great. Let everyone be equal once they're in that room.

And the hard thing is balancing your creative tendencies with being in charge of a widget factory. You're in charge of building something that is hiring three hundred crew. You have to worry if the catering isn't working out. When I watch how hard crews work on location, I really admire them. Maybe something that informs my style more so than being a woman, is my being a New Yorker. You tell me the problem and I'm going to solve it. But if you don't tell me the problem, I can't solve it. And I like to solve problems. And I think that's part of why I like being a showrunner in addition to writing. With writing, your problems don't always get solved that easily. Sometimes you can be like, "Let's lose that swing set. Yay! I saved the studio twenty grand, now they're happy." Things that concretely you can do that make you feel like you achieved something during the day, which feels good.

I'm a tiny blonde. So, I'm also aware that when I walk on set, they're like, "Who's this little kid coming on the set? Why are they in charge?" And I probably should spend more time worrying about how I look, but I'm not going to be that gal. I'm not going to wear the high heels to look taller, but I think I make up for it with my New York. I come in very much, "Hey, I'm here. It's all good, let's solve these problems." So, I think for the most part I've had crews that respect me the same way I respect them. I have had one or two instances of directors of photography who were guys, who maybe don't want to listen to me, who have their own point of view, who are more demeaning towards women then they would be if they were working with a male showrunner. I've encountered some directors, but the directors are smart and they know that you hire them, so they have to be nice. Otherwise, I have found the crews have been great and that it's my job to instill confidence in them. If they don't feel confident with me, that's something I'm not doing right.

Jenny Bicks 103

There are days where I don't want to be a showrunner. I would much rather just write. Because you lose a part of yourself when you stop being able to be creative, in terms of being just purely a writer, that you can't really get when you're running a show. We all got into it because we love writing. We're showrunners at a certain point, but we're writers first.

I love that in my TV work it's all very much about relationships amongst grownups, and then in my film work, I'm starting to get into this weird little made up world– I think maybe because of *Rio*, and the animals in it, which is– it's kind of fun, because you want to use your brain in different ways. That's something really important to me because for me, if I stop developing my own stuff I'm just going to feel a little bereft. I have to have that to stay fresh. I think the mistake is if you don't do that you can become a little too enmeshed in whatever show you're running. And it's important to keep your voice as fresh and real as you can, to feel like you still have your own voice that you want to get out there.

I write about two things: relationships and community. Whether it's about a group of friends, or a small town in Ohio. I feel very strongly about community and what it does for people, and what not having community does for people. I spend a lot of time writing about that and writing about women at various points in their lives. The crux moments in women's lives that make them make certain choices. And for men, I think I do that, too. I'm always going to be interested in relationships as the core of anything. We need each other, so I always am writing about the need to have human interaction. That is my wheelhouse and I do it well. Because that's kind of how I live my life, so I think we end up writing what our life is.

My advice to anyone getting into the business is just keep writing. I do believe that good work wins. If you're a good writer, your work will be seen by someone and you will work. My message to women is, reach out to other women. If you're starting out, find women that you can trust. And I think the one thing that we have over men – we have many things over men – is we're not afraid to reach out and say, "I need to learn some stuff, so let's go. What do I need to do?" It's still a world that is ultimately dominated by men. In the end, it's still a male industry. The people ultimately carrying those purse strings, once you get past the women who might be running an entertainment group, they're men. And that needs to change. The women are getting up there, but they're not there yet.

My advice would also be whatever style you are as a person is the style you will have as a showrunner. You might be the showrunner who's vulnerable. You might be an asshole, that's okay. Whoever you are, that's okay. It's not like the '70s and '80s when women all thought they had to wear the floppy bowtie shirts. There's not one way to be a showrunner. And I think we have to, as women, also advise other women about how to go into this industry and how to get the most out of it, and not tell them to be quiet. I think the best thing we did was stop being quiet.

104 *Jenny Bicks*

There's power in numbers. You realize the more women who are running shows, the more impact we can make. We suddenly have this ability to make change. And what's scared some men the most is we actually say to each other, "Don't hire this person. No, don't hire that guy. Don't work with this person." My sister is an English Professor specializing in Shakespeare. She told me that when women were midwives, they were called "gossips" in the 1500s. And they were outlawed from being in the birthing room at a certain point. They made them witches to keep them out of the room because they were learning too much real information from the woman as she was giving birth. Who the real father was and things like that. They have more information and more power than the men on the outside who aren't in the room. It's generally only women I reach out to ask about a director. Information is power. There are people you can call. And I think more and more that's going to become – we're going to become scarier and scarier as we get more powerful.

Brearley, the girls' school I went to, really did something. I never thought, "Oh my voice doesn't matter, or I should keep my voice down." I thank God for that, because I don't know what I would have done, and I think also a lot is how you're raised. I was raised in a home where it was fine to be who you were. It's not always the case. Let's hope it's changing again for this generation of women. I was told you can be whatever you want to be. So, you know, thank God.

JO MILLER
People Want to Hear an Angry, Menopausal Woman Screaming, So Here I am

Figure 18.1 Jo Miller
Source: courtesy of Jo Miller

Emmy-winning Yale graduate Jo Miller left her Ph.D. studies in Medieval Jewish History to eventually become a TV writer. Jo has written for *The Daily Show with Jon Stewart* and written and produced for *Wilmore* and *The Opposition with Jordan Klepper*. Jo helped conceive of and was the showrunner and head writer of *Full Frontal with Samantha Bee* from 2015 to 2017.

DOI: 10.4324/9781003298229-19

106   Jo Miller

I don't want to run another late-night show. It would just be repeating myself. But I loved every minute of *Full Frontal with Samantha Bee*. I was so fortunate to have my work as therapy during the run-up to Trump and the first year of Trump. I got paid for being immersed in news twenty-four hours a day while everyone else had to process the horror on their own time. That was a gift.

I think that election shifted what viewers craved from late-night comedy. When we started in 2015, people just wanted to watch a British guy sing in a car. Now audiences want to hear an angry, menopausal woman screaming, so here I am. From the very beginning, the voice of the show was angry and pulling no punches, but we were kind of hanging out there alone. After the 2016 election, other shows became a lot more like ours.

I cleared the decks as soon as I got that job. I got rid of the boyfriend, put all my bills on autopay, brought the cat to work. It just becomes twenty-four hours, really. That's the only way for me to do it, since you're following breaking news all the time, and there's so much of it.

Standing up a new political-satire show just as MAGA surged into power was a lot, but the *Full Frontal* staff rose to the occasion every time. They were at their absolute best and funniest when there was a crisis, and they had to turn it around fast. I'm amazed at them. A lot of our writers came to this new and just performed like Olympic athletes. The night Trump won the election, it was a kick in the gut for them like it was for everyone else. But while everyone else was getting drunk and falling apart, they sat down at their desks until two in the morning and wrote the next day's show.

In staffing a show like ours, you have to see if a writer fits the voice of the host and the voice of the show, and if they understand the difference between a comedic essay and a loose collection of one-liners or monologue jokes. Can someone build an argument? Can they craft a term paper out of jokes? The mechanics of the script aren't so important. Those can be taught. You're looking for an original voice. You don't want 10 younger clones of your showrunner—one of me is more than enough. You're trying to put together an orchestra of different instruments. I had four slots to fill when we started and I received 250 packets, which sounds daunting but it's actually not, because the unique voices pop right out. When you read the packets, you'll see 50 people making the same joke. I'm looking for the packets with the joke absolutely nobody else made. That reveals the writer's mind, their perspective, their ways of dealing with the world. And I was so lucky these extraordinary people applied for the job. Some, like Ashley Nicole Black, just happened to get the packet request through a friend of a friend of a friend. Ashley was a veteran of Chicago comedy, with top-notch training. Some people had told her she couldn't succeed in our business, so fuck all y'all. She's an absolute star. I knew it the second I saw a video of her.

People who have worked or interned on shows before have an insider advantage, so to level the playing field for the applicants, I basically sent them a little book on how to write for us, so that they wouldn't have to guess exactly what the task was, or how to format it. That way, we could just see their voices. We got scripts that looked like scripts, and were the right length, and didn't punch down. Satire involves jokes at the expense of the powerful, not the weak. That's something that can be hard for snarky liberals to remember, that it's not funny to sneer at people for being ignorant or unsophisticated. It's not illuminating, and it's not interesting.

When trying to put together a diverse room, we had to go outside the usual channels. There's so much talent out there that our system of gatekeepers isn't really set up to find. I imagine it's getting better, but when I was hiring, the agents just kept sending me men. This is *Full Frontal,* why are you sending me all men? And for people of color, it's even harder to get a foot in the door. So producers who want inclusive rooms turn to Twitter and informal grapevines. For years, Nell Scovell has maintained a list of women comedy writers, which she shared with me, and Tim Carvell and John Oliver were so generous with their recommendations. But as showrunners we need to find more ways to broaden our outreach. We also need to retain and promote writers of color. I've talked to people in WGA who have been the "diversity hire" on like 12 shows without being allowed to advance.

A lot of the best *Daily Show* writers came from a journalism background, not a comedy-club background – which makes sense because you have to be a news junkie. And some of the best potential writers think they can't do comedy. How do we tap into that diverse pool of playwrights and journalists and writers who are sitting there, being funny as fuck and not realizing it? So finding how to reach them and get them to apply is a challenge for showrunners. I didn't apply to *The Daily Show*. It was my dream job from the day it was created. I never missed an episode from 1996, but I never would have applied, because I thought there's no way I'm even in that world of talent. I'm not good enough. Well it turns out I was good enough, and I could have been doing this for my whole career instead of waiting until Steve Bodow invited me to apply in 2009.

If you're writing the show based on your instant reaction to whatever's trending on social media, it'll fall apart. Whatever outrage-of-the-moment is trending usually turns out to be more complicated once you dig into it. If you do the research, you may discover a very complicated story, but not an outrage story. Or maybe it is an outrage story, but for a different reason. You have to go where the research takes you. If that blows up your first hot take, so be it. Your fact-based take will be better.

Sometimes we start with the take, which drives the research. Other times, the research brings us to the take. I remember working on a piece with Larry Wilmore on Trayvon Martin. The argument of that piece had to be just right and true to how Larry felt about it, and so we spent a couple of days talking it through until Larry nailed his take: not "the police are racist" or "the law is racist," but "the benefit of the doubt is racist." That was the insight that the facts led us to.

My sense about comedy writers is that the dry humor is our way of processing the world around us and how we avoid despair.

108   Jo Miller

Rewrite is your last chance to get your take just right. I modeled our process on *The Daily Show*. Between rehearsal and taping Jon Stewart would sit down with the executive producers, and usually two writers who worked on the act for that night. It was mostly Jon going through the script that's projected on the wall and rewriting the whole thing. He knows where he wants it to go. Other writers and EPs were there to throw in a joke when he wanted it. We knew when to shut up, and when to provide the words. What he could do in two hours takes me like three days. There's nobody like him.

Sometimes he would come in in the morning and know his take in the 10am meeting and give it to us. Then rewrite was working out the best, most perfect expression of the take he had at 10am. So, one example of that was a recurring segment I used to work on called "World of Class Warfare." I loved the ones that Jon delivered from a place of strong emotion, and the attack on the poor by the rich was near and dear to his heart. This piece took on conservatives who were claiming that a tax on the super-rich wouldn't raise much revenue and we should tax the bottom 50% of earners instead. We were in rewrite trying to stick the landing and we didn't quite have it. Then Jon grabs a pencil and starts doing math, and he worked out that the $700 billion we'd get from taxing the top 2% equals exactly half the wealth held by the bottom 50% of Americans. We had our ending: "I see the problem here: we need to take ALL of what the bottom 50% have!" Man, I loved going to rewrite. Sitting in that tiny little rewrite basement room is where I learned everything I know about running a show.

There's a difference between attitude and a joke. Attitude is not a joke. Someone once submitted a script to *The Daily Show* with the line: "Jon gives a knowing look." Don't do that. That's not a joke. I still get a hundred packets that have no jokes, from people who watch but don't realize there are crafted jokes in a comedy show. It's not just snark or a sarcastic stance. It's amazing to me that people can't see that. A joke, in the kind of work I do, is the thing that lays bare the truth. It's the most economical way of expressing the truth that I know of. You can fit a seven-page essay into a single joke, and that's all you need to say. And sometimes it's just a funny picture. That's another thing we teach new writers: use the visuals.

On a show like *Full Frontal*, we have twenty-one minutes. It's nothing. So every pass on a script involves paring it down to its absolute essentials on a sentence-level, a word-level, sometimes on a syllable-level. If you need exposition, make it brief and make it funny.

At *The Daily Show*, the interns would gather in the writers' room at the end of their stint to chat with the writing staff. They'd be sitting on the couch and we'd go down the line asking, "Who are you? What do you want to do? How can we help you?" And the guys would all be like, "I'm Jason. I'm going to be a writer." "I'm the other Jason. I'm going to be a writer." And we get to the women and they're like, "I'm Dana. Maybe someday I'd like to write, but I'm not good enough." It broke my heart. Somewhere between the unearned confidence of the men and the unjustified self-censorship of the women will be the truth. None of you are good enough, but you will be if you practice. Women do silence themselves. When you look at a group of writers on stage at an awards show, and it's a bunch of tuxes and beards, you don't see yourself there. If there are only a few women in the room they tend to get talked over, or just not heard. I had the benefit of being older, and that's very freeing. Speaking up, fighting for your ideas, or pushing back on a take you think is wrong gets much easier when you're older. When you're over 40 it's easier to say, "That tax story sounds like bullshit to me." Being liked is less important than being heard. And Jon was always great because if somebody was getting talked over, Jon would be the one to make eye contact with them and say, "Wait, I want to hear that." He was wonderful about that.

Back in the day, being branded a "difficult woman" was the kiss of death. My comedy mentor was called "difficult" by people who didn't like taking direction from women. She's brilliant and had a strong creative vision and insisted upon it. That invited punishment if you were a woman. Meanwhile a man could exhibit truly bad behavior and it was considered a sign of their genius. Don't hire people who are going to be disrespectful of their creative colleagues. You can't have that. Sam and I resolved not to hire people who were toxic.

My ultimate responsibility to the network was quality control, and quality control means saying no to ideas that aren't good enough for the show. Which means saying no a lot, all the time. As a woman in charge, I felt I had to get buy-in for my decisions, whereas a man in the same position would be able to say, "That's the decision."

The millennials are more used to diverse spaces and more comfortable with women being their bosses. Young white men are changing, and it's great. I think a lot of problems will fade away when my generation and the boomers finally step the fuck aside and let the younger people have the reins.

I feel like a person who straddles two different eras in television. *The Daily Show* was created by two women, but in my time it had a pretty traditional, male-centered ethos. Every time someone leaves, you go to the steakhouse. *Full Frontal* was part of a new era. The writers' room was dominated by women and the men were fine with it – our guys were pitching stories about period pants. Everything was done online, where it doesn't matter if your voice is loud or quiet. There was no paper, no meetings, and we covered topics of interest to high school and college students. Generation Z were our most well-informed and devoted fans. For some reason, they got what we were trying to do better than any of the media or the adults. There's a new and better era underway, birthed by the older one. Without Larry Wilmore, you wouldn't have Issa Rae. Without Jon, you wouldn't have the *Samantha Bee* room. And we're not going back. It's all going to be better.

But the networks need to change in the same way the rooms are changing. They are still overwhelmingly white and male. Having a few women in positions of power doesn't necessarily help younger women that much, as

110 *Jo Miller*

we saw in the #MeToo movement when some of them failed to get rid of predatory staffers. When male institutions only allow room for one woman at the table, they set women against each other. I call it *Highlander* syndrome: "There can be only one." If a woman succeeds in a man's world on men's terms and kicks the ladder down behind her, that's no help to younger women. In television there are still women directors who are completely disrespected by the crew with no one at the producer level speaking up for them. Young women need to be careful of women my age because some of us are not their allies. Some of us are. Carrie Fisher would go to bat using her position on behalf of less powerful, more vulnerable women. She was amazing, and we all need to be Carrie Fisher. The next generation of twenty and thirty-somethings have a stronger concept of sisterhood, and they help each other and have other's backs. That's a better dynamic. They're not Highlanders any more.

JULIE PLEC
I Moved Here with No Experience and No Skills

Figure 19.1 Julie Plec
Source: photo by Ricky Middlesworth

Julie Plec is a creator, showrunner, executive producer and director, who is responsible for over 400 episodes of television, including the complete *Vampire Diaries* universe (*The Vampire Diaries, The Originals*, and *Legacies*), which spanned 13 years on the air. Julie is co-creator and co-showrunner of the Peacock series *Vampire Academy*, and executive producer of the HBO Max series *Girls on the Bus*, about women journalists covering the Hillary Clinton presidential campaign. In addition, she served as executive producer and director on *Roswell, New Mexico*, executive producer of the NBC series *The Endgame*, and creator and executive producer of the limited series *Containment*. Julie is a graduate of Northwestern.

DOI: 10.4324/9781003298229-20

112 *Julie Plec*

My dream was to make it in Hollywood. And it was sort of a shallow, superficial, teenage dream. It's the same kind of dream that makes a pretty blonde girl from Iowa get on the bus with her headshot. I was fascinated by all things Hollywood, the entertainment industry, movies, television, gossip magazines, teen stars, music, John Hughes movies, Entertainment Weekly. Anything pop culture, I just fed off that and wanted to be a part of it.

I moved here with no experience and no skills. Midwesterners have an extremely strong work ethic, without as much attitude as you might get from other sides. Whether you want to call it an immigrant culture or just like a heartland culture, we actually work and we keep working. We understand the whole concept of paying dues. My first job was as a second assistant, and I took it for like zero dollars. My job was to do whatever the first assistant told me to do. And he was this lovely guy named Aaron who was the least organized human being I've ever met in my life, so he was the only one who knew his own system, and he had stacks of papers scattered all over the office. And neither of us had computers, so I spent a lot of time just sitting there wondering what I'm supposed to be doing, and then hoping to not get yelled at.

Then I got an opportunity to work for Wes Craven – what I call my first real job. That's when I understood that I had a skill that could be useful in Hollywood. I learned there was an actual career called Development Executive. That was reading scripts and breaking them down in terms of development language. It was being able to say, "Here's what works, here's what doesn't, and here's what I'd suggest." After that I thought, "Well great, now I've found my way. I know what I'm gonna do for the rest of my life."

Nothing was more clear to me than that I could never be a writer because I took a playwriting class in college and almost failed, and I thought I was terrible. I spent one year as a film major and felt like I hadn't learned anything. I didn't think I could be a director because my brain didn't see things in three dimensions. Still can't, by the way, having directed. And writing was something that I actually did a lot of growing up. I would win the "Young Author" contests. I was always doing it, but to me that wasn't real. The one thing that was real, which was me having to write a play for my stupid, damn playwriting class, was so hard and so bad. And I'm like, "OK, well here it is, proof that this is not for you."

Then what happened is I spent so many years working with other writers and helping them, that I thought my skill was at helping other writers find their way. And so, if I can't put the words on the page, then at least I can help them get there. It wasn't like I thought I have this voice that must be heard. I thought, "I have ideas and opinions." And my voice would come. It was born out of the crockpot of the voices of every other writer that I had worked with over the years. Because early on I was just trying to be their voice for them. My way of creating was to funnel my

Julie Plec   113

ideas through other people as a storyteller. And that's actually what it takes to be a showrunner. Some would argue that's not true. But in terms of the way I do my job and the way I run my shows, I think you need to be able to have a voice as a showrunner, and the voice should be your own. But working your way up in television, you need to have a voice that can mimic. You need to be able to dial into someone else's rhythms and meter, and the way they put their words together, and their tone. It's sitting in a room and talking about ideas and looking at what works and what doesn't, which are development skills. It's developing an inherent understanding of structure and how a story works, which I never studied. I learned by doing. It was the same thing with directing and producing. I directed a few things and they turned out really well. And I produce every day.

I had all these skills growing up. I was bossy. I had them all to a fault. I was extremely opinionated, loved to take control of things, and loved to be the planner. I had huge ideas, and anytime there was something that came up, I wanted to be part of the planning committee. I wanted to execute it, and I wanted to be part of what the theme was and what the decorations would be and make it cool. What would make it different than anything else? I was a big idea girl always. And I wanted to be in charge. I liked being in charge because I felt like, "I know how to do this, so let me be in charge." When I would write papers, to sort of cover the fact that I hadn't really done the work, I would always approach it from as much of the creative point of view as I could so that the razzle dazzle would impress the teachers, which it inevitably did.

It surprises me that I didn't have the confidence earlier that I would do this, because it was all right there. It took me into my late 20s to 30s to rea-lize this, but it makes perfect sense. I read everything. I read trash, mysteries, Harlequins, Danielle Steel, Stephen King, *Sweet Valley High*. Everything. And I would read every young adult romance and, you know, those series that they made for teenage girls. I would read every *Nancy Drew*, and every Trixie Belden, every *Boxcar Children*. From the minute I learned how to read I was constantly reading. My friends used to make fun of me because I'd go over to hang out after school, and I'd sit in the corner and read while they were hanging out. And they'd be like, "Seriously?" You know, I'd be in class reading – trying to finish my book instead of paying attention in class. I was also a soap opera junkie – a secret soap opera junkie because I wasn't sup-posed to be watching them. The summer we got a VCR, which I think I was in sixth grade, I probably watched three to four hours of soaps a day, all summer long. So, I was taking in storytelling by osmosis. I was reading everything I could get my hands on, I was watching daily serialized soap operas, and then watching TV and seeing movies, and then reading about the business. And so, that outlier thing, the belief that, if you just consume yourself with enough – you might actually get good at something. The term

114   *Julie Plec*

"showrunner" didn't exist on my radar or make any sense to me until I was thirty. Even then, I didn't understand what they did, how it worked.

But I've run three shows at once, which nobody thought I could do. It made me mad, so I insisted that I could. Then I had to put my money where my mouth was and actually be successful at it. I can't say that's the way I'd like to work for the rest of my life, but it wasn't even that it was so busy. I suffered more, and I had more pain and despair in Season One of *The Vampire Diaries* doing one thing than I did doing three. What happens when you do three is that you have to delegate so much. For a quality of life, it's actually better to do it this way than it is to just do the one. But you're not as deeply embedded in the creative as you want to be. So, you kind of feel always one step removed, which is less painful, but it's less joyful too.

What I started to understand about showrunning is that when I asked other people how they did it, nobody had the same answer. New writers would come in and I'd say, "How did they break story on that other show?" and they'd say, "Oh, well they broke the act outs first and then filled everything in." Or I'd have friends that would go to the John Wells showrunner program, and I'd say, "Well, what do they say?" And this person would say, "Well, they say to build from the tentpole story beats." And then I talked to my friend Greg Berlanti, who's having the ride of his life, and I'd say, "What do you do?" And he would say, "I start with the emotional beats, and I target where I think I want them to land, and then I go from there."

So, nobody could tell me the science. I think the first step to being a good showrunner is the minute you understand that it is not a science. It is an art with science in it. It's not an art completely, because it does need the math, it needs management, and all those things. And that there is no right way to do it. The right way to do it is you make a good show, and it's on budget and it's on schedule, and people don't hate your guts. But you won't find many shows that have all four of those simultaneously. I've heard horror stories about highly successful shows, and the parade of assholes that live within it.

So rarely does that all exist at once. I remember calling my friend Damon Lindelof, who was someone I had known when we were both babies together – Hollywood babies, not like infants, and he was a couple years into *Lost*, and I said, "I need a person in the room that can break good story and keep the story on track. I'm dying, I don't have that person." And he said, "You're that person, you're supposed to be that person, you are the one who is supposed to be in that room." And he goes, "If I had a dollar for every person, myself included, that called up and said, I need that person – " That's the hardest job, so that's the one that we flee from the most. We try to stay out of that chair and out of that room because coming up with a story from scratch is fucking impossible. Yet, that's where it all begins. That's where the early choices are made and where you really should be.

KRISTA VERNOFF
The Key to Longevity in This Town is Knowing Yourself Really Well

Figure 20.1 Krista Vernoff
Source: photo by Brooke Blanchard

Krista Vernoff is a screenwriter, producer, and director who is a writer and showrunner for *Grey's Anatomy* and its spinoff, *Station 19*. She was also a writer and co-producer of *Charmed*, and a writer and executive producer for the Showtime series *Shameless*. Other writing credits include *Private Practice*, *Law & Order*, and *Wonderfalls*. Krista created and showran *Rebel*, inspired by the life of Erin Brockovich.

DOI: 10.4324/9781003298229-21

I was a writer from a very young age. I didn't understand that it was a gift. I thought that everyone could write as a baseline and that math and science were hard. The things that were hard for me, I thought, were the things of value. And I think that that's what a lot of women grow up with, not being taught that what they do is valuable. A lot of artists grow up not understanding that what they do is a gift and what they do is valuable. So, I didn't go to school for writing because I did it quite naturally. And I didn't understand that it was a gift. I went to school, ironically, for acting because it was so much harder for me.

I grew up in the company of artists, so I never really thought about being anything but some kind of artist. But acting made me feel insecure and neurotic, and writing just felt kind of easy. Finally, my senior year of college, I took a playwriting course, and the writing and then the producing of the play brought me so much joy and so much of what we call "flow," that feeling of being in the right place at the right time, of being enough. I had the feeling that I wanted to change career paths and really be a writer, but I was discouraged by everyone who loves me. They all thought that I was just afraid to try to be an actor, which is another thing I think happens in our culture, that women particularly are taught not to listen to their gut.

So I listened to other peoples' guts, and I pursued a career as an actor while writing on the side. And I often joke I'm the only person ever in history who was pressured by her family and friends to not quit acting. But I took a screenwriting class at The New School in New York, and then I moved to Portland, Oregon, and I worked in theater as an actor, and I was practicing writing TV shows by day. And after I had spent a year in Portland supporting myself as an actor in theater, I felt like I had proven something to myself. I had proven that I wasn't afraid of acting and that I was able to make my living doing it and that I didn't want to. I really wanted to write and I was in my late twenties by that point. I packed up all my head shots, put them in storage, and packed up my car, and I moved to LA. And I had some theater friends who had friends who were working in the industry who were willing to read my writing. I got my first job within a few weeks of having my first agent, and I have been so lucky to never stop working. It's such a rare thing to never stop working in this town. It's such a touch and go town for so many people. You get a job, then you're unemployed. And I've been really, really lucky. I have talent and an intense work ethic, but luck and white privilege had a lot to do with it.

I grew up poor. We lived on welfare when I was a child. My dad was a drug dealing songwriter who rarely paid his child support. I didn't come from what you would call a pedigree. And here's the silver lining in that: I was raised by hippie artists. The alcoholism and the violence, the drug addiction, none of that is what I would call a silver lining, but here's what I took from my upbringing: I didn't believe that money was essential to happiness. And I wasn't raised to play by the rules. I was raised to ignore the fact that there are rules. The chaos of my childhood led me to trust my gut over what everyone else has been taught to do: buy a starter house, make a pros and cons list, find a ladder you're going to try to climb, or what you're going to leverage, who you're going to try to impress. I wasn't taught those things. I was literally raised to make decisions with tarot cards. So, many times, I've walked away from a larger paycheck and a bigger sense of job security for the job that made me happier. The year I was a staff writer, I was offered twenty-two episodes of a hit show called *Profiler*, which was about serial killers. And I was offered thirteen episodes of an upstart show on Fox that was called *Time of Your Life*, which was a spinoff of *Party of Five*. It was about Jennifer Love Hewitt wanting to be a singer and moving to New York and waiting tables, which is a thing I had done. And I am so empathetic, so sensitive that I knew I would never sleep again if I wrote about serial killers. I felt as a woman and as a feminist, even in my twenties, that I would hate myself for engaging in the glorification of a serial killer story. So, it was an easy choice to take half the money for the job that felt like a job I would be happy doing, but it led to my agents screaming at me so virulently that I had to fire them. I came from an abusive childhood. I don't need to be screamed at in my adulthood. That's not going to work for me. I don't play by the rules of this town and never really have. And I think that that has served me. And I think that that's really due to both the chaos and the values of my childhood.

Never having stopped working and trusting my gut, those things are connected because I took the jobs that would give me joy, even though they would give me less money and less job security. And as a result, I was better at them. And I got hired by the people I worked with or got recommended for the next job and the next job and the next job. And what I see in this town is that people who prioritize money and prestige over joy and artistic connection get burned out. They end up being not good at the jobs that they take, and they have gaps in their career. They're doing the thing that our culture, our capitalist culture, has taught them to do. And it's not working for them because they're miserable and therefore not good at those jobs.

You have to ask yourself, "Is this job worth it? Is it worth it for me to write about serial killers in exchange for money? Or would I rather wait tables?" That was the question for me. Because I couldn't do it. I would never have slept again. And I have friends who are women, and they're feminists, and they love that stuff. They love serial killer stuff. They're fascinated by the underbelly of crime. And they would argue it's not anti-feminist, and that works for them. They thrive and they work in those rooms and they do well. You have to know yourself and you have to ask the question, "What is the cost to my soul?" Four years into my writing career, I had been writing on *Charmed* for three seasons and my dad had died suddenly during that time. I was only 30. They wanted to renew my contract, and I had just been through this unbelievably traumatic death. And the culture on that show was breaking my spirit because I had been hired to write a feminist-sister-witch-lift-up-the-matriarchy show. But then the network started chasing the male demographic. So, now the question every week from the network executive

118 *Krista Vernoff*

was, "How do we get the girls naked this week?" And I pitched a demon stripper story to try to meet that network demand. I came in pitching fairies and left pitching stripper demons.

The job I had taken that was totally aligned with my being had become anathema to my being. And so, I said "No." I didn't want to do it anymore. I was broken by it, and my dad had died. And they valued me highly because I had been good at the job, and they came to me and offered me double my salary, which was unheard of. Usually you go up somewhere between three and 10 percent a year in television. This was life-changing money, and I was definitely conflicted. So I went to Venice beach, where I grew up, and it was on the one year anniversary of my dad's death. And my dad was a tarot card reader. And I'm sitting in a restaurant on the boardwalk staring out at the ocean – and a roaming tarot card reader approaches me and asks if I want a reading. I took it as a sign. I asked this one question, "Do I go back to *Charmed* because it's so much money?" The answer was, "No, your soul will die." And I was like, "Great. Done. Sold." At my core, that's how much of a hippie I am. It's how I was raised.

And in my life, sometimes, I move really far away from that and I favor logic and practicality. And sometimes, I return to it. Mostly, I have returned to it in those moments when my soul, my body, my gut is telling me one thing and society and culture are telling me another. So, my gut was saying, "No, you can't do *Charmed* anymore. You have to go write something else." And my agents and all of our culture was like, "Are you out of your mind? This is a fortune." But I turned down the job and within a year of leaving *Charmed*, I was at *Grey's Anatomy*, which really changed the course of my life and my career. It doesn't have to be tarot cards. But the point of this tarot card story is that I sought support to trust my gut when I couldn't find that support anywhere in Hollywood. I turned down the money, and as a result I didn't become bitter and shitty at my job. More than once in Hollywood, they have tried to buy my soul, and I've said no. And the people I know who were raised with different parents, like, "you take the money, and you build" parents, some of them suffered and had less career longevity because they took the money instead of the work that was going to feed them artistically and emotionally and spiritually.

It's not about right or wrong. It's not about good or bad. It's about who you are and what your needs are as an artist and as a human being. So, that's the other thing. If your need as a human is for financial stability, and financial stability is the thing that makes you happy above all else, then maybe you just take the job that pays the most money, because the joy that you're getting is from financial stability. I really feel like the key to longevity in this town is knowing yourself really well. It's why this town probably has a higher per capita population of therapists than any other town, because we need to know ourselves in order to survive and thrive in a town that is a very strange convergence of business and money and art.

For me, activism and art has always been intermingled. The idea of separating the two, I wouldn't be able to do it. When I was eight years old and people would ask what I wanted to be when I grew up, I would say, "I want to be a movie star so that I can go on Johnny Carson and tell people there shouldn't be war." So, having a voice in the world, that is what I came in wanting.

LINDA YVETTE CHÁVEZ
Me, Fully and Without Fear

Figure 21.1 Linda Yvette Chávez
Source: photo courtesy of Linda Yvette Chávez

Linda Yvette Chávez co-created and ran *Gentefied* for Netflix, is the writer of Searchlight Pictures' acclaimed feature *Flamin' Hot* for Hulu, and co-signer of the open letter to Hollywood calling for systemic change in the industry under the hashtag #EndLatinXclusion. Linda graduated from Stanford and USC.

I grew up in LA County in a city called Norwalk, about 20 minutes south of downtown LA. My family and parents are from Mexico. They both immigrated to East LA, met there and then branched out. I grew up in a low-income, working class family, and just always loved to write, but I definitely was the one who was always practical. My parents were telling me, "Oh, you're going to be a writer one day, mija." And I was the little kid who was

Linda Yvette Chávez   121

like, "Hmm, this is why we're broke, I'm going to go be a lawyer. That's real cute that you guys think I'm going to be a writer, but no." So, I worked really hard to go to college to become a lawyer. I said lawyer because I was always really great at the humanities and didn't love math, so I was like, "What else are you supposed to do? Be a lawyer," I thought. So I always was striving towards that.

Being a child of immigrants is another part of my narrative that's really important to me as a person and to my work. I was always striving to reach that American dream more for them than anything else, to prove that what they worked hard for was worth it.

So, I worked really hard, and I got into Stanford. I was the first of my family to go away for college. My sister had gone to USC, but she stayed local. I had major culture shock when I got to Stanford because it was predominantly white. Anyone who looked like me was either cleaning the bathrooms or was working in the library. So that first year was really hard for me. I struggled a lot. But in the fall of the next year, I took a course called Social Protest Drama with Harry Elam, one of the only Black professors in the School of Theater. We read a lot of playwrights, books, and watched a lot of movies. He introduced me to Luis Valdez, Spike Lee, Amiri Baraka, and August Wilson, among others.

One of the plays that highly influenced my life path was by Cherríe Moraga, who is a queer Chicana playwright and who was a big part of the Chicano movement. She wrote a play called *Giving Up the Ghost*, and it was the first time I'd read a play that I saw my community in. I saw characters that reminded me of my parents and my cousins, and even though it was set in the Central Valley and had to do with farm workers, it was the first time I found my community in a text in that way. And it was kind of a lightbulb moment for me where I was like, "Oh, I can write about my community? No one ever told me that." Because everything I grew up reading was Eurocentric and white, and maybe there was a sprinkle of things here and there, but the majority of stuff, if it was not white or Eurocentric, was high class. It was just not the Mexican American experience that I had had. And then I found out that she was a professor and our artist in residence there. I ended up taking all of her classes for the next three years. Reading Cherríe Moraga made me realize, "Oh, I could be something else, I don't have to feel so lost or alone." I think I found my voice through her that early on because her classes were very healing and cathartic. It was very much about processing our experiences with our families, our traumas. Some of those students were children of immigrants or queer or just had different identities that were kind of all on the margins of things, and I had identified with being on the margins. And so that really set the stage for the artist that I then became, which was all of my work was fueled by social protest. I learned what art can do, how it can create, how it can heal a community, and how it can create a call to action and change minds and even change policy and all these things. So I ended up majoring in Comparative Studies

122 *Linda Yvette Chávez*

in Race and Ethnicity, and my focus was in literature and the arts in communities of color. I studied what art meant to our people, to Latino communities, Black communities, Asian American communities, and what does it mean to use art as resistance and as healing? And that became the foundation of the artist that I am. I ended up going to grad school at USC for my MFA, which was another culture clash, because I went from the womb of Cherríe's classes and art as healing, to this world of art is about money and art is about what sells. And I was like, "I just came from being revolutionized over here at Stanford with these professors, and now you're telling me I've got to put all that stuff away and just worry about making money?" It just didn't compute for me.

I'm grateful for what I learned there and the mentors I had, but after that, I ended up doing everything from directing, to working on documentaries, to working in lifestyle, and to starting a digital company led by one of my friends called Comediva. But by the end of it I started to feel like though we worked with a lot of women of color, the content was very mainstream and for white audiences. And I started to feel like I had lost that foundation of what I was going after, what my intentions were after college with my art. And I kind of had a come to Jesus moment where I left the company. I wanted to go back and really focus on telling stories from my community and remembering where I came from and what I wanted to do.

The first thing I did out the gate was revise a feature that I had written in grad school that was about by my grandmother, my mother and my tías, and it was script that I had a professor and a few people tell me, "Oh, you shouldn't write that because they're all talking in Spanish and it's about old women, they're all immigrants." Basically, "It won't sell." I've had a couple of great mentors, but there was definitely a couple where we butted heads a lot. There was a layer to the way that it was spoken about, like, "OK, I'm not supposed to tell the story," and those reasons were obviously misogynistic and racist and xenophobic. But I came back to that script and I sent it out to programs. The first program I heard back from was Sundance, and I got a rejection. I don't know what it was about that rejection. After years of trying to find ways to tell Latinx stories wherever I could and getting the door shut in my face repeatedly, that one rejection made me go, "I'm done, I'm done with this industry, I'm out." So I went on a journey of letting go of writing in this industry and my hopes and dreams with it. I kept saying, "I'm going to be a travel blogger. Screw this. I'm going to go and travel the world." I went through a whole thing, letting it go. And then a few months later I got into the Film Independent Screenwriting Lab. They called me and I didn't pick up because I knew they were going to tell me I had gotten it, and I had already made the decision to leave the industry. So, I made a deal with God and with my grandmother – who had already passed, speaking to her spirit – the script revolves around her, and I said, "If you all want to make this happen, you have to make it happen because I'm tired." So, I went through the process of the Lab, and fell back in love with writing. And then at the end, the

Linda Yvette Chávez 123

Director of Project Involve asked if I would be interested in a digital project with this young guy, Latino, Chicano, who needed someone who can help develop and write it. I was trying to get away from digital, but I needed money, so I asked, "Is it paid?" And he said, "Yeah." And that's when I met Marvin Lemus, who is my co-creator, and we wrote the digital series for *Gentefied* at that point. My grandmother came through for me.

I always talk about writing from a place of love, and the reason why you need to have creators of color or female creators, or showrunners is because the person who can relate to it the most is going to write it from a place of love. I say that with the caveat that we can write a multitude of characters, but I think when you come from a community that's been historically misrepresented with a specific stereotype about them, it's really hard for other folks to break free of that because they can sometimes write from a place of unconscious fear or bias even if they're unaware of it. I try to look for the nuance of who my characters are and why they are the way they are. For example, with Erik in *Gentefied*, the perception of men like that is that they're scary, that they're up to no good and are bad people regardless. And I grew up with those men, so for me it's like, no, that's my primo Gabriel, that's my brother Alex. I got to see sides of them that the world didn't get to see. I got to see them crying with their moms. I got to see them give me a hug and tell me they love me. I got to see them be broken by something that happened to them when they were a kid, and that's why they ended up in gangs. I also grew up with media stereotypes. So, I have to catch myself, and ask, "OK, who is Erik?" Erik is a guy who actually is very brilliant and wishes he had the ability to have what his girlfriend Lidia has. His brain works differently, and maybe the institutions that kept him down are the reasons why he can't – they're like two sides of the same coin. If things had been different for him, he probably would have ended up at Stanford, but it wasn't, it was his conditions and the institutions that kept him back. For me, the whole social protest thing is trying to change the narrative of how my community's represented in media. I'm always thinking of that when I'm creating my characters.

As writers, we grow up reading all these books and going to class and we start to make assumptions about what writing is supposed to sound like or look like, or the way the voices are supposed to sound so often, and a lot of green writers are recreating what they've read. There's like so many different versions of how my family and community talk. Early on I was trying to write like the authors I read, but I think there was a natural voice to how I would write, and I was blessed to have teachers bring that out in me. What Cherríe did for me was she really allowed me to bring my culture and my cultural voice into my work. But I think I was still holding on a little bit to the parameters of how you're supposed to write, and it wasn't until maybe eight years ago that I fully broke free.

I owned my voice and then owned who I was as an artist and walked into every room saying, "What you paid for is what you get, what you see is what

124 *Linda Yvette Chávez*

you get, and if you don't like it, you're not for me." And that was a reality. I actually came to this when I had that come to Jesus moment and left the industry. I said to myself, "If I'm going to come back into this it's going to be as me, fully and without fear," because I already went through what it felt like to let go of my dreams. I knew I can say no to this at any time, I'd be okay. I started to write, and I didn't give a fuck. The voices were fully everything that I feel I've seen or felt or am, and I did not hold that back at all. And I think it was true of the way that I present myself as an artist in rooms – as, "This is who I am. I'm going to give you all of me and I don't give a fuck if you don't like it." The journey has been about fully harnessing not only my voice as a writer, but myself as an artist. Because a lot of us have this fear around things like when is the next paycheck going to come? What if I do the wrong thing? What if this person doesn't want to work with me anymore? What if I write the wrong way? What if I don't give them what they want? I came back into the industry very fearless about my work and my voice, because I knew that I'd be okay if the industry spit me back out.

So often we're so stuck in this industry feeling that fear as writers and as creators of, "Who's going to make my dream and keep my dream going for me?" And, "Let me compromise who I am as an artist and let me compromise my work in order to keep the dream going because other people have power and I don't. So, I have to do what they tell me to do." Obviously you have to. Like, don't go yelling at people and stuff. To own the work and say, "OK, I hear your note, but in my gut I feel strongly this is what the story needs to be." But then on the flip side, to also be able to say, "I feel my resistance to this note, but what's best for this story is to not create from a place of fear in terms of ego, but to create from a place of love and what's best for the work." But really it's about not living in fear and following your gut and your instincts and staying true to who you are. There's something to that that brought me all that I have right now. So yeah, I am very happy I chose this path. When I went back into it, I definitely said, "Linda, you've always been too scared to fully go into your writing to the extent that you know you can, and this is your last shot. You get to do this one more time, if you do it, then you have to do it all the way, give it everything you have and if still nothing happens, then you have permission to quit." So that's what I did. I gave it everything in a way I had never given it before. And the reality is I ended up having everything I ever wanted.

What's interesting is that I started out my career wanting to be a writer/ director, and then I had a bad experience on my first short film with a male first AD who made me feel terrible, and by the end of it, it left me feeling like maybe directing isn't for me. I was still fragile at that time. My sense of self-worth around my work was so low that I just let it get to me. I directed a few things after that, but then I thought, "I don't think it's for me." But I've done a lot of work on myself over the years, and I think after Season One, what was interesting is I spent a lot of time on set with the DP and the directors at the monitors giving a lot of feedback, and I realized, "Yes, I can do this." And I think one of the things that really brought it home for me was Marvin, my

Linda Yvette Chávez 125

co-creator, really encouraging me. He said he could see it from day one on set, like, "Oh shit, this one's a director." At that point, we had only written together, and so when he saw me producing and then on set, he was like, "That's when I realized that you're a director, you see things very differently than other folks." And I think I was still working on my confidence at the end of the first season, but what was interesting was having a lot of crew members asking me to direct the next season. I even had our DP at the time take me aside on the last day, and he handed me a bottle of wine from the camera department and was like, "We love you; I just really want you to know that you are the heart of the series, and I really hope that you're going to direct next season."

It was those moments that made me realize, "OK, why am I holding myself back then?" It's one of those things where you have a certain Mount Everest in your life, and for me directing was that mountain. It was writing, and directing is the other mountain that I still had to conquer. I think that's where support like that and support groups are so vital when you're in this industry. You need folks telling you that you can do it. Especially as women, I feel like we just tend to shy away. Especially when you're Latina, because you're taught to be small and to serve others. It's how I grew up in terms of my extended family – you're supposed to serve, you're supposed to take care of your husband, you're supposed to take care of your children, to build a home and always sacrifice for everyone else. You're not supposed to ever center yourself because that's selfish, and all the things that women in general are told have that extra cultural layer for me. We're taught to say, "No, not me." You need a bunch of that support to be like, "Why not get your ass in there?"

Being from a working-class family, not having the money, worrying about my family along the way, that's the kind of stuff that's stopped me from getting to this point for a while. It's only forward from here. Glamour Magazine put out this article – "22 Latinas Changing the Game for Representation on TV." They had me at the top of the list. And I was like, "Why? Look at all these other amazing people on this list. Put them at the top!" Look at these other folks." Some of my best friends were like, "Linda, you did it. This was your goal. Your dream was to change the representation of Latinos in media." My life has been wrapped up in wanting to change the way that we are seen. And there's still a lot of work to do, but I think there was a moment to be able to take in the fact that the show that I created, the people that it reached, the messages that we received from fans, the thing that we set out to do was done. I feel like I accomplished what I set out to accomplish, and I'm so grateful that I didn't give up.

LISA HANAWALT
A Little Room to Play

Figure 22.1 Lisa Hanawalt
Source: photo by Kim Newmoney

Lisa is the creator of *Tuca & Bertie*, an adult animated series on Adult Swim and HBO Max. She's the production designer/producer of the Netflix series, *BoJack Horseman*. She has written and illustrated four books and co-hosts a podcast called Baby Geniuses.

My mother came from Argentina. She immigrated from there, and my ancestors immigrated from the Ukraine to Argentina. They actually meant to get on a boat to New York, but they were late. So, they took the next boat out of Genoa in Italy and landed in Buenos Aires. We're white Jewish Argentinians. My dad's just a nice man from Michigan. My parents are microbiologists, so that's had an influence on me, their interest in science and art. And the education I got certainly guided my career and they've always been very supportive. I enjoy traveling. I like being somewhere

DOI: 10.4324/9781003298229-23

different, but I don't like the process of traveling because, you know, my ancestors were on that boat, but I don't know if that ancestral trauma is real or not. I always joke about it. I'm like, "Yeah, I don't like to be on trains or boats or whatever, because it just feels like I'm fleeing for my life. I'm on edge." That's probably just how I am, who knows? It could just be my gut biome.

It was definitely interesting when I first started working in animation because I was a cartoonist. I was used to kind of going it alone. I would do illustration projects. I'd work on my own books. Then my friend Raphael sold the show, *BoJack Horseman*, which I designed, and so I moved to LA to art direct it. I really didn't know what I was doing at all, but I got this amazing opportunity just because I had designed the original concept art and because Raphael is a good friend of mine. So, it was sort of the classic story of knowing someone and just going along with an idea and saying yes to things. And then when I showed up at this animation studio, it was very bro-ey. Although I was mostly supported, there were little microaggressions that happen when suddenly, you're a female boss and men have to listen to what you say. Sometimes they don't want to. Sometimes a man would say something, and I would think, "That was so stupid and sexist." Sometimes I wouldn't respond, and then I just know this person's an idiot. And in other cases, I would gently correct them or make a joke or something to kind of diffuse what they just said and show them that, "OK, I'm smart. And I know what you just said was really stupid and demeaning to me, so I'm going to make a joke about it to let you know that I'm still in charge here and then move on." Because at the end of the day, I just want to show up, do my work, and then go home. I think I have it better than a lot of women in the industry have, meaning that a lot of mediocre men have been promoted, and I think the timing has been good for me, just kind of luck of the draw. A serendipity thing.

Growing up with an older brother and being a tomboy has helped me navigate the world. A lot of my upbringing was kind of just going along with what boys said. So, I thought, "Oh, I'm a cool girl. I'll laugh at your jokes. Like I can get the joke, I can hang." I definitely had that when I was in high school and I didn't want to be perceived as a bitch or a nag or, you know, any of the negative stereotypes about women. And as I've gotten older, I feel less worried about being perceived as a bitch. I actually think it's fine. Like I am a bitch sometimes. It's all right. But like a benevolent bitch where if you make a sexist comment, I can say something to address it and then we can move on because at the end of the day, I don't think you're necessarily a bad person if you slip up and say something stupid. But I've also had things happen at work where a guy said something where it is actually an issue. And I address it immediately. There's something wrong with this person and he's hurting people. And I've had situations where a guy is ignorant and doesn't need to be fired, but he needs to know that that was silly.

I'm glad I had the experience of working on *BoJack* first because I made so many mistakes. Sometimes I was asking for too much from people and I

128   *Lisa Hanawalt*

didn't know how to let things go. It's hard when you're expecting people to draw in your style and execute your vision. I slowly realized that if the end result reaches seventy-five percent of your expectations, that's really good. You can't be one hundred percent all the time or you're going to run people ragged, and you need to be a little bit loose and understand people are bringing their own skills to the table. And their work is going to look different from how you'd imagined, and sometimes that's a good thing. I like when people are bringing their own stuff to the table and we're all just kind of mixing together and yes, I'm the one in charge, but I'm just steering the ship and I need everyone else to make decisions as well and to contribute creatively.

I learned so much about how to communicate with people and how, if you're upset with someone, you shouldn't just write an email. You need to go talk to them face-to-face or get on the phone with them to hear the tone of voice and to reason one-to-one. You can't just fire off an email with that kind of emotion. So, by the time I was stepping up and running *Tuca*, every step of the way has felt terrifying and like I wasn't prepared, but I think at that point I knew how to talk to people and get good work out of them and collaborate. I want people to have a good time, even though it's work and work sucks and it can be draining. I still think at the end of the day, we're making a very silly show and it's entertainment. And so, we should kind of have fun making it. And I hope that that energy comes across in the show, too. That the writers and the artists had a little bit of room to play. I think that that's really important.

I'm the reason this thing exists. So, I'm the one who has to sort of gently guide it back on track a lot of the time. But that also means that when things go wrong, it's my fault. I wasn't clear in this part of the script. I wasn't clear about what this character's motivation was. For example, my supervising director from Season Two, Aaron Long, would say, "Actually we've already had three montages this season of someone cleaning an apartment." Then, I'm like, "Oh yeah, we don't need this. Let's just get rid of the entire intro and throw out these two pages that we worked so hard on." I love that – when we've worked really hard on something and then it just doesn't work, and we just have to throw it away. There's something very freeing about that. And I like when people on my team pointed out something that's just not working. I feel like, "Yes, I need you to tell me that." It's not always easy. Sometimes I really liked that one joke. I want to hang on to it. And then maybe find a way to make it work or slide it in somewhere else. But being flexible while I'm steering has been an important thing for me.

I feel like I'm a soft, empathetic person, but I also think that's a strength. And I think when I started, I heard so many stories about showrunners having these reigns of terror and keeping people working late, keeping the writers until 10pm. And I kind of still feel sometimes, "Am I not working hard enough? Am I not asking enough of people? Am I taking too much on myself?" Even in my writers' room, I didn't want to be on Zoom for more than two or three hours at most. I just feel like it's too draining. It's not

Lisa Hanawalt 129

getting the best work out of people. So, we had really short writers' room sessions. And I still don't want people working late on a Friday. I think it's important for people to live their lives and spend time with their families. And I can't work continuously for that long every day. I need to go off and do my hobbies. I play piano. I roller skate. I horseback ride. It's like I'm a kid at summer camp. But especially during the pandemic, it's about keeping me sane. So, I think that stuff's important. I think it's working. Our stuff that's coming out has been really high quality. I don't think I need to be a terror or make people feel bad or work even harder than they already work. Because it's already super hard work making a show. Writing a script is hard work, revising the animation is incredibly hard work for animators and story boarders. I just don't want it to be torturous.

I think a lot about the best way to tell stories. *Tuca and Bertie* is a place for me to tell stories about things that have happened to me or happened to friends of mine, or just things that are on my mind. I like to hide real stories from my life by changing all the details and, you know, it's represented by birds and not people obviously, but it feels very personal to me. It's a place to explore things that I'm interested in, too. I'll read a book and I'll be thinking about something and then I'll want to make an episode about that. And I'll bring that to the writers' room, and we'll talk about it and the writers will bring their own stories into it, and it'll change how I perceived the season would go. And I have a loose idea of what I want to do each season, but then there's big gaps and we fill them in and the whole thing evolves. I just love stories. I love telling stories. I love jokes. It just feels like a nice big bucket for me to throw all that stuff into. And it's on a bigger platform than I'm used to. You know, that's always been what my books were, just me throwing all my ideas into one place, and now I'm doing it in the form of a TV show, which is cool.

It can be embarrassing sometimes because the show is so collaborative that I have to bring all my stupid ideas to the team, and I have to say them out loud and I always find it mortifying. Because not only are they deeply personal, but sometimes they're half-baked and that's just part of the process. There's something very embarrassing about making all these people work on this thing that's my own fantasy that I'm fulfilling in a way. I feel embarrassed a lot of the time. I think that's one of my strongest emotions and I think it's about wanting to be considerate of other people and not wanting to take up space. But then at the same time making a show, there I am, I'm taking up so much space. Like you have to be kind of really into sniffing your own farts to want to make a TV show. So those two contradictory parts of me are pushing and pulling, the megalomaniac and the shy sweetie, I guess, are at odds. They keep each other in check, I suppose. Kind of like *Tuca and Bertie*.

The show is coming from my own feelings about living my life. It's not a show about women for women, it's a show for everybody. It has my imprint on it, and my experience going through life has been feeling sometimes

130 *Lisa Hanawalt*

vulnerable. I'm afraid of being hurt by someone. Sometimes I have been hurt. So, it's just that wariness of being a woman, which is not universal to women, but to me, it's a strong force in my life, of just wanting to live my life, just wanting to do my own thing and sometimes being thwarted or derailed slightly by bad actors or by forces outside of my control. I think that's a very human feeling.

My characters are fictional, and they're also meant to feel real and flawed. So, they don't have to do the right thing. And in fact, if they did behave correctly at all times, that would be boring to watch. We don't like to watch perfect characters. I like to watch characters make mistakes, so mine often do. And I think sometimes it's upsetting to people. I remember the first season we had arguments in the writers' room about Bertie and whether she was a bad person for fantasizing about a different man outside of her relationship. That of course is something that happens. So, I don't know if it's necessarily good or bad, but it is what it is. We have a limited range of experiences as humans to plunder our stories. But maybe by telling it with animated birds, feels different.

When our show was looking for a new home, it felt so strange to have it cut off. I had run a production so smoothly and people really seem to like it. It got good reviews. But it was totally out of my control. It felt like – whenever I make comparisons it sounds overly dramatic – but it felt a little like a natural disaster. Nature doesn't care about your plans. I was in this limbo period where I didn't know what was going to happen next and whether I'd be able to work in this industry again. Part of me felt like, "All right, well, I had my one shot and now I failed somehow," even though I don't think I failed personally. I got really sick. I got pneumonia for a few months that just wouldn't go away. My body was literally sick, but it felt like a very strong rejection of me as an artist. I want to please people; I want people to like the things I make. I want to make a drawing and I want everyone to want to put it up on the fridge. It's like a very childlike desire for being cherished, which I think is very human, but also definitely childish.

But if I'm in this industry, it's because I seek external validation to some degree. But I did a lot of other stuff. I worked on comics for a while. I continued to work on *BoJack*. My producers made this deal to move the show and it wasn't clear if it was going happen or not. I always wonder if I'm going to get another season. It's hard to feel any stability in this industry. It feels like you could be really lauded one second and then forgotten the next. And so, I'm trying not to take that for granted or forget it.

There's days working on this show where it just feels like we're in mud up to our necks and I don't know what the answer is, and I don't know what the episode's about, and I don't know what I'm trying to say. And it feels like I'm in a fog. And I don't know why that happens, but then inevitably, I sleep on it and the next day I'm like, "Oh OK, here's what I'm trying to do." And you know, the time to do that is factored into the production. I always somehow pull it together by the deadline. It feels very bipolar, the creative process, not

Lisa Hanawalt   131

to throw that word around lightly. I have moments where I'm like, "I'm a genius!" and I feel manic and I'm doing a million things and getting so much work done. And then I have days where I can barely do anything at all.

And that's always how it's been for me. It's never been different. I try not to beat myself up about it. You read all these things that are like, "Well, I wake up at 8am every day and I have my coffee and then I write for four hours," and I'm like, "That's never going to be my life." And I feel a little bit of shame about that, but I'm doing pretty well considering how crappy and haphazard my process is, so maybe there's nothing too terribly wrong with it. We'll see.

There has to be a little bit of discipline. When a script is due, I have to write that script whether or not I feel like it. I can't just wait for the muse to strike. I really have to suffer through it. I think weathering discomfort is a very important part of being a professional artist. But that said, sometimes you're feeling it and sometimes you're just not.

If I never struggled, maybe I wouldn't have much to make work about. My characters are always having some inner demons or inner battles. Maybe I need to experience that a little bit in order to write it properly or represent it visually. But I don't know if I believe that you need to suffer to make good art. I'm still kind of in the middle of figuring that out. I think if I'm a little bit uncomfortable making work, it means I'm solving a problem. So, there might be a day where I don't know the solution to the puzzle, and it feels really bad, and I feel stupid, and I feel ill- equipped to have this job as puzzle solver. But then that's what puzzles are, that you don't really know how to solve them. And then the next day you look at them, you know, you turn it 90 degrees and suddenly you see the answer that wasn't so clear that day earlier, and that's always a good lesson. And maybe it makes for more interesting work. I'm not always going for the easiest answer. Whenever I'm making work, I'm really just trying to kind of connect and communicate with other people. I'm showing them all my gloopy, gloppy insides and feelings, and hoping it connects with their own and they feel better about their own.

It's funny because I was talking about being flexible and listening to other people, but I really don't like the feeling of compromising on my own values, which is, I think it is a little egotistical, but is also important. There are times where I've had to be rigid and be like, "You know what? I slept on this, and I really believe it's important. And so, if you don't like it, then fuck you." Like, I have to be listened to, I have to feel like I'm maintaining my integrity, my own beliefs as an artist or else what's the use of any of this?

LIZ MERIWETHER
People Feeling Safe is, as a Showrunner, Your Responsibility

Figure 23.1 Liz Meriwether
Source: photo by Birdie Thompson

Liz Meriwether, playwright turned screenwriter, had her first success with the 2011 Romcom *No Strings Attached,* starring Ashton Kutcher and Natalie Portman. From there, she became the creator, writer, producer, and director for the hit television show *New Girl,* which received several Emmy and Golden Globe awards. She was known for being part of the Fempire, which included writers such as Diablo Cody, Dana Fox, and Lorene Scafaria. Meriwether has gone on to executive produce or showrun *Bless This Mess* and *Single Parents* for ABC, and the Hulu limited series drama *The Dropout* about Elizabeth Holmes and Theranos.

There was a time during *New Girl,* after the third season, where I was really struggling. The show was just so hard to do, and I was feeling really overwhelmed. I wasn't doing a great job of running the show. I was sleeping at

DOI: 10.4324/9781003298229-24

the office, and I was trying to do everything myself. It's a hard job, especially running a network show. It was 24 episodes a season, and we were shooting and editing and writing at the same time. I found myself just retreating to my office and the editing room and kind of not wanting to deal with things. I was young when the show first aired, 28 or 29.

Dana Walden, who was overseeing the show, really supported me. To have a woman in a position of power who's in the room with you is an important symbol. It does something. It's an indescribable thing. After the third season, Dana pulled me into her office and had a pretty frank conversation with me about leadership. She said she wanted me to really step up because I would sometimes go to table reads in my pajamas because I'd slept in the office that night. She said that I needed to start wearing clothes to table reads and looking people in the eye and saying hi to them when they walk in, basically growing up and being a leader. That conversation with Dana was really important. Between the third and fourth seasons, I did this listening tour of everybody in the crew. I talked to the cast and the writers about ways I could do a better job. In the fourth season, I stepped up and reorganized running the show. That conversation was a really important turning point because I think some people would have fired me, but Dana decided to give me a chance and just talk to me. That was a really important moment.

I had no experience on a staff before *New Girl* aired. I'd been a playwright, and I'd written a movie, and then I wrote a pilot. I really didn't understand writers' rooms or television. It was all kind of learning on my feet. It's strange when the show was a hit, and there was just a lot of focus on it, and then a lot of people telling me, the first couple of seasons, "Don't change anything. Just keep doing what you're doing." So, I didn't really learn until later when we weren't doing as well. Then I was like, okay, let's look at the process. Because it's a job that is not about writing, but it's a job about managing people, a lot of people, especially on the network level. I didn't know how to do that. And Dana does know how to do that. That conversation that I had with her was kind of like a wake-up call where she was like, "Hey, you're not a little kid in a room writing a pilot. You're the leader of hundreds of people, and you have to start acting like that." It was good to hear.

My experience was with playwriting, and playwriting is collaborative, but there's a lot fewer people that you're dealing with, and there's a kind of reverence for the playwright, as there should be. But television is completely different. I think you have to give up some of that. It's not giving up the artistry, but it's also acknowledging that it's a very hard, grinding job for a lot of people. In order to get your best work, you have to figure out a way that they're having a great experience too. That was something that hadn't really occurred to me. It's just not about one quote-unquote genius coming up with the great ideas.

I also started going to therapy, somewhere in the middle of *New Girl*, because it really did sort of shake my whole world upside down. This is

134 *Liz Meriwether*

awful, very LA, but I remember something that my therapist said which is, "People do their best work when they feel safe." I think that has just always stuck with me. I think in the first couple of years of *New Girl*, my focus was just really about, how do we make the best show possible? And the best show was whatever I thought it was. I think learning about how we create an environment where everyone can do great work became a shift in focus for me, and I think that ultimately allowed our show to keep going. Because I think everyone would have burned out pretty quickly. I think people feeling safe is, as a showrunner, your responsibility. You are the person to create the working environment. And I think it's really tied to the quality of the show. It took me a long time to realize, but the best work comes from a working environment that feels safe and, especially with comedy, a place where you can play, a place where you can fail. It's very hard to be funny, and I think you have to let go to get to something funny. You have to be willing to be stupid. A lot of times, it's embarrassing to be stupid and say a joke that's not funny in front of a lot of people. It's really embarrassing. And I think you have to feel like you're safe and you can fail in order to get to something great.

New Girl was on for seven years, and so much in American life changed. There's definitely an evolution with gender issues, race issues, like having a more diverse staff. There was #MeToo. I wrote an essay for the *Cut* in *New York Magazine* early in #MeToo because I had felt frustrated by the accusations made of women who had been harassed, like "Why didn't you tell anybody?" And the guilt of if you can try to stop somebody, you should try. And on the other hand, this person did something to me, and so now I have to end my career? It's a really difficult dilemma. It has an impact. A huge regret is that I didn't have a very diverse staff from the beginning. I'm very humbly just trying to learn. So much changed about television and in the culture during the seven years that *New Girl* was on. I go back to earlier episodes of *New Girl*, and there's definitely things that characters say that I would never write now. Comedy is a test that way, not to make excuses, but I just mean comedy is very tied to the year that it was written, the moment that it was written, because it's always about bumping up against a boundary or an edge and those boundaries keep changing. Some jokes that felt like they were edgy then, now I'm like, "Oh God."

On the other hand, at the time there was a lot of press that focused on comparing me or pitting me against other women creators. It was just so strange. It feels so quaint looking back, like, what was the issue? I don't even remember. The show came out in 2011. Any woman who puts something out there, it's becoming less and less of a thing, but it isn't just about the art that you're making, it's somehow supposed to fit into some narrative about feminism, which I think can be limiting because sometimes it's, "Just look at the thing that I made." The last thing I want to do is look in the mirror. We don't have to have a bigger conversation about everything. People think, "Well, you must be the Jess character." I had to constantly answer that question. I'm actually more like Nick. There's this big assumption that women have a failure of imagination, that women only write about themselves. I'm like every character. You write something, you create characters, there are pieces of yourself. Hollywood is very much about, well, women can write women and men can write men. I've been brought on for so many movie rewrites where they need a pass on the female character. And you're like, "What?" I mean, it's a job but it's such a strange mindset.

At one point recently I had three shows running at once. *Single Parents*, the second season, I wasn't involved with that much, and then I was running *Bless This Mess* and *The Dropout*, a limited series about Elizabeth Holmes for Hulu, at the same time, which was really, really hard. It's not a situation that I love to be in, running two shows at the same time. When I'm running a show, it's all-consuming for me. I tend to become obsessed with what I'm writing, and it really just becomes my life. I can't really break story or rewrite unless I'm almost fully just in my head. The show is playing the whole time. I have to fully be immersed in the story that I'm telling. That was really challenging for me. I don't know if I'll do that again, but I do love producing. That feels doable. I worked with J.J. Philbin, who ran *Single Parents,* for almost all of *New Girl*, so I had a really good working relationship with her, and it was just fun to be a sounding board, come up with the characters together and then let her run with it. I think that's definitely fun.

What I tell young writers is that your personal story is always a place to start, but I don't think it's limiting. I don't think you have to tell your story exactly as it happened. If you want to tell a story sometime in the 19th century, about some historical figure, I think it's just finding a way into it that feels really personal. Also, a network comedy, I can't remember how many episodes we did, but it was over a hundred. To be able to do that, you do have to be able to generate stories for years. So, you do have to know the characters really intimately in one way or another. I think if you're writing a movie, you can maybe go a little bit further afield. Network comedy has to be about a subject matter that you feel personally connected to you, that you feel intimately. You can't force generating stories. I usually tell younger writers to start with themselves, but I also don't think that that means it's a simple one-to-one with the character. Because television is so collaborative, and it probably is a gender thing, but I just don't think you can be a mean person. Also, if you're really precious about your work, television is probably not the way to go. You have to be somebody who listens and tries to unite people as opposed to someone who's constantly fighting and being defensive. I think that's an important thing to learn, and sometimes it requires going to therapy, right? Taking a lot of deep breaths.

I was just mortified in the beginning of my career at the readings of my plays. I didn't want any reaction. I didn't want to acknowledge that people had just listened to my writing or ideas. It's not even just criticism. I just didn't want them to even shrug it off or, I don't know. I wanted to keep it for myself. It's very hard to be constantly publicly putting stuff out there, you know? At least it's very hard for me.

I had had the same difficulties with table reads, even after three seasons of *New Girl*. Sitting there at that table and having to read a script that's a work in progress in front of a lot of people who are all judging. It's just really hard. And I think it's telling that Dana told me I had to make eye contact with people. I wasn't literally hiding under the table, which I did really do when my first plays were read when I was just starting out, but not looking at people or acknowledging their presence. I've learned a lot, and I've gotten better at it, but it's still a huge struggle for me. I don't really engage with fans of shows online. I can't. It's too hard for me. I mean, it's obviously something that I also love because I keep putting stuff out there. It's something I hate and something I love at the same time. Maybe it's because I feel that openness on the page that I'm so scared of other people looking at it. I think the times when I don't care, that's when I know I'm not doing good work. It continues to be a torture, but when I'm doing good work, I'm the most scared and unhappy. I've never really understood people that are just like, "I don't care," but to each his own.

There's a really good network now of women that do this. I'm still good friends with the women in the Fempire. And I have friends who are showrunners, women I reach out to for specific questions about show-running. My best friends probably don't have anything to do with television writing, but I think it's so important. It's such a weird job. So few people are showrunners. It's a really strange, isolating job that you can't prepare for. You absolutely have to find other people that have done it and talk to them because there is no perfect one way of doing it. I always tell new writers, "There's no perfect way, and you'll never get to a place where you feel like you've cracked it." You just have to constantly be relearning and relearning. I'm always in the process of trying to figure out a better way of doing things. I think when you give up that there's a perfect way of being a showrunner, then that's when you can actually be. It took me a long time to not look around at the male showrunners that I knew and feel that I was less than. It was important to change my thinking into, "I'm a different kind of leader. I'm a different kind of person," as opposed to, "I just don't have the skills that I need to do what they're doing." It was a lot of work to realize that this is the kind of leader I am, and that's not a problem. This is who I am and that's what I can bring to the table. And it's enough.

LIZ TIGELAAR

I Had to Stop Myself from Being So Wide-Eyed and Grateful All the Time

Figure 24 Liz Tigelaar
Source: photo by Ricky Middlesworth

Liz Tigelaar was most recently the creator/showrunner of Hulu's *Tiny Beautiful Things* and *Little Fires Everywhere*. Prior to that, she was the showrunner on *Casual* and created the CW's *Life Unexpected*. She has written for many shows including *The Morning Show, Bates Motel, Nashville, Revenge, Once Upon a Time, Brothers & Sisters* and *American Dreams*. She got her start on *Dawson's Creek*.

DOI: 10.4324/9781003298229-25

138 *Liz Tigelaar*

I believe that the real work of writing begins in the writers' room. And by work, I mean we talk – about everything. We talk about our exes, our sex lives, our marriages, our career mishaps, our most embarrassing moments, our confessions and fears, which ultimately leads to our story. So much about being in a writers' room is about sharing these moments – the messy, imperfect ones. It requires vulnerability. Which speaks to why having women at the helm is so great. In general, women are less afraid to be vulnerable because we practice doing it all the time.

I always say that a great writers' room should feel like the world's best dinner party – you could just sit around and talk for hours and be fascinated by each other. I remember my dad once came into the writers' room on *American Dreams*. I'd invited him because it was so vastly different from his work and he wanted to see what it was really like. Then he got there and people had watercolors out, someone was painting, somebody was talking about being cheated on, somebody had something dramatic happen with their kid. I'm sure I was telling some dumb story that I'd 100% censored because my dad was there. Anyway, at one point, he leaned over, and said, "Did you guys just take a little break just now?" And I was like, "Oh, no. When we take a break, we go, like, nap in our offices or walk laps around the lot." This didn't look or sound like the writing process, but it was all part of it: creating that familiarity, comfort, and safety to really be able to open up and share. I've been in rooms where all you did from 9am-6pm was talk about the show. I remember thinking, "I have been at this show for like a month. I don't know anything about these people! Not the superficial things but the deep things. How do you feel about your mother? What have you never told your spouse?" Those revealing, personal moments – that we all relate to – are usually what a story comes out of. You have to be open and vulnerable and willing to share the flawed parts of yourself, not the perfect parts of yourself because no one wants to sit in the room with that person. You have to share the fucked-up ways you think and feel – that you almost are scared to admit – because that's where the story comes from.

When you go into a pitch, you can't always share what you'd share in a writers' room. You don't know if it will be a receptive space. I remember collaborating with someone I'm a huge fan of and going out with a deeply personal pitch, that had to do with grief and loss and wanting to hold on to her mother who had died. And we talked about this real-life desire to actually want to take a part of her mother and keep it – like a toe or a thumb! And we knew we wanted that to be a part of the story but we didn't know if people would be receptive to that, especially with a comedy. Like, was it too dark and twisted to have your dead mother's thumb in your freezer? If we didn't really feel a deep connection in the room, we knew to skip over the thumb – the room wouldn't get it. But when we felt in it and connected, we'd pitch it. And everywhere we mentioned the thumb, the pitch sold. Because it was so honest and revealing and raw and that's what people connect to. Which to me, is the whole point. People are looking to connect to what is deep and real. It's not the

Liz Tigelaar 139

happy, bubbly parts of us that are looking to connect, it's the dark, fucked-up, human, "Oh my God, am-I-the-only-one-who-feels-this-way?" parts that are looking to connect. That's why writers' rooms get so close because you feel like you're seeing and sharing all these parts of yourself and each other that usually stay in the dark. And when you have that trust, you also have safety – where you don't have to worry about bad pitches or bad ideas or where it's not competitive, where in your best-case scenario everybody's throwing a ball and everybody else is diving to catch it, instead of just putting their hands up and letting it fall to the ground. Or worse, smashing the idea into a million pieces.

I think what sometimes people don't understand, and it's taken me a long time of doing it to think I understand it, is that the work – *the writing, the story* – is actually happening even when you're not working. The breaks in the room to stop focusing on the beats on the board, the times when you literally step away – like going to the bathroom, everyone comes up with a story-solve in the bathroom, because they aren't thinking of the story for a second, they just needed to pee! All of that is making space for the ideas. Whenever it's been a long day and you're stuck and your boss says, "Should we stay and order dinner?" the answer is always NO. I believe no good has ever come from staying at work longer. Go home, do something completely unrelated to work, actually have a life experience so you have stories to tell. To me, that's so much more productive. It's not endless hours in the room with diminishing returns. I've discovered you can be efficient in the room, set goals and still have plenty of time for the room to be fun. The room is such an important place – it's where it all begins – and it's a place to protect. When it works, there is nothing better. And when it doesn't, there's nothing worse. The showrunner's job, first and foremost, is to run that room.

Winnie Holzman was my biggest mentor and still is in many ways because of how much I admire her. I worked as her assistant, and I absolutely loved it. I think it's still one of my favorite jobs to this day. She was writing *Wicked* at the time and was working on *Once and Again*. I would sit there and read *My So-Called Life* scripts and had this epiphany – that's probably obvious to most people, but felt wholly new to me at 25. Up until then I'd always thought that it was somehow indulgent to just write your own story. Obviously, you don't have a million stories, so even for job longevity, you can't really just write your own story over and over again. But what I realized from Winnie is that it's not indulgent to write your *voice*. That's what you should be doing as a writer – that's your greatest tool. And I think that's what I realized Winnie did. When I went back and read or watched *My So-Called Life*, now knowing Winnie, it made me look at it so differently. All the ways that Angela Chase pontificated were the same ways Winnie pontificates. And the way Winnie thinks, and the way Winnie connects things – the kind of Winnie-ish insights she has, the Winnie-isms she uses – it all opened my eyes to how to use your voice. When I was a baby writer, I was told to write a pilot of my own – as a spec, as a sample – and I immediately thought, "I don't know what to write. I don't even know what

140   *Liz Tigelaar*

my voice is," because up until then the only writing I'd done was on *Dawson's Creek* and my job was to try to sound like *Dawson's Creek*. And Winnie said, "Well, Honey, why don't you write about a person who doesn't know their voice." And I did! And it worked! I can't say the pilot went anywhere or got me an actual writing job, but if I go back and read that pilot now, I see that same voice that's with me today. It was really great advice.

So now, over time, all I want to do is hone and complicate and deepen that voice. And you know when it's time to move on and keep growing because what used to challenge you doesn't anymore. If I get on a show that I think I can write in my sleep, there's obviously a relief to that but also a sadness because you know it's not going to push you to grow. And I always want to grow. Back in the day at a certain point, I could curl on the couch, pour a glass of wine, get out my computer and – pow, pow, pow – a *Revenge* or *Nashville* fight scene would just pour on out of me. It felt fun and easy and like I was good at that because it harkened back to the types of things I used to watch. But then I looked at the kind of stuff I was watching now. Shows that were amazing to watch but would have terrified me to write. *Bates Motel* was a good example. I was obsessed with the first season of that show. To the point where, when I got a meeting to staff on it and was sent all the episodes to watch (before the public could watch them), I had to really weigh whether I wanted to watch or not. I thought that them hiring me was such a longshot that I didn't want to ruin the rest of the season for myself – but of course, if I didn't watch, I was afraid I'd tank the meeting by being in the dark. Ultimately, I watched and miraculously got hired. And I spent the whole season being both incredibly happy and incredibly stressed because of how outside my wheelhouse so much of the show felt. But I loved every minute of it because I could feel my writer-insides expanding. And that's what it is. Honing your voice is really expanding it.

I've been in two deals under ABC Studios – one a decade ago and one now. I think we've grown together. My first show, *Life Unexpected*, even started as an ABC Studios show and then the list of ABC shows is extensive – *What About Brian, Brothers & Sisters, Dirty Sexy Money, Once Upon a Time, Revenge, Nashville, Astronaut Wives' Club*, lots of development too – I mean, this place has been my home. But what's interesting being at one place for so long – and selling to one network for so long – is that you start to intrinsically know what they are looking for, so you start to shape everything toward that. It's not as if anyone is saying you have to do x, y, or z, but you start to think to yourself, they are going to *want* x, y, or z so I should just do that now. But what you've done is you forgot to explore *a* thru *w*! You start to anticipate and then you start to self-censor and that's when you know it's time to go. That you are stalling out. That you've put yourself in a box. After my first ABC deal ended, that's when I went to *Bates Motel* which led me eventually to *Casual,* and *Casual* blew open everything for me. It showed me all the different ways of storytelling, the simplicity of silence, and that I didn't need to delineate between comedy and drama. And while I was there

Liz Tigelaar 141

to bring some tentpoles of TV structure to the show full of feature people, it taught me to both impart what I'd learned about structure and abandon it. Which was thrilling and terrifying. In a way, that show was as scary to me as *Bates* was. And also so so valuable. Not only did it forge my relationship with Hulu, it would be a key piece in expanding myself in the direction of shows like *The Morning Show, Little Fires Everywhere,* and *Tiny Beautiful Things.* Which of course brought me right back to ABC Studios (now ABC Signature) but I came back in this new, un-self-censored, much more expanded, I think deeper way.

It's funny how people are snobby about shows and storytelling but what they don't realize is that the tentpoles of a great story are the same. I was so adamant about this that one day R.J. Cutler made me write it on his whiteboard at *Nashville.* I was dissecting an episode of *Vampire Diaries* and then dissecting *Breaking Bad* and although they are very different shows, when you break down the structure, you find the same thing. *What does your hero want? What's in the way of that by the end of act one? What did they do to overcome it in acts two and three? And what twist at the end of act three creates a bigger obstacle that they didn't anticipate?* Then – *How does it resolve? Do they actually accomplish what they wanted to from the beginning or does what they want change based on what happened in the episode?* It's a very formulaic structure. And they both are structured to not give the audience everything that they want. I mean, I learned this from *Days of Our Lives* in the '90s. If everyone wants something, don't do it. Withhold it. And fight every single way to keep what they want to happen from happening while just giving them enough to keep wanting it. Easy, right?

I agree with Stephanie Savage in that it takes chops to break a soap. She's brilliant. And it does. It's funny, someone once asked Kerry Ehrin about how different it was to write *Bates* then *Parenthood* or *Friday Night Lights,* and she was like, "It's all just a family drama." Which I thought was a great response because she's right. It's true. In all cases, you have to create characters that are flawed, that you root for, who are going to get in their own way enough to sustain a series based on those flaws. And you have to still find a way to entertain people in a compelling way by hooking them into a story and making them care. Feel. So, whether it's network or cable, hour or half-hour, comedy or drama, soap or procedural, act breaks or no act breaks. That's the same across the board. That's the challenge.

I did my first pilot for the CW, before *Life Unexpected.* I was 29 and it was actually UPN's last pilot (and Spelling's, which is crazy) and one of CW's first. There was a male director who was kind of given the pilot and it was full of male producers, one of whom I really loved and continued to work with over the years. But it was a really tough experience for me. We all went up to Vancouver to shoot it, and it was so exciting and incredible and my whole family came to visit but I felt this *feeling* – like thank you for your script, but now, little girl, go away. Go approve hair and make-up or pick out what backpacks and purses the girls should be wearing. But no one

142 Liz Tigelaar

would involve me in the big conversations – like how are we shooting the scene that's the whole premise of the show or when are we rehearsing the opening dream sequence and what's that going to look like? At one point – I think literally on a night we were shooting a sexual assault sequence – a male producer said to me, "You know, you just don't seem like you're having any fun." And I just wanted to burst into tears. Honestly, I probably did cry to the one producer I felt like I trusted. And I said a less articulate version of, "This is the most spectacular, fun thing to ever happen in my life. If I don't feel like I'm having any fun, it's because there's a group of men not making it fun. I'm fighting to even get to participate in the thing that I created, the thing that came from inside of me." And that's what it felt like every day. A fight to be seen or heard or just regarded at all. And back to the opening that I had all the questions about. It was this simple opening that was a dream but was supposed to feel real.

Our main character – a teenage girl – was playing dodgeball against a brick wall in gym class, and the dodgeball thrower was taking out the people around her. So people were getting plucked off one by one. And she wasn't getting hit. Which at first felt like a relief. Until she realizes – she's invisible. Like no one even sees her or notices her enough to even bother to hit her. And then we see, she's just part of the brick wall, completely blended in – and then wakes up from this nightmare. So that was it. Pretty simple. Just a handful of girls and a dodgeball and a brick wall. But when we went to shoot it, all of a sudden, all these extras came in, like dozens and dozens, and everyone was dressed in really short Catholic school skirts with high white knee socks (even though they were supposed to go to public school). And their white button downs are tight around their boobs. And I see there are smoke machines and the gym is dark, and I'm like, "What's happening?" And I find out we are shooting in slow motion. So basically, the dodgeballs will be bouncing slowly, the girls who are throwing them are sexy and sneering, and hundreds of people are in the stands cheering like it's an Ultimate Fight or something. It wasn't at all what I'd pictured or written. And I felt really confused and unsure. But they tell me, don't worry, once we have the special effects, it'll be great. And I'm like *what special effects?* So cut to post and I see the *effects*. Basically, the sexy sneering girls throw the slow-motion dodgeballs at the terrified sexy girls and when a dodgeball makes contact with the terrified girl's body, her body shatters into a million pieces – like glass! The women shatter like glass. They sexy shatter. Into a million pieces. Their bodies shatter. That's the story. And I watched horrified. It felt misogynistic, it felt violent… and it didn't feel anything like the show. It felt like a male fantasy. And maybe it was a generational thing. Maybe it was a male/female thing. All I knew was no one had asked me and I felt small and alone and sad. Which was an awful way to feel about the greatest career accomplishment I'd had at that point.

Things were different on my next pilot, *Life Unexpected*. I met and developed the show with Gary Fleder, who had a deal at ABC and from the start,

Liz Tigelaar 143

Gary was such a collaborator. And I could tell from the very beginning how protective of writers he was – at least he was super protective of me. I was 31 at the time and he treated me like I was a peer, whose voice and input mattered. He had a VP of his development company, Mary Beth Basile, who was about my age, and the two of us became attached at the hip. Gary had so much respect for Mary Beth – who despite being younger wasn't afraid to say her opinions, to challenge him, to question and of course to support. Their partnership was respectful and inclusive – they were a team and the three of us became one too. Because of that, *Life Unexpected* was completely different. And not just because Gary was different from the last director I'd worked with. I was different, too. I had to stop myself from being so wide-eyed and grateful all the time. All those stock answers of "I'm just so happy to be here. I'm so grateful someone's doing the show." I felt all those things, I felt that gratitude of course, but I chose not to lead with that all the time. I decided I wasn't going to be some wide-eyed, little thirty-year-old who's sooooo excited her show is getting made. I was here to do something. To say something. And of course, Gary is going to come in and elevate it and bring a thousand more things to it – but it's not going to be in spite of me, it's going to be with me. I knew I had to come from a stronger place because the system, the process, will try to take your strength and power away. But running a show forces you to plant your feet and not topple over. You have to have a million hard conversations a day. You have to do things that you don't want to do – that you wish someone else would do for you. You have to give people bad news. You might have to fire them. You have to say no. You have to say hard truths. You have to do many of the things that we are taught to avoid doing. And it never gets easy, but it does get easier.

Certainly now, I would probably be able to speak up at an earlier stage than I did on my first pilot and I hope now someone would listen. But back then, would it have mattered? Honestly, no. And I remember knowing that. I figured there were tons of experienced people around me. And if they thought this was a good fit, then it must be. I remember thinking, "What do I know? I haven't even done this before." But now, having more knowledge of the industry, more experience and a track record – that shifts things. Of course, I'd never be in that position again. But I'll probably be in other ones that feel challenging in their own ways, that I will have to learn to navigate as well. In the end, I'm grateful for that first experience because it was my first. And I learned so much. If the show had succeeded, I would have been running a show with no clue how to do it. And if you're lucky enough to get a show on the air, you ideally do want to be capable of running it. And capable of being a person who can speak up and have a voice. So, it gave me a lot more time to learn how to show-run and learn how to speak up.

What's so great about so many more high-level, female writers is that you look across at women who just get it. And there's a knowing between us. As women, we know that we are all juggling a million things – be it big careers, marriages, caring for kids, caring for parents... and women just get it done.

144 Liz Tigelaar

That's how it was on *Little Fires Everywhere* – a sea of working, creative moms. We all wanted to give every ounce of ourselves to the show while we were there and as soon as we were done, we raced home to give every ounce of ourselves to the people waiting for us at home. For me, if I'm away from my son, it better be for something that fills me up creatively, that feels vital to my being. I look at the women my age in writers' rooms. Especially the moms. They are jumping up the second we're done, they have their purses and keys in hand, ready to race home to start their other fulltime job. Whereas the dads – there's no rush there, no urgency. They'll finish an email in their office, browse around on their computer. Women don't even pee. They just go. They race out to keep living their lives, to keep experiencing all the things, so when they show back up the next morning, there's even more story to tell.

MARTA KAUFFMAN
I Wanted to Prove it to Myself

Figure 25.1 Marta Kauffman
Source: photo by Eric Charbonneau

Marta Kauffman is the co-creator and co-showrunner of *Friends*, and the co-creator and co-showrunner of *Grace and Frankie*. She also created many other shows including *Veronica's Closet*. Marta has won numerous Emmy Awards, an Icon Award from the Hollywood Critics Association, and a Lifetime Achievement Award from the Producers Guild of America. Marta recently endowed a chair in African and African American Studies at Brandeis University after beginning to understand how she had internalized systemic racism and in an act of allyship over regret for the lack of diversity in front of and behind the camera in the shows she has created.

DOI: 10.4324/9781003298229-26

146 *Marta Kauffman*

When I was a little girl, I used to put on shows for God with my Barbies. A friend of mine said that for a lot of women, if you look at what they did with their Barbies, you could see what they were going to do in the future. She used to make clothes for Barbies, and she's a costume designer. It starts somewhere. I don't know where the drive came from. I'm sure it was overcompensation for insecurity because I'm a writer, and we're terribly insecure and crazy. But I've also always been highly driven.

My job is a thousand things at once. I go down to the set for every rehearsal and master to make sure the scenes are working, leave my notes, and if it seems in great shape I don't have to go back inside. I might come back for someone's coverage, so I go back and forth all day. We're doing everything at once. We're editing, listening to score. There was a day that I had something to do on every single episode. But I stay in the writers' room as much as I possibly can. We often split up into two groups. Sometimes one group is working on putting together the beats for an outline, and the other room is working on the next episode. It depends on where we are in the season and what needs to get done. We just sort of divide and conquer. People are heard better in smaller rooms.

It's a tricky thing to be heard as a woman because often guys tune out women's voices. You just don't put up with that shit. I also won't put up with sexism. I won't put up with guys talking over women. It's really important to make sure they hear it. This is how I do it. Say, "Wait a minute. I just want to go over that again and see what you think about it. It's an idea I kind of like." To not allow it to be the way women are treated in a room. You have to stand up for yourself. On *Friends*, it was very important to me to be seen not as the girl, but as Kevin Bright and David Crane's equal partner. David and I used to talk about how Kevin would be called a good producer and decisive, and David was the nicest guy in show business. I was either tough or a bitch. Now if I were a man, then I would've been called a good producer. This isn't just a writers' issue. It's across the board. The script girls, secretaries, they don't get paid as much as men. As far as what women need to do, it's a couple things. One is that they need to write and create their own content because that's where we really get to show our voices. In doing that, there will be more stories about women. What sells is what draws you in. It makes you want to hear more about a character. Things haven't changed enough, and as women writers, we need to prove that stories about women want to be seen. We aren't nearly as far as we'd like to think we are. I think women still have a harder time getting started.

My last production company before Okay Goodnight was called More Horses Productions. The reason it was called that was I used to ride as a kid, and when I was sixteen, I had a really bad accident, and I became phobic for twenty years. One day David Crane and I were in New York on his mother's balcony watching the finish line of the New York City Marathon, and we were commenting on how people can do whatever they set their minds to. We each chose one thing we never thought we would do and said we're going to do it within a year. Mine was to get back on a horse. His was to run the marathon. We both did it. I then got back into horses, but the reason I called it More Horses was because it was about new challenges and facing fears, the things I felt the strongest need to reinvent myself with when *Friends* was over. But *Friends* ended when I was turning fifty, so that was coming anyway, I think. And I guess it would be really boring to not keep trying. You'll fall on your face, but get back up and try something else.

After *Friends*, when David and I decided we wanted to do different things, I started writing hour-longs, more than anything to exercise the muscle. I did documentaries. I sold a couple pilots, but they didn't go to air. *Friends* was one of the greatest experiences I ever had in my life, but I also knew that I wanted to go deeper. That was important to me for the next step in my career. I'm not a good joke writer, but I can be funny, which is different. I do more that comes out of character, but I'm never going to write the joke. The joke writers, God, I don't know how they do it, but they have this wit and this ability to put disparate things in a sentence that suddenly are hilarious. The important thing is, as far as I'm concerned about joke writing on *Grace and Frankie*, is that it can't be there for the sake of a joke. It has to connect to something.

I think being a showrunner for me, this is not true of everybody, but for me it is a lot of mothering. I try not to make them feel guilty. There's multitasking. There's conflict resolution. There's encouraging people to think on their own, even to make mistakes. I like to be the person who, with wardrobe, for example, let them do the work and say, "Here's what we love." Rather than say, "Here are seventeen choices," because that means you don't trust your designer. Try to keep the conflict to a minimum, which is also my rule in my house. Be kind.

Writers' rooms can be brutal. I've heard stories that if you had a bad idea, you had to put a dollar into the pot. We did that with a pot, but that was if you called a character by the actor's name. But showrunning isn't just the writers, it's also the set. I want a place that's happy. I want a place where people look forward to coming to work and are proud of the work they do. In order to do that, I have to be that person who acknowledges everyone and says good morning and knows everybody's name. It just lets people know I'm happy you're here to work, and I appreciate you. I steer the ship. Your vision is the core. It's like the mission of a school. Everything comes from that mission. My job is to keep people in that bubble of "this is what our show is."

From pitching on, I think you have to start with, "What is the heart of the show?" With *Friends*, it's about "the time in your life when your friends are your family." Everything came from that. We knew with *Grace and Frankie* that we wanted to do something powerful about women and sexuality and starting your life over at any time. We wanted to empower an age group that's dismissed. Everything we do has to come from that. In terms of pitching style, I tend to be very animated. I script it and then know it within an

148 *Marta Kauffman*

inch of its life. Scripting it is also an opportunity to understand what your show is and to really get a sense of, "How do these characters help that story? How does the setting help the storyline?" Everything comes from that single nugget. You write the pitch around that nugget. You write the script around that nugget. And the nugget doesn't change, but everything else does as soon as actors breathe life into it. You have to hold on to that nugget so that you can mold it. You want actors who elevate the material to something you didn't even realize it was. We've been very lucky. Casting is key. Hopefully, I've figured some of it out. There are always curveballs.

Even the ending of a show goes back to the nugget. By the end of *Friends*, they're starting their own families. That was a natural, organic growth for the characters in the story. It made it not easy, but simple, because it was built in. You look at something like *Six Feet Under*. That ending was built in. I think for my shows, it wouldn't be wise to frustrate the audience at the end. In some way the end has to be satisfying. It can be emotional. It doesn't have to be funny. It doesn't have to have everything work out with a pretty bow, but it's got to be satisfying. I didn't know where *Friends* was going until we got there. I don't plan my ends before the middle is finished.

I certainly see the relationship between *Grace and Frankie* and *Friends* in this sense: they're both about friendship and love. I don't do edgy. I don't do dark. I try not to write people that you're going to be annoyed by. I want to write people who you'd want to welcome into your living room while you're in your robe folding laundry. I think TV is very intimate that way, and I think that is something that is comfort food-ish. In terms of my characters, there's a desire to be kind. They don't have to be kind to each other. They can't just be assholes for the sake of being assholes. For me, a lot of what I see in comedy are a bunch of assholes. They're just mean. And for me, they don't act like people.

One of the things that we had hoped would happen with *Grace and Frankie* is that people who might not necessarily watch a show that has two gay men in it will watch the show and see them as people and not as gay men. You always have this little hope that you can affect even one person's outlook for the positive. It's pretty cool. And I get to work with my daughter Hannah Canter who is a producer on the show. It's the best. She kicks ass. She didn't think she wanted to go into the business for the longest time. She thought she wanted to go into academia. She's responsible and really smart production wise. We don't fight. She can be stubborn, but I'm sure I can, too.

A long career success is a little bit like lightning in a bottle. I felt that way about *Friends*, too. The first season of *Grace and Frankie*, it was so hard for me emotionally. And I didn't realize until the last night of the show why it was so difficult, and it had to do with *Friends*. It had to do with competing with that. I desperately wanted the *Friends* writers to see me as a writer, to see me separate from David. Success feels surreal, period. Someone says that word and I wonder, "What does that mean?" Because what I experience is getting up every morning at five AM to be on set at six forty-five. I'm really driven. I don't want to have an empire. I have no interest in that. What I want is to be working on passion projects. Things I love. Things that I care about. Things that are meaningful. As I get older, I feel the sense of time passing very quickly, and there's still a lot to say and do.

MARTI NOXON
Let Go of Being Liked by Everybody

Figure 26.1 Marti Noxon
Source: courtesy of Bravo

Marti Noxon is an Emmy-nominated writer, producer, director and showrunner. She attended the University of California, Santa Cruz, and was a writer and executive producer for *Buffy the Vampire Slayer*, *Private Practice* and *Grey's Anatomy*. She was a consulting producer for *Mad Men*, *Angel* and *Glee*. In addition to writing the features *I am Number Four* and *Fright Night*, she wrote and directed her first film, *To the Bone*, which sold at Sundance to Netflix. She's the creator-showrunner of *Sharp Objects* for HBO, *Dietland*, *UnREAL*, *Girlfriends' Guide to Divorce* and *Point Pleasant*. She recently completed a multi-year producing partnership with Netflix, where she worked on *The Woman in the House Across the Street from the Girl in the Window*.

DOI: 10.4324/9781003298229-27

Marti Noxon 151

Whenever I'm teaching or talking to a group of young women especially, I tell them "Don't box yourself in." I don't feel like for this generation of writers, what used to be labeled "boy stuff" and "girl stuff," is as much of an issue. But for years it was women who got hired to write romantic comedies and soft drama. Fortunately, I came up in the *Buffy* world and I had "genre cred." That gave me a wider choice of material to work with both in television and film. But that was just pure luck that I didn't get shoved off into, "You go do girl stuff." Ironically, now I'm doing mostly aggressively feminist content, which isn't necessarily genre. It's just where I am right now.

For its time, you could absolutely call *Buffy* aggressively feminist. Which is rife with contradictions now that people know the atmosphere there was toxic toward women in some serious ways. But that's another story. Fortunately, today there are more women showrunners and more shows run by women that are hits artistically as well as commercially. They speak to an audience who are starved for that kind of content. What is different for me is that there are more homes now for the kinds of shows that I'm interested in writing.

My first show, *Point Pleasant,* was just a perfect storm of all the things that I didn't know. It was an incredible learning experience, in great part because nobody really knew what the show was. Even the network was confused. Still, I decided to accept the offer to run it. And, of course, pretty soon I was also confused about exactly what we were trying to do. The network would call and say maybe it's kind of like *Desperate Housewives* meets *Lucy, The Daughter of the Devil.* I was always trying to please them, and figure out how to make the show good. And then we got canceled. One of the executives said, essentially, I'm paraphrasing, "You were so agreeable, thank you for being so easy to work with, I also think it might have been to the detriment of the show." And I was like, "Oh shit."

The interesting thing was, that once we knew that we were on the path to getting canceled we kind of went wild and the show got better. We didn't care anymore. They stopped noting us to death and we started to have more fun. And the show got better but it was too late. It was dead. But I should be clear: I don't hate getting notes, per se. Feedback is essential. I know when I've gotten a good note, and I'm grateful for it. The problem in this situation was that nobody knew what a good note was. Because nobody knew exactly what tone we were trying to hit. *Desperate Housewives* is very different from *Lucy, The Daughter of the Devil.* So, it was a hot mess. Plus, I had given birth and a day or two after she was born I was sneaking away to the bathroom to look at a title sequence so my husband didn't know what I was doing. Then I was bringing my daughter to work with me and breastfeeding at the office. It was complete madness. There was a lot of crying in cars. I'm not a big crier. But, you know, when you're hormonal like that you're a big crier and you can't help it.

152 Marti Noxon

It was a big network show. My name was going to be co-creator for the first time. I was so lucky to be able to say, "I'm bringing my daughter in or I can't do the job." The need to be close to your baby is primal. It can be wrenching to be away from them. There was a moment when I thought, "This is part of the patriarchal plan." The fact that most women can't bring their baby to work through those preschool years is a weeder, meaning it weeds out women who would stay in their jobs but feel they can't because of their kids. If men had babies there would be mandated maternity leave for every profession, child-care services in every office, breast pumps that looked like super cool Star Wars contraptions and Nike would make "birthing wear."

I didn't give up on my career when I became a mom. In fact, I doubled down. I realized that at that moment in time, full-time television work wasn't for me. I started writing film. And consulted on some shows three days a week. I was very lucky that my film career kicked in, and for three or four years, that's what I did, and had way more flexibility. When you work from home nobody cares if you go out to dinner, as long as you turn the work in. Which is why screenwriting can be really appealing to moms. I think until recently I felt I had to apologize for having children and still being ambitious. Look at all the men who are fathers and have multiple shows or who have shows and do movies at the same time. Men who build companies. Nobody asks them how they juggle parenthood and those responsibilities. So at a certain point, I stopped apologizing. And I'd argue that I have really deep, strong relationships with my kids. Still, sometimes I worry that they'll be on a shrink's couch someday saying, "She loved to work. Did she love it more than me?" But I think it's more possible that they'll know balancing work and family isn't a gender thing. It's a life thing. And they definitely know how strongly I feel that one of the best blessings you can have in this life is to know your purpose here. To feel passionate about what you get paid for. So, I hope that I live that example. I talk to my kids about how to just keep trucking. And that I wish for them what I've been so lucky to find.

When you're new to the business, there's so much fear. I remember staying in a job long past when I should have left. I was afraid I wouldn't find another job and I look back now and I'm like, "What was that about?" You know? Some of it was very "dark night of the soul" where I was working on network television for 70–80-hour weeks and I had a small son and daughter at home. My now ex-husband would bring them to work sometimes, and we'd have dinner together and then I'd cry, and I'd go back to work. In that situation I was working on something that was popular, but it didn't reflect stuff that I understood very well emotionally. I could connect here and there but the biggest lesson for me was that every time I said yes to something where I didn't have that gut feeling, "Oh, I know what the show is," I would end up in hot water. One way or another.

I was hitting a wall in terms of exhaustion and then the (2007–8) writers' strike happened. And I met Matt Weiner on the line (also a very problematic person but, again, that's another story.) We exchanged a couple emails

Marti Noxon 153

because I was already just agog over *Mad Men*. Just to hear him talk about the work and what he was doing and to start that dialogue was really inspiring. At some point during the strike, I was like, "I did not get into writing to make a lot of money." That was not my goal and now here I am with this great overall deal. And I'm asking myself "how did I get here and do I even want to be here?" Before *Buffy*, I had no real experience of the TV industry. When that show ended it was like all of us got thrown out of a car at 70 miles an hour. Because we'd had this family, functional and dysfunctional, and we made a show – *Buffy* – that we loved. There was very little outside interference (because it was so successful). So, after it was over I had a kind of rude awakening. That's not your experience when you get into the big bad world of network television.

Once I was running a show myself, I learned that the more agreeable you are, in some ways, the less they respect you. I just wanted everybody to like me and to do a good job. I was really sacrificing, not realizing, that my job wasn't to be liked. My job was to protect the show no matter what. But you can't protect something if you're not sure in your core what it is. So that's when I quit doing TV full time and I wrote a spec feature for myself. My one rule was: "Do not write to entertain. Just tell the truth." I didn't have an outline. It just was totally different from anything I'd done. That script kind of woke me up again in terms of the stuff I wanted to say. It became a calling card for other work. And it got me back into the feature business. Eventually, I couldn't even do the consulting because it was just like my whole brain and heart was someplace else.

Somewhere in that whole experience I also had this epiphany, which I wrote into the first season of *Girlfriends' Guide to Divorce*, which was, none of the showrunners or creative people who I had great respect for were universally liked. It didn't mean that lots of people didn't love them. It just meant that some people didn't, because they were fierce defenders of their work. I thought, "Oh, I've got to let go of being liked by everybody," and I think that's often a female cross to bear. Men aren't generally conditioned that way. So it was, for me, really stepping out on a limb and saying, "OK. The rules are: You don't commit to something you don't feel deeply about, and know what the show is so you can fight for your baby. And, let go of this idea that you always have to please everybody. You can't."

In fact, my trying to be so agreeable was standing in the way of people thinking of me as an artist. It was because I was so accommodating and I'd think, "Well, we'll just try and make that work." I was on a call the other day and they were questioning a storyline and I said, "You know that I don't challenge notes that often, but I'm going to say that I think it's working." By using the "no" card selectively, it's more powerful when you do. And often the note-givers go, "Oh, she has a point of view." They're relieved because they're working on 1000 other projects and they can barely see straight. Of course that's not always the case. Sometimes you can stand up for your work and it's like you're talking to a super computer that keeps spitting out different algorithms every day. It's indifferent to your passion. But that has nothing to do with your gender. That's just a fact of the business, especially now with all the data that gets thrown at us.

Still, saying no can be challenging, especially if you're as deeply entrenched as I was and still am to certain degrees in fitting in, and being a pretty, pretty pony. And wanting people not to say that I'm difficult. On *UnREAL*, with two shows running at once, making 23 hours of television in five months, I lost it a couple times. I mean, I lost it bad. F-bombs were dropped. Somebody came away from one of those phone calls saying, "I never want to have that conversation with Marti Noxon again." And I have to say there was a part of me going like, "Fuck yeah, finally." Finally, someone's a little bit afraid of me. Because they paid me to do a job. We're not talking about abusive behavior. We're just talking about losing your shit occasionally. I've had these experiences where I pushed back the littlest bit and my agent got a call complaining about me, saying I was hard to work with. I think I'm somewhat complicit because I come off as if I'm always going to play nice. I do think there's something where if you identify as a woman, it's like if you're going to be a good girl from day one if you present like, "I'm just here to do your laundry."

Here's a funny thing, every time I've been in a meeting with certain women, there is the water bottle ritual. Everybody gets a bottle of water. Period. Almost every woman I know picks up the bottle of water when they leave and they throw it away, or they ask an assistant. They say, "I'm so sorry, would you throw this away for me?" Every time I'm in a meeting with a bunch of men, they walk out, nobody's cleaning the effing table. It just shows you it's so deep, this feeling that we're not allowed to leave a mess.

Despite it all, I feel like I've found my voice. Or finally found what I'm really engaged in talking about. I learned so well from *Buffy* and other experiences like *Mad Men* and *Grey's* and *Private Practice* that you can be really entertaining and have an agenda. I do think that right now my agenda across the board is talking about sexual politics. *Sharp Objects* appealed to me because the thesis is about women and women's violence, which is not in any way motivated by the men around them. It acknowledges that women have anger and violent feelings and explores what happens when those are suppressed. How corrosive it can be and, in this case, literally dangerous.

Gillian [Flynn] wrote *Sharp Objects* as a kind of Western. A character comes back to the town where bad things happen and it turns out the source of all the bad stuff is women doing it to each other. And, to me, even though that's not a pro-woman statement, it's acknowledging part of the fullness of our character. There was an article a couple years ago that challenged the idea of the strong female lead. That all that meant at that point was, "you put glasses on her and say she's important," even if she only has six lines and doesn't know how to drive a car. The dimension to female characters has been so limited unless you were talking about independent film or literature. My goal for the future is to keep putting all kinds of characters out there with as much complexity as I can... Like, in *Girlfriends'* the men are as real as the women. They have as much dimension. And they're not all to blame. They're not the bad guys.

As a feminist I also want to show that the world that we've created, where we reduce people to these ideas, is bad for all of us. The more I can explore that in any genre and just keep open the idea of what a person is, and it extends to race and class. We just do so much compartmentalizing of who people are. That's a wall that I want to beat on as much as I can. The core source of so much is that people want to be loved and they want to have their essential needs met. The more we make people "the Other," the harder it is to have those things.

I'm gonna make another broad sweeping generalization though. Women tend to engage in a kind of conversation with other women and other people that sees many dimensions of a person or situation. I think that many women probably have an emotional IQ that can encompass more than one truth about a person. Or five or six truths about a person. And that's why so many diverse female voices on television are being recognized as important. We're in a world now where you don't have to appeal to 33 million people. That makes it feel like it's like a land of opportunity for so many people, not just women. But people of color, anybody who's been sort of locked out of the conversation in a certain way, the conversation's just getting bigger and bigger.

Of course, you still have to Trojan horse stuff in. You can't just be like, "I'm writing a show about feminism with a capital F." Although I say that and it's exactly what *Dietland* was. A feminist howl of rage. Which is probably why it only lasted one season! However, with *UnREAL*, we created this tasty soapy show about reality dating shows that was subversive because, underneath the gloss, our thesis was that these women are creating an unrealistic fantasy that is hurtful to themselves and other women.

At some core level we're still teaching each other that love is supposed to save all. And that having romance in your life validates you in a way that nothing else does. The women and men who lose in those beauty contests are subject to humiliation and bullying by the general public. That message is so destructive. But I wanted all our characters to fall for it. Because we do.

MEG DeLOATCH
I'm Authentically Telling My Story

Figure 27.1 Meg DeLoatch
Source: photo courtesy of Meg DeLoatch

Meg DeLoatch recently created and executive produced the award-winning Netflix multi-camera sitcom *Family Reunion*. She worked her way up in comedy on shows such as *Living Single, Family Matters, Malcolm & Eddie, Bette*, and *One on One*, then created UPN's romantic comedy, *Eve*, and showran TV One's comedy series *Here We Go Again*. She also wrote and produced on shows such as *Brothers, Austin & Ally, Born Again Virgin, Raven's Home* and *Fuller House*. Meg recently ran *The Neighborhood* for CBS under her overall deal and is now developing original shows for them.

DOI: 10.4324/9781003298229-28

When I created *Family Reunion* for Netflix, I really wanted to do a show about an American family that's authentically Black. And that just makes people feel good when they join them. They feel like they're a welcome part of the family. Our show started out of Netflix's kids and family division, so we're definitely kids-centric. But at the same time, it was critical for me that I created a show that parents wouldn't cringe having to watch. I'm looking to do one of those throwback shows where the family might get together and go, "Let's watch together."

I was very blessed with our actors. They're Hollywood royalty, and they bring their own special class and gravitas that is Loretta Devine, Tia Mowry and Richard Roundtree with them. I got really lucky, putting it all together and going, "This feels right." And then, bam! You put them in a room together and they made it right. I was the showrunner of *Eve*, and then I've run a couple of pilots as well as shows for some of the smaller networks, like TV One, but it had been a while, so this was a wonderful opportunity. What makes *Family Reunion* special is that this is the very first time in my career where my thoughts aren't being filtered through someone else. Yes, they give me notes, but I'm authentically telling my story, and it's wonderful.

About a year-and-a-half before Netflix asked me for a family show, I had gone on a wonderful family reunion to Columbus, Georgia, my mother's hometown. And it was such a great experience. But at the same time, I just could not imagine living in such a small town. It was some-thing that just stayed with me, how much I wanted to be closer to family, yet how I knew that it wouldn't work for me. So when they came to me, I flashed back to that time. And much like how opposed to it my character Jade was, that is how I would be if you said, "You've got to relocate to Columbus, Georgia right now." I'd lose it. It's very much a classic fish out of water tale.

It's now a more woke Hollywood. But I spent my entire career coming up on Black shows, with mostly white writers on staff with white showrunners. It would be so frustrating if you don't have the final word. And I get it. I'm happy to be somebody's follower when I'm not the showrunner. I can pitch my heart out to you when I'm pitching for the star of your show, who's a Black woman. I can give you a joke, a story or whatever, coming from the point of view of someone with a similar background. But if you are filtering that through a completely different life experience, it may not be funny to you or relevant to you. And the result is a character who comes across as inauthentic to those audience members who know better. And even for those who didn't get it, they might have gotten some insight and said, "Oh, that's interesting. Maybe I'll look into it, or, maybe I'll have more of an understanding going forward about that." And it cheats the actor, who's often grappling with something that doesn't work for them. More than any-thing, I think it just cheats the community. Because you don't really know my story, and you haven't walked in my shoes. You're not telling my story,

158 *Meg DeLoatch*

but you're telling the world that it is my story. And that's a lot of what Hollywood has done, over and over.

A lot of people talk about how they're really down on cop shows right now. If there's not an equal representation of Black people, who are often being targeted by the police, it just looks like what you're seeing is a bunch of delinquents out there who need to be rounded up and put in prison. So, it's a really big deal. I think we have to recognize the power of Hollywood and the power of television, around the world and in this country. Some people don't have a lot of contact with people of color. If all you see of us is what you're getting filtered from Hollywood, and all those images are either subservient or menial workers or criminals, that's problematic. It's problematic if all the Black heroines look a certain way. We need to open up the universe, and the world, so that people will recognize that there are all different kinds of Black people. But I am encouraged. I see people talking the talk, and I guess what we'll have to do is see if they walk the walk. To make this more than a moment, it's about accountability, and it's continuing to remind, and fight and push. It seems like all of the studios and networks have kind of come out saying, "We stand with Black Lives Matter." Okay, so, did you mean it? You know, let's check, show me the money.

Once upon a time, if you dealt with a serious topic or issue on a show, it was always called "a very special episode." I didn't really want to explore issues from that point of view, but I also wanted *Family Reunion* to be grounded enough that it lives within the reality of everyday life. That was really important to me. I don't like those shows that sanitized race out, for example. No, Black is not the only thing I am, or that the McKellan family is, but if you remove it completely, except for having Black actors and sanitizing it, it doesn't have that sense of authenticity. It was really important to me to open ourselves up and explore our culture as worthwhile of being shared and celebrated. And then to acknowledge that, even within the light and joy of this Black family, there are some sorrows, and some of those sorrows have to do with being Black in America.

One particular episode, Season One, Episode 10, "Remember When Our Boys Became Men?" dealt with the McKellan boys being racially profiled by the police. It was very painful to shoot. And I didn't realize it until it was done and aired, but it was very painful for our audience as well. We did everything to make them fall in love with those children on the show, and then those children were robbed of their innocence. And I realized that struck a chord when a blogger who had written a piece and had raved about the show – she thought the show was great, until Episode 10, and then, according to her, "Hollywood writers couldn't resist indulging in the mythology that the police are bad and out to get Black people and blah, blah." Research revealed that she's a conservative blogger. And what I could read between the lines was that I had made her mad because she loved those boys. And she was mad that the police were mean to those boys. And I made her mad at the police and that didn't sit well with her politics. I'd written that episode after seeing news footage of a young Black boy who was walking down the street in his neighborhood with another boy, and somebody called and claimed that one of the boys had a gun. This little boy was about ten years-old, and he was sobbing hysterically with his hands up, trying to do everything the cops told him to do. The cop was actually trying to calm him, saying, "Hey buddy. It's okay, buddy. Keep your hands up, buddy. Okay. Get on the ground, buddy, lay down flat." And this little boy cried and cried. I saw that and it upset me so much that I brought it into the writers' room. And then it started a lot of conversation about similar situations others had seen or experienced. And then ultimately somebody said, "We should do this episode." At first I was reluctant. Unfortunately, this is a conversation we have to have in our family. This is something that happened to many people we know. And so maybe we go ahead, and we go there. And we're honest about it, and we're not trying to do anything but tell our story. Honestly, we're not trying to make anybody feel any kind of way about the police. We're just going to tell the story of what happens sometimes to young Black men.

Family Reunion is on Netflix, and I'll give Netflix credit. They gathered a group, a roundtable of female showrunners, and made a video for promotions. I shared a story about a negative experience I had with Netflix's HR. Because one person claimed that I was intimidating, the Netflix HR person suggested that I go around to every department head on my show and ask if they were afraid of me, and if so, to tell them not to be. I refused to do what that HR person suggested because I felt that I was being made into the angry Black woman, you know, that trope. And while anger really had nothing to do with it, it was sort of the way it was being shaped into. I had a very frank conversation with my agent. I said, "Well, you have to understand the narrative they're building is that one." Nobody was afraid of me unless they weren't on top of their job game. There's nothing to be fearful of with me. I'm not the scary showrunner. I'm the no-nonsense one, but I'm not scary. I'm very touchy feely in general. But if you allow other people to sort of build the narrative about you, as women we have to ward against that very quickly. We have to be aware and go, "No, no, no, that is not what is happening here. And if I were a man, you would not be saying this or doing this" and kind of calling it out. And you kind of learn that over time because you see how people treat you and you go, "If I had spoken up sooner, maybe this wouldn't have happened to me." And to my surprise, Netflix didn't cut it out. You know, they let me tell the truth, they didn't edit it. That they acknowledged that they made a mistake. I think that that's a good corporate environment, recognizing, "What we did to Meg and how we tried to hamstring her was not the way to go. She didn't like it and she's telling the people on our platform about it but we're not going to censor her." It was heard and it was addressed, and it hasn't happened again. So, I have learned to read a room very quickly and call out very directly what I see. And if I'm wrong, please, correct me. Let me know. But what I see is that I feel like you're marginalizing me and I'm not going to allow that.

160 *Meg DeLoatch*

There's a special something when you feel like you're dealing with sexism *and* racism. I like where I am at this time in my life to be able to call it directly as I see it, as opposed to having to roll my eyes and whisper about it. When the pandemic came and they started talking about all these underlying conditions and distress that people of color have in this country that are breaking them down, I understood. Because when you're holding it in all the time, instead of calling a racist, "a racist" to their face, it does break you down a certain kind of way.

I feel good because I feel like I'm living a positive life. I feel that I'm giving as much as I'm taking. I definitely don't feel like anybody is undermining me now. I feel really grateful to be where I am right now. I'll be honest though. I recall my very first year of being a showrunner, on *Eve*, one of the things they wouldn't do for me is, even though I'd legitimately worked my way up the ladder, they would not give me the title of Executive Producer, even though I was the showrunner for the first 13 episodes. I was not even the highest paid writer on my staff. It was my creation. My show, and I was the showrunner. And Peter Roth, the head of Warner Bros. at that time, called me, and he told me I had one of the best run shows at his studio. And I was a brand new, not yet official executive producer or showrunner, and after *Eve* ended, I never got another offer to run a show again from them. I just can't help but think things would have been different if I came in a different package.

I feel like I got into this business knowing that writing is never a steady thing and learning to save my money and just do a good job, and hope that that will eventually lead to the next opportunity. Whenever there is some significant announcement, like when Netflix and Ava DuVernay said, "We're only hiring female directors on this show," I hear anecdotally so many men grumbling and mad and suddenly claiming they can't make a living. "They're taking my job." And it's like, "You had all the jobs," you know? "So now you give a third to women and it's such an imposition?"

I'll never forget I wrote a pilot years ago and the producer I wrote it for loved it. It was good, it was funny. It was all that. And yet, when he decided to start talking about possible writers for hire, he said to me, "You need a couple of funny Jews." And I'm like, "I pitched this, I sold this, you love it." And I was insulted as a Black person and as a woman. I did say to him, "Well, I'm funny." And he said, "Yeah, but you're a woman." There's this inherent bias that women aren't that funny. And then of course the whole bias against, for whatever reason, people of color. It's maybe less against us and more about, "I want my friends in the room," or "I can't have this culture in the room that I want if I have these people there," maybe. Unfortunately, because the people who are in charge all look alike, it doesn't have to be organized. It's an inherent bias.

I remember Eunetta Boone. She was a showrunner who passed away recently. I think I was the first Black female showrunner for the Disney Channel, but it was on a pilot that didn't go. I was overseeing someone else.

Meg DeLoatch 161

Eunetta actually was the first Black showrunner and female they'd ever hired. And that was for *Raven's Home*. How long has Disney Channel been around? And she was their first Black female showrunner. Now I don't even know about Black men. I just know someone told me she was their first Black female. But that was 2019. And in 2021, I was the first Black female showrunner of a comedy on CBS. Crazy. I think just like when the writers' room for *Killing Eve* posted their pictures and people were like, "Where the hell are the Asian people?" I think that change is coming. I don't think it's going to come as fast as I'd like it to. It is going to be about holding people accountable. And speaking truth to power.

Family Reunion won the Writers Guild Award in the Children's Episodic category. We won the NAACP Image Award for Outstanding Children's Program three years running, and then Netflix submitted us for the Daytime Emmy Award for Outstanding Children's Program and the Academy decided, "We don't think you're a kids show." And they threw us into the best comedy category up against all those fantastic adult shows that are out there like *Veep* and *Schitt's Creek*. And I said, "But why aren't you doing this to *Fuller House*?" You know, I wrote on both shows, they're similar. And they said, "We grandfathered them in." And, you know, even the phrase "grandfathered" has a very charged racial history. That is what the Southern states would use when they didn't want Black people voting. They instituted laws that said, "If your grandfather voted, you can vote." So illiterate white people could vote, not Black people because of course their grandfathers had been slaves. I wrote an essay about what happened with the Academy in the *Hollywood Reporter*. I'm pretty bitter about it. My show was completely disenfranchised because they decided it couldn't be in that category.

Fox built their network on Black television shows and then dumped them. And then here comes WB and does the same thing. And then UPN, and then CW. It continually happens. And we just sort of have to roll with it because it does mean jobs, even if it means ghettoized jobs. But maybe in time the Academy will become a little bit more diverse. I never joined the TV Academy because I felt like I wasn't an insider, and I joined because of my show being put in the submission, and none of the Black writers on my show who were eligible, all these years, none of them had joined the Academy. I think that says a lot. And then we finally joined, and this is how our show is treated.

Another common problem is that writers of color are getting stuck at staff writer and story editor, and they can't progress. And staff writers don't get paid for scripts. There's definitely a big issue there that speaks creatively to having power, but also financially people's careers are just stalling out, they're unsustainable. That's a problem. So even if you manage to get onto some prestige drama, but you're only allowed to be a staff writer, you're still getting the low end of opportunity. It's terrible. And some of the magic of what we might be missing if we don't open up and hear other people's stories and feel that they're valid, it's a shame. How many times do we want to see young boys coming of age or *American Pie* kind of movies, but not a Korean boys version?

162   Meg DeLoatch

Or whoever? I'm sure universally they might share very similar themes, but there might be some really cool, different kinds of experiences and stories that could come out of that. I think especially to younger viewers, you know, like people 40 and under, I think it has really changed, for the better, having an interest and an awareness. Before *Empire*, when was the last time there was a Black family drama on the air? As many Latinx people as there are in the world, let alone in the States, there's still not enough programming. This is a huge audience, but really being underserved. And then someone told me that *black-ish* was originally left off of ABC's fall schedule. There was some hullabaloo and then they ended up putting it back on.

You get sick and tired of getting passed over for the job that you should have. The opportunity you should have. If you're hungering to share your story and to be seen and not allowed to, it's a different kind of pain and oppression. I think with me there is the eternal optimist. There is– at least now– enough of a longevity to expect that if I take a job that I will be heard whether or not heeded.

I maintain a really complete sense of self, of understanding that this is where I am, which is, I've gone a lot further than a lot of people, but I haven't gotten to where I think I thought I should be. But that's not due to my feelings, not trying or working hard enough. It's due to forces beyond my control. And now I've hung in there long enough that maybe I'll be a part of this sort of new wave of change in Hollywood. And if I have something to say, you should hear it. And I'm a really good showrunner. So even if I'm not creating a new show, I can certainly write and I can execute a show. And I've got a skill, not everybody can do it. I can do it on time, on budget, and without chaos. And it's crazy to me how many people who are given far more with far less to recommend them don't do that, and yet are allowed to continue to do it year after year.

MELINDA HSU
Foster an Atmosphere of Possibility

Figure 28.1 Melinda Hsu
Source: photo by Elisa Haber

Melinda Hsu was the executive producer and showrunner of *Tom Swift* and co-showrunner of the CW's *Nancy Drew*. Melinda worked her way up from staff writer and wrote the groundbreaking *Lost* episode "Ab Aeterno." She also wrote for *The Vampire Diaries, The Gifted,* and *Touch*. Melinda helped found the Asian American Writers Brunch, is involved with CAPE and Harvardwood, and has brought her team to volunteer with Amnesty International, Got Your 6, Young Storytellers, My Friend's Place and other local organizations. Currently, Melinda is in an overall writer-producer deal with ABC Signature.

DOI: 10.4324/9781003298229-29

164   *Melinda Hsu*

I grew up in a very task-oriented household. I was rewarded for super achievement. That led me to be very organized, goal-driven, and very good with deadlines. My parents were born in China, but they emigrated separately. They fled the Communists in 1949 separately and went to Taiwan and struggled there, you know, poverty, hardship and so on. They got to the States on scholarships, were introduced to each other, got married, and here I am. My dad was a college professor, and he taught at the University of Maine. My mom the other day said that she noted similarities between me and my dad. Once he set his mind to something, he would just make it happen somehow. It was nice to be compared to him, how he just set his eye on a gold ring somewhere and went and got it. So, I think that's kind of how I got here.

People say to me sometimes, "You didn't have any connections when you came to LA, your parents learned English in their twenties, you had no idea that this was even a job, and now you're showrunning." I think what it was for me, was that I never accepted a reality that would not result in this, which also included many years of struggling in the wilderness. People not returning my phone calls, working terrible day jobs, and being completely broke with student loans. I remember this one trip to the grocery store where I was like, "I think I'm going to splurge on eggs this week." I said that if I ate one egg a day, then I wouldn't run out of eggs for the next couple weeks. I remember being so excited about breakfast in the morning, because I literally was not eating a lot because I was that broke. This is not to be like, "Poor me." If it had come to it, I could have begged my parents for money. I could have run home, and a lot of people don't have that. But I definitely was broke in the literal sense for a while, for a long time actually. But I just didn't give up because I just didn't want to do anything else. I really wanted to be a feature writer.

When I met my former husband, at the time we were dating, he had been working for a literary agency, and he understood how Hollywood worked in lots of ways that I did not. He kept putting these ads on my desk when we were living together. Like, "There's this thing called the Warner Bros. Writers' Workshop. You should apply for this." And I was like, "I don't watch TV." Finally, he cajoled me into applying because I was like, "Well, I guess I can bang out a *Law & Order* spec." I started watching *Law & Order* because it was on TV all the time. I sat down with a yellow pad, and I charted the whole episode and realized, "There's a very clear structure to this. I can do this." So, I wrote a sample like that, and it got me into the program. Also, they were very open with us when we got into the program. They said, "The 13 of you who've been selected for the program, you weren't always the best writers, but you were really good in the interview, and that's more than half the battle." At the time I was kind of like, "Thanks." But now, I realize it was a huge compliment because it is more than half the battle to be able to converse with people and be pleasant to be around for ten hours in the conference room.

I definitely was very shy for the first job I had, terribly shy. The second job started to get better because I was just a better fit for the show. I started to realize that my pitches are getting traction. The showrunner responds to how my brain works. That was just a chemistry thing. Sometimes you're hired, and you turn out to be as good of a fit as you seemed to be in the interview. That doesn't mean you're brilliant. It just means you're a good fit for that show.

After that, I started to build on the confidence of that job. I started to pitch pilots and go give these half-hour, forty-five minute storytelling sessions where it would just be me trying to convince somebody to pay me quite a lot of money to write a script, to hopefully pay me even more money to turn it into a TV show. That's where my salesmanship started to radically improve, partly through feedback. My agent was great about giving me feedback about those meetings, body language, how you present yourself, how you speak, how you stick to your own script. You have to stay on your own message in these meetings. You can't just chat. You have to go in there and close it.

Initially when I was pitching shows, I got notes that said, "Somebody told me that Melinda reading the pitch pages looks like a third grader giving a book report. She goes so fast, and she doesn't look up." It's a funny thing now, but it was not funny at the time. I'm terrible when I read, so I started to memorize completely. I've found that when I'm completely off book and going from bullet points, instead of trying to read something that's completely scripted for me, I'm way better on my feet. I think I just learned to be a better actor in some ways, or a better presenter. So, part of what I learned in the pitching process is that you have to snap your fan (like at the end of a Kabuki performance). Sometimes you've got to tell them, "This is where you get into it, guys. This is it." It was pretty fun to learn that.

I got some great advice very early on from Ed Solomon, the guy who wrote *Men in Black* and *Bill & Ted's Excellent Adventure*. He was very generous. This was when I was working for a webzine, back when that was a thing. I asked him what his advice was for writers. And he said, "Don't be one of these people who writes endlessly and never finishes. You have to say to yourself, 'I'm done with act two. I'm not going back. I'm going to continue and complete act three.'" So, that was that. This was after film school, but it clicked with how I was hardwired anyway. But he also said, "When you rewrite, don't just rewrite to make it different. Rewrite with specific goals in mind. Pick five things. 'I'm going to make it shorter. I'm going to make it funnier. I'm going to bring out the love story, and I'm going to give this character a better backstory. I'm going to punch up the action sequences throughout.' If you do those five things, your next draft is going to be quite a lot better and not just different."

When it comes to getting off the page and managing people and the larger process, I'm very mellow, but if push comes to shove, I'll totally take charge. But my style is more to build consensus and be quiet for a while. And then, when necessary, assert myself forcefully if the situation calls for it. One of

166   *Melinda Hsu*

my favorite Tao quotes is "When there's a good leader, the people say, 'this person did it for us.' When there's a great leader, the people say, 'we did it ourselves.'" So, that's always my goal, to feel like you barely even noticed I was there. The reason that it works so well is because I was leading in a really quiet way, in a way that empowered people, and leaned on collaboration. It's not even me bringing out the best in them. It's creating an environment where people want to bring out the best in each other, which I think we've been successful in at *Nancy Drew*.

The other guiding principle I have for leadership is another Tao quote. It says something like, "All the rivers run down to the sea because it's lower than they are. The sea gains its power from its humility." When you don't try to take credit or enforce your own way, if you tell people that you trust their judgment, they'll feel called upon to really shine. And then, you'll find that you can trust their judgment and they will respect you. I've worked for people who have very domineering, bullyish personalities, and it really stunts the creative process. I've seen it firsthand; I've experienced it. It's very unpleasant to work for somebody who threatens, intimidates, disparages, criticizes, talks shit about. Very quickly, you're like, "Fuck this. Why would I try any harder than what is necessary?" People will always perform competently, because when you hire somebody, almost always, you've hired somebody who is extremely competent and way beyond the pay grade or the title. So, they're never going to do anything less than very competent, but they might give you a lot of resentment and feel demoralized, like, "Well, what does it matter? They're just going to piss all over it anyway." Versus somebody who is excited to contribute. They will go so spectacularly above and beyond your wildest imaginings of what the scene could be, or what the production design should look like, or what the costume could say about the character. It's thrilling when you let people free to do their best work.

I read this interview with the director Kenneth Branagh, and he said that his job really is to foster an atmosphere of possibility, which I think, in its purest form, is the job of the showrunner. There's no way that any single human being can do all the jobs that are involved in a TV show. There are showrunners who will be really control freak-y about all sorts of things. And I think people pick their things that they're manic about. I'm really interested in props. I love props. I also give these crazy-detailed sound mix notes. Like, "I feel that the jingle of those keys was too heavy for what the keys looked like in his hand," or the opposite way. I feel like I could see in their body language that they were sighing a little bit. "Can we get just a little bit of an exhale?" I'll do that kind of thing. I don't know if it drives people crazy, but I enjoy doing it. To me, it enhances everything. If you're going to get that extra 0.5% out of the episode in the sound mix, why not go for it? That's what everybody's there for. So that was the environment I started from the get-go.

I think that it was a real benefit from my slow march through the ranks because I have seen a lot of people get promoted too quickly. I also needed to mature a certain amount as a person and as a professional. I think that

Melinda Hsu 167

there were a couple of pilots that I sold, had they gone to series, I would have been in the EP position a lot earlier on than it ended up being. And I think I probably wouldn't have been ready in different ways. If you divide my career into thirds, and maybe I'm starting the showrunning third now, but in act two of my career, I definitely had some really dysfunctional workplaces that were very difficult, but also taught me a tremendous amount. Some of those dysfunctional places also were great hands-on learning experiences, but also taught me about what I did not want to submit people to when I finally got the chance. So, it was really valuable.

Now, I'm less shy. I'll speak up pretty firmly. There's a side of me that a producing director from Season One calls "Firm Melinda," if I get provoked or if I feel like this is really not right, what's going on, or I feel strongly that this is a negotiation point that is bullshit. The charm of "Firm Melinda" is that she comes out of nowhere. I wasn't realizing that I was getting provoked by this rep. I wasn't on the phone with the rep, but internally one of our executive producers said, "They're asking for more money, even though we just gave them a best and final offer." And I was like, "Well maybe, but then again, no." That's not allowing my assistants to charge overtime and mileage. And we can't even give them a lunch stipend for fifty bucks a week because of COVID costs, which are at least $80,000 an episode. "No. Best and final means best and final, go fuck yourself." It was actually quite a bit firmer than that. I hadn't realized that I was on the ramp then, but that's definitely different from the old shy Melinda. I think part of it is just having to choose your moments, kind of like Double Dutch jump rope. You jump in, make a pitch, and get out. You have to be forceful enough to be heard, like literally heard physically, but also concise and to the point, catchy, and then out. Actually, one of the great things I did for myself during my trek through the wilderness in the second act of my career, when a couple of things weren't going my way, was that I started martial arts classes. A lot of things from martial arts are very applicable to writing and careers, and just life in general. If you're hitting the heavy bag, you have to hit and then pull your fist back, so you don't get hit by the recoil. Pitching is like that punch and retract. Punch and retract.

I started in procedurals, then I started to gravitate more and more towards genre. Once I had the credit after writing *Lost*, I could start to be choosier, but not always. There was definitely a year where things did not pan out, but that was a really instrumental year because I started to really reevaluate. That was when I started the martial arts classes. I started to reevaluate what I want to do in general in the world, the kind of footprint I want to leave, I guess not to be too grandiose about it, you just start to look at the big picture and the overall, the bird's eye view of your career. I started to get much more intentional about incorporating public service into what I was doing. When I interviewed with Julie Plec, I talked about the martial arts classes and how you reach a point where you don't step back. That was one of the things that my martial arts teacher taught me. I was really intent on having public

168 *Melinda Hsu*

service be part of whatever job I entered into next. And I started organizing public service outreach outings for the writing staff. I was like, "People go to Palm Springs and drink, and there's nothing wrong with that, but couldn't we also volunteer at the runaway shelter," – which we did – "as a bonding thing?" To just kind of get connected to the community that's a half mile away from our cushy office with all the free food.

I'm very intentional about the work environment I create in the office as well. When I had my first kid, it was definitely a different era, with women and pregnancy and childcare. I had a great arrangement because Patricia Arquette had a nursery on *Medium*, and even so it was very difficult. I found myself in jobs after that, pretending that I didn't have a baby so that people would think I was a man, basically. It was definitely like, "I can stay just as late as anybody else. I can work weekends just like anybody else. I never have to go do a thing at school. Never, ever. I have people for that. I don't even have kids. What are you talking about?" Even in some jobs, I would not dress in a feminine way because I wanted people to think I was a man, not in the literal gender swapping way, but I just didn't want them to have any reason to take my pitches less seriously. It sounds terrible to say, but that's what it was.

I found that during the interview process, it was not helpful to say that you have a toddler or a baby at home, and they can't ask you that. I'm proud to say that when we were interviewing for *Nancy Drew*, we were very, very supportive of people wanting to have families and being moms. People can nurse their babies if they want to. People can take time out to pump. People can use the nursery that we've got set up. People definitely should go be with their kids if there's an event happening, all those things. It feels radical, but it shouldn't be because people work harder when they feel like they're treated like a human being here. It's seen as a strength that I have a life outside of this job, and it's not like you have to have kids as a prerequisite. We also have people who are single, and they have lives, and I support that too. I want people to have lives. I don't want people to come in and feel resentful, out of ideas, burnt out, and tired. There are other jobs I've been on where all your energy gets focused on how badly you're being treated, and then the work suffers. Essentially enlightened self-interest, but I also think it's the right thing to do.

I try to be guided by that principle. In my first year on *The Vampire Diaries*, when Sarah Jones was killed in the *Midnight Rider* incident in Georgia, I was also in Atlanta in that part of February, and it just happened that the accident happened while I was there. Without exaggeration, the devastation and the emotional impact that it had on the crew was really life-altering. Writers use this word "devastated" so casually, like, "Nancy was devastated that her clue trail didn't pan out." But when you actually see what it looks like when people are devastated, it's really tough. The crew members were her closest friends. I only met her once myself, but she was great. I didn't know her personally beyond having worked with her a little

Melinda Hsu 169

bit. But her best friends were still on *The Vampire Diaries* crew, and I was friends with them. And going to the memorial and hearing everything that people were saying about her, and all the things that were posted on Facebook, and the whole Safety for Sarah thing was operating out of our DIT tent on *The Vampire Diaries* set while that was rolling. So, I thought, "It's not right that the last time everybody's going to talk about this person, this particular spark of light, is at this memorial service." I asked Julie about it. Julie was terrific, incredibly supportive, and so were Warner Bros. and Local 600. Sarah's birthday would have been September 22nd, so I wanted to organize a walk-a-thon and awareness raising. And so we did, and that turned into the Sarah Jones Film Foundation, which I'm really proud of. It turned into this really kind of transformative event where, out of this awful needless tragedy, we found a way for people to build community and also do a little bit better on set.

It feels awesome to be able to create a better work environment. It's so empowering. I've been in hiring situations where I've said, "I can't possibly pay you what you would normally get, but I can offer you this ethos and environment." I explain the way I run a show. For example, I bring in a coach on the first morning of the writers' room who discusses how the first process in making the show is to reach consensus, a group agreement, and establish norms and protocols for creative interactions and decisions. That's a really basic thing that most companies would do, and writers' rooms almost never do it. They kind of just throw a bunch of strangers together with a couple of best friends of the showrunner and expect everybody to just figure it out as they go, like kind of suss out the pecking order to take the temperature of the room and find out through the grapevine how this show-runner likes to work. It's like you've been dropped into a secret society, like an escape room. You have to figure it out and you're not allowed to ask for hints. It was crazy to me, so I was like, "Why not do this? Let's all be on the same page. Let's hire a coach who actually does this for a living to get us to do some team building exercises, and just think outside the box and to kind of notice about ourselves what our approaches are." And it works, because I've had people choose to work with me, for a lower rate than what they would normally get, because of the environment I promise.

It definitely feels like I made it through, so that I could create this environment. I put up with some bullshit along the way, and now I get to create the job that I wish I'd had, but that's okay. I think if I had not been through that amount of bullshit, I probably wouldn't have had the specifics for the things that I wanted to create. I don't demonize people I've worked with before. Sometimes people have blind spots, and they may not even know. They don't know what they don't know. It might not occur to them. Then other times, yes, I think people could have done better, but that's a whole other subject.

MICHELLE NADER
Open Your Mind to All the Possibilities of What Could Be

Figure 29.1 Michelle Nader
Source: photo by Lio Mehiel

Michelle Nader showran Season Two of the single camera comedy *Dollface* for Hulu and the last season of the multi-cam sitcom *2 Broke Girls* for CBS, after working her way up in television comedies for more than 20 years, writing on *Spin City, Caroline in the City, The King of Queens,* among others. She has created, developed and showrun multiple shows for CBS, NBC and Fox. Michelle is currently the showrunner of *Deli Boys* for Onyx/Hulu, developing pilots for Fox (*The D.L.*) and Netflix (*Old Friends*) and writing a feature to star Ellen DeGeneres about three friends who used to be like "Charlie's Angels" in the early 80s and are called back into action.

DOI: 10.4324/9781003298229-30

Michelle Nader 171

It was a novelty to have women writing on a show back in 1995 or '96 when I started. I didn't even know that we were part of an experiment or part of a movement – that "women really needed to be part of the staff." But I realized it when my partner and I got hired for *Caroline in the City*. And then we went to *Spin City*. We were the token women on the show. They didn't expect us to be funny. They expected us to know story, "How would a woman feel?" We were like, "Well, what about the jokes? I write jokes."

On *Caroline in the City*, I had no idea what I had gotten myself into. I'm a writer, and I used to be a reporter too, but this was like, "Oh shit. These people are really funny and really fast." It's a minute-to-minute proving of your worth. I couldn't think that fast, and I thought I was smart. I remember my eye twitched, and no one could see it, but I could feel it for a solid – from like pre-production, all the way to once we got into production, I was like, "It stopped, it stopped." But I was still so freaked out. But you just have to let go of the fear. You start to get more primal. I learned that it's instinctive; you have it in you. It's a very pressure-filled job. I didn't know I needed to perform on that level as a writer. So that took me a while to get accustomed to, and then I did. It takes years to master it. And I really wanted to be great at jokes. That was my goal on *Spin City*, because Gary Goldberg had hired a bunch of us in our 20s and we didn't know what the fuck we were doing. And we were there for the duration. We had beds brought into the room. And I thought, "What did I sign up for?"

Friends was the huge hit of the '90s and that was the culture that I grew up in. And I think that's why *Spin City* and shows around that time thought that if you didn't stay until 4am, you were doing something wrong. But we never did anything worthwhile after 8pm. Your brain just can't work. I worked on some shows where we worked on Saturdays! And I thought, "We're not going to be better on Saturday. You're not going to make a better show on Saturday." But at the same time because I was there 18 hours a day, I listened to how people formulated jokes. And I love telling a good story. Then the jokes are so much easier to come out of that because the best joke in the world, if there's no story behind it, it just falls flat. And you don't wind up using it. Or it doesn't shine as it should. So, I learned how to think in jokes, formulate jokes with the joke people – because on every show there are the story people and the joke people – and there was nothing more satisfying than to get all those guys to laugh.

Eventually, my writing partner and I split up, because it's just hard to have a partner. And as much as I love her – we're still friends – I really loved this world of multi-cam sitcoms. I took to it. And I didn't think I would. And then I went on to do *Dharma and Greg*, and then went back to *Spin City*. I might have gone to *The King of Queens* after that, then I started getting my own development stuff, went to NBC, developed *Kath & Kim*. And then ran another show, *100 Questions*, which wound up being like six questions.

172   *Michelle Nader*

Then I came to Warner Bros., developed one year and then I met Michael Patrick King, who was developing *2 Broke Girls*. I worked from the pilot on, then I moved up to showrunner.

In some ways I think that female showrunners are more natural at doing the job. I can get my son ready for school, I can be doing construction on my house, I can be trying to look good, I can be trying to be social and have a boyfriend – certainly not a husband. And run a show. And we get it all done. We get it all done somehow and it seems like we're just built that way.

I did learn a lot from men – because I never worked for a female show-runner, ever, because there weren't any – what not to do. How not to be. You have to encourage the people around you to want to pitch stuff. Not to shut them down. And also, to care about their ultimate product because I do still believe in writing. Some shows room-write. I don't love that because I feel like, when I take the script home, and I see when other people take the script home, they're going to discover stuff. In the room, we're definitely going to discover stuff, because they'll have so much time with the script after it's written to hear it, and rewrite it, and to get that collaboration. But there's something to be said for a writer writing a script and figuring out those problems and something emerging. I believe in that. And then they're invested in the final product. I think the best shows come from one person thinking about what the show is. And I think that is a little bit of the auteur thing but at the same time, as a showrunner I am trying to guide everybody. I need everybody in there, all those different voices. That's the difference maybe, me as a woman, I'm very eager to hear what everybody else has to say. As opposed to, "Nah, not that." I'll make the ultimate decision, but I want to hear what everyone else has to say. And then I can make the decision, as opposed to preempting what might be the best idea ever.

It was a big thing for me to be stepping into Michael Patrick King's shoes really, filling those expensive shoes in the last season of *2 Broke Girls*. So, I was like, "Listen guys, I'm not this crazy, but every joke has to be an A joke. Just be bulletproof." So, we just went through the jokes and through the jokes. And I went over it and over it. That show is a beast because the more you give it jokes, the more it wants. And it just never ends. CBS is the last bastion of these kinds of shows. No one was going after jokes the way we were on *2 Broke Girls*. As much as everybody has been saying networks, network shows are over – they're not over. They're not going be over. When I go home to Philadelphia, and I hear things and see things, it's not just my shows they talk about. They talk about network shows. Those are the shows that those people care about. *2 Broke Girls* was the biggest show in China. Internationally, that's a whole other game.

Moving up within a show, taking over from a creator-showrunner, I know how I approached it was: "I don't want to alienate him, because it is his show, but we can't both do this." I will say that one of the show's directors was a huge support to me. He gave me the best corner man speech. He was like, "Everybody loves you; everybody wants you to succeed. You can do

Michelle Nader 173

this. Do it, I'll stand behind you whatever you do. If you don't want to do it right now that's fine, but you gotta do it." I needed to take over this group and have their respect and have the authority creatively and otherwise, to make the decisions that would be best for the show. Because I have seen it in other experiences, not just my own, where the creator doesn't step away and the current showrunner is just going back and forth trying to please that person and also manage the day-to-day. That doesn't work. For sure, if you're in any business, if there's no strong leader with a real vision it's going to be watered down and not be as strong as it could be, so you have to go through that one hard moment. And it happened throughout the year at various times in various instances, where there was tension between what he wanted and what I wanted and where the show was going and what direction he wanted. And I will say, he didn't fight me even though he disagreed with me, but ultimately – and it's funny, because when he was running the show, we would fight over things and I was like, "You know what? It's your show, you get to be right." And now I get to be right. And again, the female-male thing, I don't know if it helped. But we've had a friendship that sometimes suffered because if you're doing 22 episodes of a show, it's an immense ball to roll up the hill.

2 Broke Girls did jokes that are written as jokes that a stand-up would do but in a character's voice. The actors have to find a way that makes it sound like the characters would say it. Single camera, they don't have this pressure of getting the laughs. They can just talk and it's the situation that's funny for them: the absurdity of the situation. Absurdity isn't funny, it's just absurd. The degree of difficulty is highest for sitcoms. The number of jokes and how hard it is to get these shows done is the least appreciated, the least celebrated. I don't know if it'll ever get the respect. Shows that don't have story, we took a lot of shit down, and I think people were like, "How dare you?" We had a line where Sophie, Jennifer Coolidge, says, because she's bored, "I have Hulu, I have Netflix, I have HBO, I'm about to HBO Go out of my mind," and then she says, "Alright, I guess I can give that Aziz Ansari show another chance, they say it gets good after the 11th episode." We could never get away with waiting to Episode 11 on a sitcom because we have an audience. The audience that comes on Tuesday nights to see a taping, we listen to them, and if the joke isn't like "shit your pants funny," we gotta beat it, and we beat it. And I don't always go by the audience, I don't live or die by the live audience. But you know when something is working and when something isn't. And we all tell ourselves lies as comedy writers: "That'll work, they just don't get it, they just aren't smart enough, this audience was dead. They're German, whatever…" and sometimes we're just like, "It wasn't funny, it doesn't work. We were laughing all week and it's funny to us, but it doesn't work." So, we'll change it. On the spot.

Not everyone is suited to the multi-camera form. Not everyone likes it; it is an old form. But when they are good, they shine. I think you have to be funny, in order to learn. If you're not, you can't do it. I've learned how to craft

174 *Michelle Nader*

a joke. Some of the writing staff would be comprised of stand-ups; they knew how to craft jokes. So, I would listen to how they formed a joke, and how do you open your mind to all the possibilities of what that could be? That's not just obvious, what regular people would say to each other if they want to be funny or clever. You have to absolutely open your mind a million times to a million opportunities and then form it. And when enough of these people are around and you see it happening, you begin to learn it from them, and I did learn it from them. And funny people are so smart. I mean, if you don't have a little bit of an off sensibility, in the timing, get that sort of offness about everything, you're not going to know what makes people laugh.

I still consider myself more of a story person who can pitch shows and do jokes. But it's not like, "The joke guys are the men, and the story guys are the women." There are women stand-ups, Laura Kightlinger, Morgan Murphy, Liz Astrof, on our staff, brilliant joke writers, those people are like the Navy SEALs of jokes. They're just like BOOM, they're crazy good and crazy fast. They're writing on the floor and the audience loves that, seeing how fast we are. Some of the writers, we go to the stage knowing that on Tuesday night, we're probably going to pitch some jokes, so they prepare, but it's those stand-ups that are in the moment, that are the touch up people.

Somehow as we get older, we feel like sitcoms are too simplistic, it's just kind of a bias. Everything is so fast-paced now. I wonder if a show like *Everybody Loves Raymond* were around now, could that sustain itself because they did five scenes. It was like the *Family Ties* model – Alex does something wrong and then he makes it worse. It was like three scenes basically, and then *Seinfeld* was like thirty scenes, a lot of scenes. *2 Broke Girls* did, relatively speaking, about nine scenes. When I watch *Stranger Things*, or something I want to binge, it's great. But if I get scared or something I literally will turn on *Seinfeld*. And I think *2 Broke Girls* is in that model where you're like, "I just want to go to a place where I know what's going to happen and I'm just going to laugh." It's like comfort food. When I see a multi-camera show on a plane – any show – I'm happy to see it because it just makes me feel, in this crazy world that we live in, a little bit of, "I can relax. I don't have to work hard." It brings me back to my childhood of feeling happy. Now, if sitcoms were going to go away, I would be sad. They are like little plays, and everybody can understand them. They're archetypes. I look at it on paper, it's the opposite of simple. It's on this level of experience, you buy into this surreal world where we say, "This is what we're doing, come with us."

On *2 Broke Girls* we did a table read with all the actors on a Wednesday, and then Thursday we'd see it on its feet, we do a run through, and if it holds up, doesn't hold up, usually it holds up, and then we'll redo jokes. And then Friday the network comes in to see it at noon, have some notes, and then Monday we do pre-shoots and Tuesday we did our audience show. And Wednesday we do it all again. For 22 episodes, we'll do three episodes on, a week hiatus, three episodes on, a week hiatus, and then we do 2, 2 and 2,

Michelle Nader 175

because as you go, we eat up our lead. It's a hiatus for the actors, they don't have to work, but the writers are always working. We never have a day off. And it's so funny because the actors are always like, "What did you guys do, did you go anywhere for the hiatus?" And we're like, "How many years do you not know that we're in the room, dying slowly?"

We usually start pre-production in summer. I'm still relatively healthy looking but by September, it's yoga pants, black boots. You just have to get into your mentality of in the trenches, like you're not wishing your life away but it's a lot. You can't have a social life. I don't really have a social life, even though I try never to work late, by the time I get home, I'm still doing work on scripts, dealing with casting. I'm always dealing with the next script of the week, so it is a 24/7 job. But the way I manage it is to manage it and not bring everyone down with me.

I can do stuff in the mornings, at night, and I'd like to keep the writers doing what they do best, which is coming up with stories and coming up with jokes. Everybody's there for the show taping unless we get really behind. I'm very much about getting the script in the right exact spot so we have the best exact chance of winning each week. It's like a game I have, like we have to get this in the best shape possible because so many things can fall apart if it isn't. I feel like I'm the curator. I'm the person that's always listening to everyone and saying, "We shouldn't start there." It's hard for me sometimes now to write, like I'll have to be really close to the screen, because I'm always looking at the back row so much. So now sometimes just doing jokes is harder for me, because I can't get into what I used to when I was coming up on a show, which was just thinking of jokes and thinking of lines and thinking of stories and that's what the showrunner would choose from. And now, although I do it, it's a different head.

Michael Patrick King calls me a gangster. He says I am a gangster, because I'm decisive, like, "That's not right, nope, no thanks, no cut it, fire him, they've got to go, that's not right." I feel like I've had to fire lots of people along the way, and I've had to say no most of the time, so you have to find a way to be humane about it but not be precious. And I love celebrating. I laugh really loudly when I love a joke, but everyone should know that I don't take any time off. I told a staff writer, "Listen I'm always working, you should always be working." Always be working, always be thinking of the next joke, you're just starting, this is a tough business, this is a very demanding business. When I see someone's not doing that, that just bums me out. I just have a different mindset – and I think it's a generational thing, because I do not see that in young people – I don't see people submitting to the process, like an assistant the other day was like, "I was wondering if I could get an episode?" Like, "No you can't get an episode, why would you get an episode? Just because you're around here and you're getting coffee, you think you can get an episode, you deserve that? No, that's not happening," and I wasn't mean about it, I was just like you have to do a lot of work before that. It takes years and years of being a writer's assistant to become a writer. It takes years and years of being an actual writer to be a writer.

As a showrunner, you're a dictator. I happen to be a benevolent dictator, but still a dictator. And you have to, because there are too many decisions. It can be a collaboration until a certain point when you have to make a decision. I am very clear, like, "I don't like this." But I'm not shaming anybody. I'm just the person who has to decide whether something is working or not. I think my writers are all brilliantly talented, but I'll just say that I think they can come up with something better. You do have to have a nose for it. You have to sniff around and then something will happen. And I think experience is everything. To me, the showrunner is carrying the comedy from the idea to the writing, to the show night, to the actors, to the editing. You can't drop any of the formula, you have to know what the comedy is and keep building it. It's having that comedy voice in your head that's guiding it.

I grew up in South Philadelphia around mobsters and I saw people get killed. I remember talking about that kind of South Philly mentality. And I did try to kill my stepfather. He was hitting my mother while she was pregnant. So I guess I am kind of a gangster but a non-violent one.

I didn't have a dad. I had uncles. My uncles were my Lebanese half. But so, my uncles, and a few other things, are why I wound up doing this. I wanted to be Pauline Kael, a film critic. How I got into movies was that as a kid I couldn't sleep at night, and I would just watch old movies. My mother dated somebody who was really a genius but an alcoholic and he turned me on to Pauline Kael. So I had that, then my uncles would sit around and they were always funny, and they would joke around. I realized early on if you weren't making the joke, you were the butt of the joke. So comedy and movies were something wired in me at an early age. It's funny I realized, I'm actually tearing up a little, but I thought of it because back when I made my uncles laugh, that was the laugh that I wanted from the writers I started under. To make people laugh. That was the currency. Then getting back to the gangster thing, growing up in South Philadelphia, I dated the person that went on to become the head of the mob and I was like, "Either I'm going to be a mob wife, or I'm going to go and get educated." That's when I started reading books like *Pride and Prejudice*. I wound up going to Penn. Nobody I went to high school with went to college. I remember seeing that old boyfriend, who was the one that became the head of the mob, when I went back to South Philadelphia, and I rolled up in my car and he's like, "I hear you're on a hit," and I'm like, "Well, you know a hit when you see one." He laughed. He's probably in some ways more successful than I am. Certainly in his world. And I think the gangster in me has helped me to be a showrunner because you have to have a certain sense of like, "I'm the boss and I like to be loved but I don't need to be loved." I'm not after love, and I feel like a nice person, but at the same time, not to a fault where I won't get the job done. My priority is to get the best show done to make something great and for people to be happy because we're so lucky to be doing this, and I never forget that. If I didn't love doing this, I wouldn't be doing this anymore.

Michelle Nader 177

I still think I'm finding my voice. I don't think I have, in some ways. I haven't actualized it until I get my own show in which I feel like I've done something somewhat personal, then I'll feel like I got there. I feel like I've found a way to use my voice in shows and I think the DNA is clear. People will say, "Oh that's your joke," or "That's your imprint." But to me, for a writer, it's always a work in progress. At different stages, I've had different pilots that represent different parts of me, different parts of my life that when I look back, I'm like, "That's terrible I don't even know who that is."

We had to do a table read right after the 2016 election and people were crying. I was crying and I had to give this speech. I looked at all these faces and I had to lead in this moment, and this was the first time I was like, "Ok this job is more than just doing comedy. I have to lead these people who are looking at me for how to feel better in this moment or what to feel about this." This was the actors and the writers, and the executives and I just said, "We're going to do this today, through tears and we're going to laugh through the tears because this is what we do for people and this is what we're going to do, stick together. And know this won't be our future forever. I mean I hope. Or I will die." Everyone slowly started to laugh, and fortunately by the end, it was a good script. It was right what we needed in the moment. So, we started in tears and ended laughing. A show like this, a silly sitcom, is actually a great antidote for the world. People want to check out and laugh, and that's what we do.

It's been incremental for me to get where I felt, "I can do this," but every day is like that. Even now, when I'm writing a script, I'll think, "Wait a second, how do you write a script?" I have no idea how to make it happen. Every day is like a new struggle, to decide how to write out the script. Every day I'm like, "OK, I'll just write one thing down." The blank page is the most awful thing you can face. But even with rewrites, you're like, "I think I know what I want." But it's only in the execution that you know you can do it. For anybody who wants to start out doing this, forget about breaking in, I have no advice about that for people – but you really do have to just do it and just understand that you can do it.

We have to help each other. I'm going to do whatever I can, from whatever pedestal I've been given as a showrunner or as a director. If I create the next show, I'm going to give it my full. I'll always write about women, that is one thing I feel strongly about. I think we're all kind of shedding those ideas of what a woman is and should do. That's kind of wish fulfillment for me, because the girls I'm doing this for, they are young and they're like the littlest feminists and they're badasses. I'm just much more interested in women and their relationship to each other and to men and not from a male perspective. As I'm getting older, it's shitty that you don't get the opportunities men get. There's plenty of guys I see who are ok, but it's like, "Oh yeah they knew that guy." We should get to do that. I might be the only woman on a network, multi-camera wise. It's just about that break-in point, that's where it all has to start. And I think that women who have broken in have to help open that still very closed, tiny vein of entry for the next generation.

MONICA MACER
You Gotta Be the First One Out on the Dance Floor

Figure 30.1 Monica Macer
Source: photo by Mark Levine

Monica Macer has run *Queen Sugar, Gentefied, MacGyver,* and written for *Nashville, Lost,* and *Prison Break* among others. African American and first-generation Korean American, Monica grew up moving around the US. A woman of faith, Macer spent 14 years climbing the ladder, often repeating levels, before being given her shot at showrunning. Monica graduated from Vassar College.

I really feel like so much of who I am and what I do are the gifts that my parents gave me. My father always knew I was a creative kid and that I probably wouldn't have a normal 9 to 5 job. In college I directed a play, *The Colored Museum* by George C. Wolfe, and my dad came to see it. And that's when he knew, "She's going to do something artsy." I remember graduating and having student loan debt to pay back, and there was a job fair in Philadelphia – featuring jobs at schools, banks, non-profits etc. So, I thought,

DOI: 10.4324/9781003298229-31

"This is the responsible thing to do. I need to go to this job fair. And get a *real* job." So I put on my little suit from The Limited and was getting ready to leave. My dad was going to drive me to the train, but before we left, he stopped me in the hall and said, "I thought you wanted to direct." And I said, "I do." And then he looked at me and said very matter of fact, *"Then direct."* It was his gift to me. Basically, he was saying, "Look kid, I know you have student loans to pay back." Because he had loans to pay back, too, but growing up, he didn't have the opportunity to follow his dream. He really wanted to be a teaching tennis pro, and that was something that he was eventually able to do in retirement. My dad was an auditor for the federal government. He liked numbers, but he really loved tennis. And so, he wanted to give me the gift of pursuing my dream, and that changed everything for me. So I walked back upstairs, took my suit off and started looking for theatre directing internships in New York.

My mother was also very influential in my career and supported me for years while I toiled away in the theatre. One year she even rented an apartment in San Diego for me while I worked as a directing intern at The Old Globe Theatre. My mom cooked every meal for me so I could just focus on "the work." We lived together for months, as I assisted directors on two back to back productions (one was *Hedda Gabler*) – and I never would have been able to afford to do that on my own. But those two credits on my resume were priceless for an up and comer like me and I owe it all to my mom.

Growing up, I went to 13 different elementary and junior high schools. We moved around a lot because my dad was working for the Department of Energy, so I lived in Oklahoma, New Jersey, and Houston, Dallas, and DeSoto, Texas. So, a lot of times, I was the new girl. I was constantly trying to find my tribe in school. What's so strange is that transient upbringing prepared me for this career because in TV, *tomorrow's not promised*. Your show could get canceled, your lead could get sick, and you might have to go on a really long hiatus, or you could not get "asked back." So many things can happen. Take *Nashville* for instance. After the show's fourth season ABC canceled it. And we all went off and found other gigs. Then a few months later, *Nashville* was resurrected and picked up by CMT. So, you just never know. Moving around really prepared me for the ups and downs of this business.

As a TV writer, I've worked in a variety of genres. And honestly that was a conscious decision, because being Korean American and African American – I never want to be put in a box. My family is very multiracial, very multicultural. And when we roll through a restaurant together – we get a lot of befuddled looks. It's interesting. I'm used to having a very rich and diverse family life, and I think that made me not want to be put in a box as a writer. I like genre. I love action. I love writing character AND soap. And I want to continue to write in ALL of these genres. I think of it like dinner – I wouldn't want to eat the same thing every night. I love steak and potatoes because I'm from the Midwest originally, but I don't want to eat that for dinner every

180 *Monica Macer*

night. And I don't want to eat pizza every night and I don't want to eat Korean Barbeque every night – even though I love pizza and bulgogi. And I think as a writer, I'm constantly trying to challenge myself and reach my full potential. So, wherever there's a weakness, I want to shore that up because I want to be able to paint with all the colors of the rainbow. And working in various genres helps me to stay in fighting shape and flex all those muscles when needed.

Early on in my career, I was trained by the writers on *24* (as their writer's assistant for Seasons Two and Three). So, because of them – namely Joel Surnow, Michael Loceff and Howard Gordon - I have strong action writing muscles. I was able to pour that into *Lost*, which was a really big room of about a dozen of us. It was very hierarchical in a traditional sense, where the upper-level writers spoke and I waited for the lull in the room before I could pitch, so as not to disrespect anyone. I was given a large realm of authority over the characters of Sun and Jin because they were Korean, which was a blessing as a staff writer. After Season One of *Lost*, Damon Lindeloff said to me, "Your DNA is literally imprinted on those characters," which was such an empowering thing to hear as a very new writer. Then on *Prison Break*, Karyn Usher was my mentor. The advice that Karyn gave me in the room – and we were the only two women on staff – was, "This is an action show. You're tweeting like a bird in the room and your pitches aren't landing. You need to learn how to bark like a dog. Bark like a dog when you pitch and then folks will start leaning in. Because right now, they can't hear you on that *tweet, tweet, tweet* frequency. You're trying to be so polite – DON'T. Pitch like an alpha male – with energy and enthusiasm and as if you're speaking in all caps. Be like, 'AND THEN SCOFIELD COMES IN THE ROOM!'" That was a huge gift because it worked! And her advice made me much stronger in the room. On *Lost,* I didn't have that boldness. But after *Prison Break*, I definitely had more confidence.

When I was producing my first episode of *Prison Break* (by myself) in Chicago, I kept calling my boss (the showrunner) and saying, "Oh, they're asking about this, and what should we do?" And then after the fifth call or so, the showrunner said, "You know what Monica, producing is making decisions. Don't call me unless the building is on fire." Click. Basically, he was telling me, "Just do it. You have incredible department heads and a great line producer who will be there to guide you through the experience, but *you're the writer*. Empower yourself, make creative choices that we've talked about in the room that uplift the vision of the show." So that was also a huge gift.

I'm an introvert, but I have become an extroverted introvert because that's what I need to be to do this job. As a showrunner, if no one else is talking, I have to be able to lead the room and put beats on the board until everyone else can catch the vision. You have to be able to do it yourself. If no one else is going to show up to the party and dance, you gotta be the first one out on the dance floor. It's like, "Oh okay, no one's going to do the electric slide and my aunt paid a lot of money for my cousin's wedding and this DJ? I gotta get on the dance floor…" – I always joke that on the Korean side of my family, they always come to me or my sister first if we're at a family wedding. They're like, "YOU start the electric side." And I say, "Okay, Auntie. Yeah. Let's do this." My husband always asks, "Really? Do we have to do that?" and I nod, "Yeah, we have to, they paid a lot of money for this wedding. They want everyone on the dance floor." So, it's kind of like the same thing when you're running the show. The studio has paid a lot of money for the show, you might have to be the first one to do the electric side.

I'm a woman of faith. When I was a kid (before we started moving around), we lived in Chicago Heights and my dad made sure we went to church with my grandparents. My grandparents' church was this tiny, little church on the South Side. My grandmother was the rock of our family and if you had a problem, she would grab your hand and pray for you and say, "Don't worry about it, baby." My grandfather was a deacon in the church, and I remember going with him as a kid to visit the "sick and the shut-in" (folks who were too sick to come to service) to encourage folks or bring them a little treat. He'd sit and talk to them for hours and just be there for them during some dark times. My paternal grandparents and their faith had a strong influence on who I am and how I treat others.

I'm also an encourager. I don't like to see people down. I want people to enjoy what they're doing. I feel like I've been given this incredible gift of being a writer and this amazing career. The gift that my parents gave me – to do what I feel called to do, that's why I like mentoring because I want other people to realize that it's possible. It might take a little bit, you might not get staffed right out of college or grad school, you might have to be a PA and then an assistant for a minute, but you will get there if you keep working. *"Just keep swimming…"*

This industry is a marathon. It's not a sprint. And it's my faith and my family (especially my husband Sterling and my daughter Dylan) that keep me grounded and able to survive the challenging times, the ups and downs and periods of career uncertainty. And to be completely honest, it's helped me overcome some really abusive bosses and toxic situations. And while I've had some truly horrific experiences in this industry – I've tried to take those experiences and learn from them. Mostly how NOT to treat people. Thankfully, because of who I am and the experiences I've had – I try to make the writers' room an inclusive and safe space for everyone. And as a showrunner, I want to be a safe space for people on staff and on the crew.

For me, every show is an assignment. I'm thankful that I get to be the showrunner of *MacGyver*, this badass action mission of the week: where we save the world every episode. It's a gift that I'm ready to receive at this point in my career. I've been doing this, coming up on 17 years now. It's exactly the right show at the right time for me in my career. I came up writing action, trained by the writers of *24, Prison Break, Teen Wolf, Knight Rider*. That was the strongest muscle I had for the longest time in my career. And then I made a choice and said, "I want to write character." And then I got

182 *Monica Macer*

staffed on NBC's *Deception* under Liz Heldens – a great showrunner who has since become a good friend, and *Nashville* under Dee Johnson. And I became a stronger character writer because of them. Dee Johnson was the first showrunner of color that I worked for and the first Asian American woman that I've been able to work with. And I learned so much from Dee – she always said, "It's character first." So now, because of Liz and Dee, I feel like my character muscles are as equally strong as my action muscles.

When I took the job on *MacGyver*, I said, "Nobody cares about running and jumping, if you don't care about the PEOPLE who are running and jumping." So, I would love to lean more into character, lean into the love triangle. I'm an action writer who does character. And that's what *MacGyver* is. Because at this point in my career, I want to laugh AND write strong characters. But I also want to blow stuff up and have awesome car chases. For me, the full circle is the action. Because the last few years, I'd been doing character, character, character shows and decidedly took a step in a cable and streaming direction. But now, I'm really excited about the opportunity of coming back to network on a huge, high octane show with car chases and explosions and "Oh, we get to save the world every day... *with science.*"

But becoming a showrunner only happened when I met with Ava DuVernay for Season Two of *Queen Sugar*. Even though I had a job on *The Breaks* for VH1, where I was the number two – I got the call to interview with Ava for the showrunning gig. I didn't need the job, and I didn't think I was going to get it. So that took the pressure off me and allowed me to be honest with Ava and say, "This is what I love about the show. And this is what I would love to do next season." I didn't have that fear that comes when you *really* need a gig, so I said at the end of the meeting, "And girl if you don't hire me, no sweat. I'm still going to watch your show." And I really meant it. And then it worked out. When I met with Ava, she asked me about my post experience. And thankfully, I was able to say, "I ran post for my boss, Liz Heldens, on *Deception* so I've done everything from playback, to scoring sessions, to sitting with the editors." And Ava said, "You are the only Co-EP level woman that I've met with who has that much post experience." And when I got the job, Ava admitted, "That's a large reason why you got the job, because I'm going to be in New Zealand and all over the globe, shooting *A Wrinkle in Time*. I need someone who I know can do it." From the start, Ava empowered me, and it was life changing to work in an atmosphere where there were so many people of color and women in leadership roles.

Queen Sugar was the first time someone said, "And now you're the showrunner." And it took a woman of color to do that. I know that I was on other "showrunner lists" before that, but nobody had pulled the trigger and taken a chance on me yet. When Ava hired me, I think I'd been working in the industry for 14 years. When it comes to the showrunners of color, I'm sorry, the system is broken. *14 years?* Realistically, it shouldn't have taken that long. But people of color and women are not matriculating up the ladder. They're repeating levels and being held back, because of the choices that are made at the top. And the folks at the top – the ones who decide who's ready and who gets those coveted jobs, they don't always look like me. And that can be really discouraging.

So, someone asked me on a panel, "How did you feel when you took over *Queen Sugar*? Were you nervous?" And I said, "No. I felt perfectly prepared." When you climb the ladder for 14 years, your bosses are constantly delegating to you. It's kind of the old school way. You should be ready to run a show after 14 years. People now are getting shows left and right only after a few seasons under their belts. Some with very little production experience. And great for them. *Are they prepared?* I don't know, time will tell. But I know I was grateful to have had all of that experience on many different shows with many different bosses. When I had to repeat levels – (namely staff writer and co-producer), I would get down on myself and think, "I just did a network, 22 episode show at staff writer on *Lost*, now I have to repeat it on *Prison Break*?" But that was a rule back then with studios. If you hadn't done 22 episodes with THEIR studio, you had to repeat THAT level. But Karyn Usher told me, "That's a good thing, because when you're up for your next job, you'll have 22 more episodes than your peers. It will pay off in the long run." And it did.

When I go up for a job, I want to find a point of connection. That's what we do as storytellers – connect with our audience and connect in the room. It all comes down to that. I like to connect with folks and get to know them – *find out what makes them tick.* I like telling stories and entertaining. I want to move people and I feel so honored that I get to do this every day. It's a really exciting time right now because as a nation we're being forced to reckon with the lingering wounds and mistakes of the past (especially when it comes to race and gender). So now there's a huge spotlight shining on us – which is an opportunity for change, not just in our country, but in our industry. And I feel like we just need to lean into it.

NATALIE CHAIDEZ
My Lane is Transgressive Women

Figure 31.1 Natalie Chaidez
Source: photo by Laura Burke Photography

Natalie started her career by winning a Disney Writing Fellowship and worked her way up on shows such as *New York Undercover, Judging Amy, Heroes, Terminator: The Sarah Connor Chronicles*, moving up to showrunner on *Hunters*, which she created, *12 Monkeys, Queen of the South,* and *The Flight Attendant*. Natalie has developed multiple projects including an adaptation of *Chicano*, and an Isabel Allende book, and is currently on an overall deal with Warner Bros.

DOI: 10.4324/9781003298229-32

I did the Disney fellowship program the first year that it was created, back when it was little known and everyone used to call it "This weird minority program." It was incredibly valuable training. I was mentored by three executives – a female Latina executive, a male Latino executive and a Black executive. They really took me under their wing and it was transformative. I don't think I would be where I am today if it wasn't for that program. And part of it was that they did say, "We're going to treat you like a regular writer who's on a deal, so you have to pitch as if you're pitching something that we would actually buy." And so, I pitched for almost half a year. And I cried on those days because I had to go in every Friday and pitch, and it was just so demoralizing. But it was great training. I learned how to pitch and how to take rejection. I finally pitched something that they ended up developing, and then I wrote that script for them that year, and they picked me up for a second year. At that time, I was just writing movies and they helped me get an agent, and that kind of launched my career. That was like 30 years ago.

There's two parts to the skill of pitching. There's what you're pitching and then there's the way you're pitching it. So there's the idea, and then there's the presentation of that idea, which has to be communicated really simply and is like a hook of a pop song. It has to resonate quickly. But I was very shy. I didn't know anything about Hollywood. I didn't understand the culture. So, part of it was just learning to speak that language, which I'm frankly still learning. These past couple of years have been really helpful in terms of me learning how to pitch, and learning what makes the project go. You need a critical mass of power behind it to push it through, usually. So those are lessons that I'm still learning even this many years later. Sometimes you're only pitching to places that you think might be right for the idea. You're not going to take the Isabel Allende project, which is sort of in the YA genre, it's not hard edge, and try to sell that to FX. That's just not a show that they're going to make. So, part of it is just matching the material to the network. Part of it is also knowing what they've bought before. This thing that I sold at Freeform was originally set in the '90s, but they had just recently bought a couple of things set in the '90s, so then we retooled it to be in the present day. That's an example of just knowing what their appetite is and knowing what they've already bought, and then we were able to sell it because that was something that fit their slate better.

I do visual presentations, pitch decks. They're very important, particularly when you're pitching something that's maybe a genre piece or something that's hard to visualize or super stylized. Everybody pitches with a deck these days. With *Chicano*, my mother's family is Mexican American and I grew up in East LA, which is where the project is set, so I included my family pictures to say, "This is my family, my family had the same journey as this show and as the book." Sometimes there'll be other stuff you include, like with the Asian American girl gang story I did, the writer/director added

186 *Natalie Chaidez*

pictures of his family and immigration pictures from Vietnam. When people saw them, it really made that connection. It was really cool.

I absolutely love genre. The Isabel Allende project is a genre thing. It's fantasy. So, I'm still working in that area, but my lane is transgressive women. Everything I write about is kind of that same story over and over and over. Sometimes that's *T2 (Terminator 2)*, and sometimes that's a story about a track team, which is a movie I have set up at Lionsgate. So I do love genre, but I feel like it's definitely not the only place I can tell the stories that I want to tell.

I think one thing that's kept my soul alive in television is following things that interest me in my life. So right now, I'm skateboarding. I don't know why. I just want to skateboard. I'm terrible at it, but I'll go down the street and I'll go to the park. I'm old, so I can't do anything. But I feel like those journeys as a person have just reaped incredible rewards professionally. I skated roller derby for eight years. Actually, I'm retired now. It was the most amazing experience and I met the most powerful women. My feature writing partner is actually a Black woman that I met doing derby who has a PhD in film studies, and now we've launched our feature career together. It was just a beautiful world. There was so much acceptance and closeness. I absolutely loved it. Then I left because I had concussions, so I couldn't play anymore, but I miss it. I miss it dearly. With derby, I was able to write about female athletes. I met my feature writing partner. I want to direct, and I met the DP who I just shot a music video with. So, I've found that just following those passions has really fed into my life as a writer and into my career in a really cool way. Anything that I'm really interested in sometimes develops into a project, sometimes it develops into a relationship, and sometimes they take twenty years to come to fruition. Like this movie that I sold that's going to get made at Lionsgate was just something I carried with me that I was interested in and read about. And it just took a really long time to find its moment in Hollywood. It's just really exciting right now to see that people are now interested in the stories that I wanted to tell at the beginning of my career, when nobody gave a shit about us. It's just really moving.

There are worlds that you can explore that people care about now that you can sell, and that people are interested in. There was very little space for that twenty or twenty-five years ago when I started, when the Latino character was the sidekick, where there wasn't a show about us. There wasn't an *Insecure* there, there weren't all these other shows with female leads. So, it's been amazing to walk into a WGA room and have all of these faces you would not have seen twenty-five years ago. Obviously, there's still a lot of progress to be made, but it's still inspiring.

When I started in the business, there was just flat-out racism and sexism. So maybe it's because I've just been around longer that I know how much has changed and I'm grateful for it. And I'm not saying there still aren't obstacles, but we've made progress. Twenty-six years ago, there was no one.

There were maybe three female showrunners, and I can't even think of one Latino showrunner. I don't think there was one. There's still a ways to go. There are definitely rooms you walk into where everybody is a white exec or is a male exec...there are still those spaces, and there's definitely a lot of racism and sexism. I experienced that on my projects. I experienced it in the notes. I'm just saying it's come a long way since I started when it was blatant in your face stuff that would just get you arrested these days.

To maintain your voice over time is really tricky in television. You need two skills – you need to be very original, but you also need to "write the show," in a lot of cases, mimic the showrunner's voice. So those are often two very different skills, and sometimes people can do one or the other. And I think what happens through the process of notes is, there's so much explaining, particularly if you've worked in institutions that don't let the artists just do whatever they want. So, you go through various notes until those voices are in your head. So, then you'll read younger writers who haven't had all those edges knocked off of them and they feel more original. There are people who are able to maintain that all the way up to the top, because they've had this great career where they started right out the gate and had this tremendous success, like Sam Esmail with *Mr. Robot*, or Issa Rae or somebody like that, and that sort of carries you through. But for a lot of people, you have to work inside the system for a long time, and it can be very challenging to keep your soul as a writer and remember why you're doing it, and remember what excites you and just keep your voice.

I kept my voice by always doing something else that was mine. It might have been a movie that I was writing, it might have been something that I was developing, and it might've been something that was just a part of my life like derby that feels wild and fresh, something that makes you think, "You guys can't fucking take this from me." So, it's just a matter of keeping in touch with that part because the rest of it is jumping through other people. They want that wild voice and then they want you to jump through the hoops. So, for me, it's been about carving out that space for myself as a writer and as a person to protect that part of me, that 1) I know is marketable, and 2) is what makes me happy.

I've had two writers who I consider my mentors. One is named John Wirth and he's a veteran television writer-showrunner who I met on *Sarah Connor Chronicles*. And I really respected his management style, his integrity, his respect for writers, and he became a great personal friend and mentor and has always been incredibly supportive. And when I got my first job showrunning, I would call, I would email, I would ask for advice and he would always get back to me quickly and with great advice. He would make the attempt to listen. The other mentor is Jim Leonard, who's a playwright and a TV writer-showrunner. I think with Jim it was more in the writing. From John I learned a lot of management stuff, and Jim was the one who would look at my writing and circle it and say that's the wildness, that's the part I want to hear more of and see more of. He taught me a little bit of a

188 *Natalie Chaidez*

looseness because he came of age as a playwright, and I came of age as a writer inside the TV system. So, they've both been a tremendous support over the years.

I grew up in a very challenging environment. Both of my parents were criminals, incarcerated drug addicts. So, by the time I got to Hollywood, I was like, "What the fuck are you guys going to do to me that I already haven't been through?" I was already a lot older psychologically than I was chronologically. And people in Hollywood kind of talk tough, but I'd already been around really tough, scary people. So, I think I wasn't scared because I was like, "There's really nothing you can do to me that I haven't been through already...what are you going to do, stab me? I don't think so." I was already coming from a place that was really hard, and in a way, it was really good preparation for Hollywood because it's all about power and protecting yourself. So, I already had that kind of self-protective resilience going into it. I think I was also protected because I'm light-skinned? I might be part-Hispanic, but I look white to people, so I can go in a room and I'm not facing that kind of discrimination that darker Latinos or Black people go through. I know that people have been in terribly abusive rooms, and my heart goes out to them.

And I have been part of trying to change culture in my own way. I haven't been perfect, but you know, I think it's a systemic thing in rooms where you have phrases like, "Oh we're going to gang bang that script." We're never going to say, "we're going to gang bang the script," we say, "We're going to tampon that script, we're going to plug up those holes and stop the bleeding." The men, they hated it. But I was like, "You know what? You guys can just deal with it, and you're going to remember that one day someone made you tampon a script and understand what we've been going through over the last twenty-five years." And yes, I have been told many times, "You're not capable because you're a woman. You're not capable. It's too hard. You're not capable of this because you're a mother." For me, it was just a matter of getting in touch with that defiant, transgressive "fuck you guys" attitude. I can do it, and I'm going to do this no matter what. Keeping in touch with what's inside has been what's gotten me through it, even when things get canceled, "Your show's a flop," or "Your show's a hit," then you get fired. I've been on all of those ups and downs, and it's just about trying to come back to that place inside of me of like, "What do I want to do?" And I get a new idea and then I feel fresh as a baby, because that's what I want to do, those ideas excite me. I was actually told by the first female showrunner that I worked for that I was hypervigilant because I grew up in this dysfunctional world and that made me perfect for Hollywood. And that I sensed danger around every corner, and where it actually is.

I know there are still obstacles, but I've been really heartened by the changes I've seen even in the last few years. I was sexually harassed early on in my career. I was someone that, when I first got to Universal, the assistants would tell me about a lady who came around and gave hand massages. And

I was so naive, I thought it was a lady who massaged writers' hands. Of course, it was a hand job lady. I started out in a culture that told me there's no beautiful Korean women. Someone told me that to my face. Shit like that, the stuff I saw when I first started, it's not all gone, but I do think that there is a little bit of accountability now. It was the Wild West when I started, men could do and say almost anything, and there was no accountability at all. Now I feel like there is some accountability and I'm really happy about it. I'm really proud because I think that this came about because of people speaking up and being resilient and moving forward and being tough enough to hang in your jobs. I'm proud of us. I know we have a ways to go, but I'm really happy to see where we are as female showrunners and where we're going.

NKECHI OKORO CARROLL
Everyone Deserves the Right to Dream

Figure 32.1 Nkechi Okoro Carroll
Source: photo courtesy of Nkechi Okoro Carroll

Nkechi Okoro Carroll is a writer, producer, and one of the founders of Black Women Who Brunch. She is the executive producer and showrunner for the CW drama *All American*. She also created and now showruns the spinoff *All American: Homecoming* in addition to the new NBC drama *Found*. Carroll's other credits include producing and writing for *Bones, Rosewood,* and *The Resident*. Nkechi worked for many years as a trader/analyst at the United States Federal Reserve, while writing and acting in her off-hours. She graduated from UPenn and received a master's degree from NYU.

From a very young age, I've always had to adapt. I was born in New York. We moved back to Nigeria when I was young, and then after my parents got divorced, we moved next door to Cote D'Ivoire. I think part of that was underneath my love for writing and creating characters because I got

DOI: 10.4324/9781003298229-33

exposed to so many different types of people in so many different settings at such a young age. I went to boarding school in England because, especially in West Africa, that's what a lot of the families did. My sister really wanted to go to the UK. So, the UK is where we went. While I was in the UK equivalent of eighth or ninth grade, I first fell in love with Shakespeare. I ultimately joined the Oxford Youth Theatre, but it didn't take me long to realize that my love of Shakespeare wasn't so much about performing it, but it was the words and the way they moved me.

I knew I wanted to be able to use my words to create worlds and settings and laughter. Around 13, I set my heart on becoming a writer. Of course, coming from a traditional Nigerian family, my options were doctor, banker, lawyer. I did end up choosing banking, and I had a real, genuine love for economics. But I'm sort of very much a left brain, right brain person, so I was very strategic about pursuing both dreams. I went to school for economics. I followed the banking route, and that led me to New York. Even in college, I stayed very active in the theater community. I directed and wrote plays at the University of Pennsylvania. When I graduated, I stayed true to my word, and I used my economics degree to get a job at the Federal Reserve Bank of New York so that I could be in New York and be near the theater scene. That became my life for the majority of my twenties.

It was wake up in the morning, go to the Fed, do whatever trading I had to do in the morning in the fed funds market. Then in the afternoon, I do whatever economic analysis I have to do to send to DC. Then it would hit 5:30 pm, and I would leave work and go to whatever black box theater we were throwing up our production for that month. We'd go right into rehearsals for plays. I was writing, directing, some of them I was even acting in, and then I would circle back home. Sometimes with enough time to make it home and sort of catch a nap and make it back to work, and sometimes it was shower and change in the gym at work and go right back down to my trading desk. And of course, you're young, so you feel like you're invincible. I was like, "Who needs sleep? I can pursue writing and economics at the same time." Now I'm like, "Oh my gosh, kill me if I can't find my bed."

That was where I developed my unhealthy love for caffeine and continued my love of theater. But I was also an avid TV watcher. Even more than movies. I loved TV. I always tell people that everything you need to know about me, it can be figured out by my equal love of *Buffy the Vampire Slayer* and Shakespeare. Those two shape who I am so much as a writer. I was obsessed with TV shows like *Alias*, *Grey's Anatomy*, *The West Wing*, and of course *Buffy*. I was fascinated by the TV art form of writing. I couldn't really afford to leave my job at the Fed, so I just decided I was going to put myself through my own writing masterclass. I took a break from the theater and after work, I would go home and download whatever scripts I could find on the internet. Then I would watch the episode and would just spend all this time breaking down these scripts as I watched them on TV. Then when my material was at a place where it wouldn't completely embarrass me to send

192 *Nkechi Okoro Carroll*

it out, I basically came home, I had been married for all of about a year, and said to my husband, "I think we need to move to LA. I really want to pursue writing." And God bless him. He said, "Listen, I'm a teacher. I could teach anywhere. If you're saying LA is where you need to be to pursue this, then we'll do it." And we moved out to LA a year later.

About three months in, I realized, "Oh, I'm not one of those people who functions well as a starving artist." If I didn't know where my car note was coming from, I couldn't write anything. I was one of those people who needs to know that water, rent, the car, are taken care of and, you know, bills are paid. I was like, "Okay, not-sleeping artist is my thing." I went back to work full-time and also worked on my writing after work.

I had called the Federal Reserve and asked about working out of the LA branch. I covered Asia from Los Angeles. And I went back to work with the deal I made with myself, which was nights and weekends, we're shooting short films. We're going to acting classes to study character work and meet actors and sort of flesh out our characters that way. I started doing extra work on my vacation days from my job at the Fed on *Alias*, on *General Hospital*, on *The Guardian*, because I only knew the theater scene. It always used to confuse my assistant at the Fed because she'd be like, "People use their vacation days, and they go to the spa, but you go to do 12 hours of extra work." And I'm like, "Yeah, cause that's how I'm learning."

I knew nothing about what it takes to put a TV production together. I would sit next to the focus puller and be like, "Okay, so what's your job?" And that was how I taught myself the art of making TV shows. On nights and weekends, we would shoot short films with people I met in acting class. Ultimately one of those short films did really well on the film festival circuit and landed me my lit manager. After I signed with her, less than a year later, I got my first showrunner meeting, which was with Hart Hanson. They were doing the *Bones* spinoff and were looking for writers. It was my only show-runner meeting. My first and only one. I was still working at the Federal Reserve. Hart notoriously is not a soap fan, and my writing samples were all soaps because I was convinced I was going to write the next *90210*, or the next *Grey's Anatomy* or *Private Practice*. And it felt like all the ingredients that shouldn't have worked to land me my first job, but Hart ended up hiring me on *The Finder*. A couple years later I'd asked him, given his reputation for how he feels about soaps, what it was about my writing material that spoke to him. And he said it was my characters. There's something about people's voices and how they approach character that is harder to teach. He used to say he could teach someone how to structure a procedural but having a unique voice and a message and a way to bring characters to life, that is harder to teach. So, Hart gave me my first job as a staff writer on *The Finder*. That only went one season, and then he brought me over to join the *Bones* family after that and continue on with them from Season Eight on. That was when I actually officially quit my job at the Federal Reserve, the day after I got staffed on my first show. That was in 2011 in July, and I've been blessed to work ever since. In fact, when I left, when I resigned, because I got staffed at my first show, everyone was so shocked because I worked at the Fed for a total of 14 years. Seven and a half in New York, six and a half here in LA. It was a lot of time. I actually really did genuinely enjoy it. I loved working at the Fed. I just knew it wasn't my passion.

I planned my big economic career, and I could never quite let go of the writing dream. I just kept working on it. I never stopped doing it. In hindsight, those two fields and my love of them from such a young age, I think it's actually what probably makes me the showrunner I am today. As opposed to just sort of ascending on the literary creative side, I've kind of done both, the business end and on the creative end. And you need both of those skill sets as a showrunner because the thing you have the least amount of time to do as a showrunner is write. Everything else becomes running a multimillion-dollar corporation. That's practically what a TV show is. I have 250 employees between the cast, crew, writers, production staff, post-production staff. I'm a little bit of a type A, my friends would say a little OCD control freak. If I didn't know what every line item on a budget was, it would just drive me insane. It's something I need to know. The producing aspect of my job isn't just producing from a creative perspective. It's producing from a real-life corporate perspective and being able to wear all those different hats as the boss. And then still carve out time to shape storylines and shape the vision for the season and write episodes and rewrite other people's episodes. My desk is the last desk that any script or outline or anything goes across, and I have the final pen before it makes it to air.

Carla Kettner, Gina Prince-Bythewood and Greg Berlanti are some of my mentors. I feel like I very much lucked out in the influences in my life, that kind of shaped who I am as a showrunner. My showrunning style is, are we telling a good story? I want my shows to feel like they're leaving the world a little bit of a better place than I found it. Who knows whether I'm actually achieving that or not, but that's the goal behind everything I do. I believe that TV carries so much power. Even growing up for me, especially when I left the States, so much of what I learned and kept up to date on American culture came from TV shows. Our kids spend so much time watching TV shows that even subliminally so much of the messaging they receive and their point of view on things comes through from that perspective. As a mom of two boys, I feel like, "Oh, the TV is a way for me to also have some conversations with them that are a little harder to start from scratch at home." If I start it through the TV show, then I could follow it up. And I do believe that there are other shows that are doing the same thing and other shows that are leaning towards the aspirational humans, who can be the best we can, and those are the TV shows that I often gravitate towards watching.

I feel like my show is part of a call and response from a number of other shows that are equally doing the same thing about the types of conversations they're leaving in the room. Shows like *This Is Us*. I loved that show for the family connection, the family conversations they have, and Beth and Randall's marriage. In ways it's similar in terms of the mother-son relationship

194 *Nkechi Okoro Carroll*

between Grace and Spencer on our show and the broader sense of family, both the family you're born into and the family you pick. We share common themes with *This Is Us*, in both the traditional and non-traditional family arcs that we do on all three of my shows. Even when they make mistakes and mess up as part of everything they're doing, it's coming from a good place. The challenge is always making sure that the stakes feel real and high enough, that you're emotionally connected to the story and want to see them make the journey through. When you're doing an emotionally driven family show or teen show, the stakes can at times feel like they're not as high as the stakes that are inherent in a procedural show, and that's usually the challenge. The solution to that is, everyone has different problems in the world, and to that person, those problems are do or die to a certain extent. You can't tell teens in high school that everything isn't life or death. They say, "Someone broke up with me. My life is over." And you try to have that conversation with your 14-year-old daughter or son to tell them their life is not over. They don't believe you in that moment. And it's the authenticity of what the stakes mean to those individuals, into their emotional life and staying true to that. Inherently you'll find that being able to write the emotional life through that becomes easier than one initially imagined.

What *All American* has to say to the world is that everyone deserves the right to dream, and dreams are achievable. And that at the end of the day, your relationships with your family and your friends and the whole sort of village can really lift you up, and you can achieve it together. Something that *All American* seems to do well is give people hope and give people the permission to dream and to dream bigger than their circumstances, and to be better friends and allies to each other. I say I make *All American* in part for my sons. My oldest son especially, he's also a student athlete, and I try to use Spencer unapologetically to help my son see the world from a better perspective. And then also to help the rest of the world, who sees my son and sees a young Black male as something to be scared of, to think differently. Even if it's one household at a time, if we can make even one person stop before they cross the street the next time they see a Black male or not react in fear and actually think like, "Oh, that could be someone's son. That could be your doctor, lawyer, banker," whoever, but see them as a whole human as opposed to just something to be scared of, it makes a difference. I think the show is achieving that level of discourse, which is something that we're extremely proud of because those kinds of conversations help keep my sons alive.

As for the industry, the only way we can really change it from the inside is if we all start being more of a community. That's how Black Women Who Brunch was started, as a mentoring group for Black female TV writers. Lena Waithe, Erika L. Johnson and I started it. That first meeting was a dozen people in my living room. Five years later, we were at 162 women. Everything that happens in the group is confidential because we want it to be sort of a sister circle where people feel like they have a safe space to talk about anything that they're dealing with in the industry, and we give each other advice. During one of our retreats, we took a picture of all of us, and we posted it on social media and that's how *The Hollywood Reporter* saw it and then featured us in an article because everyone is always saying they can't find Black writers, and here was a photo of a hundred of us. Inspired by us, my friend and colleague, Diana, partnered with a couple other writers to start a Latina version of the group. And the Asian American Writers Brunch was also allegedly inspired by our BWB group. It's been fantastic to see all these affinity groups coming together to sort of help each other and support each other. With five hundred or so shows out there, there is enough work for all of us. We can all rise together and do this.

I was lucky to work with two of the best showrunners before I left to do *All American*. There were always other women on the staff, other people of color, whether they were Black or Latino. I was able to get Lena Waithe hired on *Bones* very early in her career, one of her first staffing jobs. I remember hearing a couple of the writers joke like, "I can't believe you fought so hard for her. What if she comes in and replaces you?" And I asked, "Why me? There's 14 other writers in a room. Why aren't you scared she could come in and replace you?" But as the only Black woman, the assumption was, "Oh, aren't you worried that they're going to think she's better than you?" But there's more than enough of this for all of us. But you would hear stories about people saying, "Oh, we don't have any more diversity money." And I would think, "Do you have regular money? Because that works too. And you would use that money on a non-diverse hire, so what is this diversity money we don't have?"

My mentees have encountered, "Oh, we love her, but we've already hired our diverse writer for the staff." And I'm like, "Why are they in their own category?" As opposed to just, you need more writers for this room, and you really loved their material, and so you want to hire them. It started to feel like, unless you were coming from a diversity program or diversity funding, which technically made you free for the show, it was hard to get showrunners to really consider you, without thinking more broadly about what the repercussions of that are on a global, more systemic basis. As a showrunner, it can't just be about the bottom line on the budget and getting the show finished on time. It's also about how you're cultivating the writers and about making decisions that do not systemically impact one particular ethnicity of writers. And you need studio executives and network executives who are also focused on this and pushing it to be on all sides. But you have enough people not focusing on it, and you end up with what we have in the industry now. It's something that needs to be addressed on a systemic level where showrunners are being held accountable if they're not thinking about it. That's how the studios and the networks can show that it is also a priority to them. What I hope is that the success of a show like *All American* pushes executives and buyers and TV networks and studios to take more chances on all sorts of diverse storytelling, whether it's from a female lens or a different ethnicity lens, that it just broadens people's minds to the idea that there's more stories to be told. The movement that this whole industry needs to go towards is to stop going for the traditional content where our leads are white males. The truth is audiences just want the stories. They will emotionally attach to a good story with really good characters. If it connects with them, it connects with them.

RAELLE TUCKER
Is This a Net Positive for the World?

Figure 33.1 Raelle Tucker
Source: photo by Danielle St. Laurent

Raelle Tucker grew up in Ibiza and was a finalist for the second season of *Project Greenlight* in 2003. She then worked her way up on staffs for *Supernatural, True Blood,* and *Jessica Jones,* among others, before creating and showrunning *Sacred Lies* for Facebook Watch, which expanded possibilities for impactful interaction with its audience. Raelle is a founder and a driving force behind Mentorship Matters, an initiative to increase opportunities for emerging writers of color in Hollywood, and the showrunner of *The Power* for Amazon Prime.

DOI: 10.4324/9781003298229-34

198 *Raelle Tucker*

My parents wanted to escape Reagan's America in the early 1980s and live somewhere where they could smoke hash in public, basically. So, I grew up on the island of Ibiza in Spain, riding a horse to school. Later as I got older, a motorbike. All of my friends were drug smugglers, drug dealers, wannabe DJs, go-go dancers. Those were our main options – those were the role models we had.

But I was always different. I started writing and directing my own plays when I was about eleven. I formed a theater company at my school – this hippie school in a house in the countryside with about 80 students total – from kindergarten through high school. It was a unique school – many of our teachers were not certified, smoked black tobacco, and drank cognac in class, and we could not afford books, so we had Xerox copies of books. But they also gave us a lot of freedom to be creative. I started writing, producing, directing, acting, set designing – pretty much teaching myself how to do these things through trial and error. My plays would sell out the local 500-seat theater because there was nothing else to do on this tiny island. This is pre-internet. No one even had televisions or telephones in their houses in Ibiza back then. We were very isolated, so my plays were big events. By the time I was 16, I thought I was a huge star. Everyone knew my name; they wrote about me in the local paper. I had this skewed perspective of how easy it would be to succeed. So, I dropped out of high school at 17 and moved to Hollywood. I figured I simply needed to do what I did in Ibiza, just on a bigger scale.

Of course, I was in for a rude awakening. I waitressed in LA while running a small theater company and writing really bad plays and then really bad screenplays. Eventually waitressing became exotic dancing. It started as a way to pay my rent and fund my plays, but I became fascinated with the theatrical aspects of stripping and pole dancing. This was the mid-1990s – no one was talking about burlesque at that time or teaching pole classes to rich housewives. I choreographed my shows, put together elaborate costumes, told stories through my dancing. Even if most of the guys in the club didn't get it. I was really naïve – I thought I could "revolutionize" the sex industry, just like I thought I could take over Hollywood right out of high school. I eventually went back to Ibiza and opened my own burlesque theater strip bar there called *The Blue Rose* with my older sister who became a dancer, and we convinced my hippie parents to invest in it. But that's its own wild story – and I'm hoping to make it a documentary someday.

All the way through that, I was still writing screenplays and television samples. I connected with a UCLA theater major named Sera Gamble – who decades later would create and showrun *The Magicians* and *You* – and we started writing together. We co-wrote a play that went on tour called *Will Strip For Food* – a marriage between our theatrical backgrounds and experiences in the sex industry. Sera and I were both in our early 20s, and we were both sort of lost. We were each other's best friends and teachers. We tried everything we could to break in – including submitting to writing contests like the second season of *Project Greenlight*. And our screenplay *Cheeks* placed in the top three scripts. We got to go pitch the script to Matt Damon, Ben Affleck, and Chris Moore at Sundance. That was the very first time we ever pitched – on HBO with these Oscar-winning movie stars and, like, six cameras in our faces. It was honestly fucking terrifying. We lost the competition, but that was probably a gift – we would have made entertaining reality TV, but it most likely would have destroyed our future careers. But *Project Greenlight* was good to us. It helped us get signed by agents at the United Talent Agency, and those are still the same agents I have 20 years later. After the show, Sera and I started getting meetings to pitch movies and TV series. But for that first year after the show aired, I was still working at a strip club in downtown LA at night. And during the day, I was going to meetings at Warner Bros., Paramount, and Fox. A lot of the executives that were meeting with us at that time just wanted to meet with the girls from *Project Greenlight*. I think it was a kind of gag, a good story, and they didn't take us seriously.

I guess, in retrospect, it may have helped us that we were so under-estimated. Everyone thought we would be reality show idiots when we walked in there. It didn't take a lot for us to be impressive because we were serious. I mean, we had been writing for years at that point, producing our own plays, and we had real samples. We got our first staff job on a show called *Eyes* working for John McNamara, which ABC canceled mid-season. But that experience was completely life-altering for both of us. I walked into the writers' room, and I was like, "Oh my God, everything I've ever done in my life makes sense. This is exactly where I belong." It just felt like home to me. But after running theater companies and directing and choreographing, I was used to being in charge – I was so vocal and loud and obnoxious, and I had no idea that wasn't what I was supposed to be doing as a staff writer. Thankfully, my showrunner didn't fire me. He thought it was funny, I think, and he kind of encouraged it. In retrospect, I'm completely embarrassed and sorry for all the other writers that had to sit with me in a room and go through that learning curve with me. And I'm so grateful John McNamara took a chance on me and let me learn on his show.

When I got into the business 20 years ago, I was used to being the only, or one of the only, women in the room. I was determined to make it, despite my lack of education, connections, and privileges. What was clear to me, but unspoken coming into a writers' room back then, was you had to be the kind of girl that men liked to hang out with – you were not allowed to be offended by anything, ever. You needed to be funny and easy and a little bit sexy – but not too sexy. And you could never be emotional. I was often told that I was too earnest, too emotional, that "it's just TV." Meanwhile, my male counterparts were allowed to get angry and be passionate and defend their ideas. But we were playing by different rules. All the women I knew at that time, we shaped ourselves into something that was acceptable to the boy's club we were trying to break into. Like every one of us did, and I don't think

200 *Raelle Tucker*

many of us were fully aware that we were doing it. But I'd been a stripper – I was ready to turn myself into whatever I needed to be to succeed.

Sera and I staffed on the first season of *Supernatural* after *Eyes*. I took that job knowing that I didn't love horror, and after growing up in Spain with no TV, I didn't know much about American pop culture. I also have always gravitated toward writing female protagonists. And this was a show about two dudes in their 20s, driving around in a classic car, making jokes about TV shows and bands I'd never heard of while killing monsters of the week. I knew I had almost nothing to offer the show – other than the fact that Sera and I were going to be the only female writers on staff that first season. Sera is a brilliant writer and probably more adaptable than I am, and she thrived in that environment. She went on to become the showrunner of that show eventually. I did not thrive in that environment. I could not bring any of myself or my sensibility to the storytelling. The show was very successful, and Sera was succeeding, and I was trying really hard not to bring her down. I almost quit television after working on that show for two years. And by the time I left, I was thinking, "Maybe I'm just not cut out for television, I'm not good at this." It was really scary because I couldn't imagine what else I would do with my life.

Sera and I broke up as a writing team. It was like a divorce, and I was scarily depressed, heartbroken, and totally certain that I would fail without her. I holed up and somehow managed to push through the self-doubt to write my first television pilot spec by myself. It was a very personal story, inspired by people I grew up with – about a father and daughter drug smuggling team. It was edgy and weird, and most shows on TV were broadcast procedurals at that time, so I had no idea if it would connect with anyone or if it would be the end of my career. That pilot got me a lot of attention. And then Alan Ball wanted to hire me on *True Blood,* and it changed everything. I finally realized, "Oh, I just needed to be able to bring more of myself to the work. I'm not built to work with everyone in every environment, and I can't succeed everywhere, and that's okay." The more authentic I am, the more truthful I am, the better my work is, and the better I'm received by the right people. I learned a lot from *Supernatural*. I learned how to write genre, which really served me going into *True Blood*. Even though that was not a classic genre show, it was much more of a soap opera and a comedy, Alan hired me partly because I came off a genre show. And *Supernatural* taught me how to break 22 episodes of story efficiently – that's a tough thing to do. I learned a lot, and the showrunners there were kind enough to let me out of my contract and not say terrible things about me. That job was the hardest of my career, but it was a gift – without what I learned there, I'm certain I wouldn't have the career I have.

I think it's so important to hear about experiences like that – the failures – because I know that there are people who have been in my writers' room who have felt that they weren't thriving, and I hate that. When I felt like I was failing, I would just piss on my showrunners because it was a lot easier to blame them for why I wasn't succeeding on their show. Now I understand it differently. I imagine showrunning is much like parenting – all show-runners are reacting to the experiences they had coming up that shaped them, both positively and negatively. And they are trying to build environments that are healthy for their process and their show. No matter how hard you try to be fair, not everyone is going to fit in, work the way you want to, tell the kinds of stories you want to tell. Artists with strong voices and strong points of view aren't always the best on a writing staff because they usually won't be happy until they're doing their own thing their own way.

That was definitely the case with me. I rose up the ranks from staff writer to showrunner and spent 10 years writing on other people's shows. I learned a lot, but it was never easy for me. Partly because I think my best work, the most rewarding work, comes from a personal, raw place. There wasn't always room for that on other people's staffs. My goal now is about trying to write from an authentic place, writing toward something truthful and vul-nerable, because those are the stories that have the power to touch people. They feel real. In order to create that kind of vulnerable, emotional, personal work, we have to create an environment where people are allowed to be all of those things in a safe space. That is easier said than done since even showrunners who might be more comfortable with expressing emotion in the workplace have all been trained by the old-school boy's club coming up. It takes courage not to do what you've been taught, to question the established way of doing things and forge your own way of creating.

That said, there is also always a danger of creating an overly-intimate, permissive culture in a writers' room, where people aren't respecting pro-fessional boundaries and forgetting that we are also here to create a market-able, profitable product on a schedule. Finding the balance, creating that space where being emotionally vulnerable and deeply invested is rewar-ded – and also understanding that this workplace needs to be productive and safe – is the challenge. It's challenging for a showrunner to achieve – and I think it is challenging for a writer coming on to a staff to navigate what is acceptable and expected of them when it's an ever-moving target. A writer on staff has to be able to shape themselves, at least to a certain extent, into what their showrunner needs them to be – and sometimes that's just not a good fit, no matter how talented they are.

There are a couple of tricks I've learned along the way in terms of how to attract the right people. Everyone says, "I have a no asshole policy." But if that were true, our business wouldn't be full of so many assholes. Do your due diligence on who you hire – check references. That's important home-work to do, to hear what everyone else's experiences have been. It can also be dangerous because somebody may have been a bad fit in one environ-ment, like I was on *Supernatural*, and then go on to be a great asset on another show. There is no formula – the subject matter and the way a showrunner runs their room can greatly impact someone's ability to do their job well. So you have to take that into account and ask a lot of questions.

202 *Raelle Tucker*

I'm also really honest with every potential staff writer I meet with – I tell them up front what I think I'm good at as well as what some of my weaknesses are as a writer and a boss. And I ask them to do the same – to be candid about what they are good at, what they think they can work on, and what a healthy work environment looks like to them. If they aren't able to answer these questions, it's a red flag to me. It's almost like a first date – a relationship probably won't flourish unless we're both being honest and open about what our needs and deal-breakers are.

For the actors, weeks before we start shooting, I send an email to the entire cast explaining the way I want the set to work. Even the day players. And I'll send every actor every script way ahead of shooting, whether they're in the episode or not. I want them to know they are trusted partners and have a role to play in the bigger picture. I tell them, "I welcome your thoughts and feedback about your character, but I ask those thoughts to be delivered in a way that doesn't upend the process – and respects the work the writers and all the other departments are doing to create and prep for these scenes." I don't allow major changes to the script on the day. I ask them to send me any thoughts they have the week before each episode shoots – and I give them clear deadlines with dates for that feedback.

Most actors are rebellious by nature. They're people who had to forge their own path and break down these massive barriers to get here and are expected to do outrageous things every day on camera. Putting a personality like that in a box and giving them no voice is generally not going to work well. I think the thing most showrunners are afraid of is that if you open these gates, you're going to get five hundred calls in the middle of the night, you're going to be flooded by requests and opposing points of view, and you're going to be bombarded by bad story pitches. I just haven't experienced it that way – the direct opposite. When I've been able to make actors feel like respected partners, they have usually reciprocated that respect by only coming to me when something was really important to them.

I'm also very focused on meeting deadlines and on doing things at a rigorous but steady pace. Ideally, if a show is well-managed, everyone gets time to do their best work, and no one is feeling rushed or blindsided. When people feel safe and taken care of, they don't have to second-guess everything because they know there is a plan with clear parameters that we are all adhering to.

I believe a great script is a shootable script. I come across a lot of very high-level TV writers these days who don't have any production experience, so they don't actually know what that means. They're writing night scenes on a boat on a lake of fire. Scenes with animals and babies, five hundred extras. Or fifty locations in an episode, elaborate sets we would have to build that we only spend one scene in all season. Just not thinking about the budget or how a crew is going to achieve any of it on a TV schedule. Being imaginative and dreaming big is great – but being a showrunner means taking those big dreams and whittling them into something that can be made on budget, on time, and actually look cool with the resources we have. That work starts in the writers' room, challenging writers to think about budget when they are building their episodes. That's when we have the time to rethink intentionally, instead of in pre-production when suddenly the cool set piece can't be done and we have to compromise on the spot in a way that doesn't always serve the story best.

Part of the problem is that studios don't want to pay for lower and mid-level writers to go to set and produce their episodes anymore, which was the norm back when I started in TV. So, writers can go through entire careers in writers' rooms and get all the way to executive producer without learning what it really means to be a producer. I keep hearing from line producers, "We've never worked with a showrunner who actually writes for production." They just get handed these impossible scenarios and have to try and make them happen, or they have to say no, which no showrunner likes to hear. Collaborating with your line producer is part of what it means to be a showrunner, and the more you can do that on the page ahead of prep, the better your show will end up looking.

I worry that if TV writers aren't being trained to produce and write responsibly for production, we'll lose even more authority and trust with the studios. My nightmare is that TV becomes like the film industry or the UK system, where they don't really have showrunners. Writers just hand in their scripts and walk away; non-writing producers and executives make all the decisions. I think this would be devastating on a creative level to our industry. All the best, most groundbreaking shows in recent years have been made by showrunners who had a strong vision and the power to push back and fight for their vision. Imagine what *The Sopranos* would have been without David Chase or *Breaking Bad* without Vince Gilligan. But these showrunners are writers who paid their dues for years in rooms, learned the skills to produce TV that works, and earned the respect and authority to protect their vision. Unfortunately, the way the system is now, most writers aren't really being trained to become showrunners – and many believe they should skip six rungs on the ladder and run their own series because they wrote a good pilot. I'm not saying some great shows aren't being made by first-time showrunners. But my showrunner friends and I are constantly being asked to come in and fix shows that can't get scripts done on time or need massive reshoots and rewrites – shows that weren't developed with a showrunner at the helm because we were too expensive. Saving a show like that can be a thankless job – it's not anyone's dream. And it ends up costing the studios way more money than just hiring an experienced showrunner from the beginning.

Stories have the potential to change the world. I know that sounds earnest and grandiose, but I truly believe that. Exposing audiences to people they would never interact with in the real world and allowing them to empathize with an experience outside of their own is beyond powerful. It can be life-changing. My father was gay and dying of AIDS in the early 1990s, and I witnessed firsthand how people treated him before and after shows like *Roseanne, Ellen,* and *Will & Grace* started bringing gay stories into people's

204   *Raelle Tucker*

living rooms. Television, in my opinion, is the most powerful tool we have to create real social change.

I ask myself every time I work on a show, "Is this a net positive for the world?" And if it's not, I don't do it anymore. After two decades of being lucky enough to get to tell stories in television, I feel like it's my responsibility now that I have some sort of control over my work to do something that's making the world better, even incrementally. We talk about this in my writers' rooms a lot – either we're building the world we want to see, or we're shining a light on what we want to see change in this world. Every decision we make has some significance. From the people we choose to hire on and off screen to the way a character behaves in the story – these things have a positive or negative ripple effect. I want to be intentional about that, and I think we all should be.

We are in this incredibly privileged position to have a small degree of influence over millions and millions of people. I don't think we should be frivolous with that. At least I don't feel that I can be frivolous with that anymore.

I don't think what I do is going to be for everyone. From the shows I make to the stories I want to focus on to the environments I create to work in – they are not for everyone. I have worked in rooms where the highest form of wit is cynicism, and people just delight in it. And that's not something I'm interested in. I find cynicism to be a kind of cowardice. I think it's easy to act like you don't give a shit and make fun of everything – I mean, there is certainly an artform to doing that cleverly, but that's not what inspires me. Being heartfelt and earnest takes real vulnerability, which is scary, and some people will ridicule you for it. But I think audiences, especially right now, are hungry for stories that don't make them feel like they need to take a shower after they've gotten through an episode. Stories that lean toward hope. That doesn't mean we can't explore dark, fucked-up topics, but I choose to focus on how we survive those things and find empowerment on the other side. I think there's an audience for that. And I think there are writers, directors, and executives who hold the same values I do and want to help make those shows.

I've found that becoming a showrunner brings your biggest flaws as a human being to the surface, makes you confront all those things that you hate about yourself and that you're afraid of. At least once a day, I think I'm an uneducated hack and everyone is going to wake up and realize that. I get defensive. I lose my patience in ways I'm not proud of. No one wants to be a bad boss, and there are days I'm probably a bad boss. It's such a high-pressure role but also a weirdly intimate, vulnerable creative process that you are asked to do with so many personalities involved. Politically, there are things you need to protect and people you need to protect yourself from. You're expected to be both a strong-willed artist, an expert of your craft, but also a flexible collaborator. You're supposed to generate original art on a budget and deliver it on a crazy, intense schedule. You're supposed to pour your life into making these shows, but you're never supposed to lose your temper, or, God forbid, cry.

It's kind of amazing to me that anyone can do all this without turning into a monster. But it's really important to me to try not to become one. When they stop making my shows, if I'm remembered for anything, I hope it's as someone who tried to do something heartfelt and purposeful with the gifts and opportunities I've been given – and helped some talented people up the ladder along the way.

SARAH GERTRUDE SHAPIRO
Fear is the Enemy of Creativity

Figure 34.1 Sarah Gertrude Shapiro
Source: photo by Tom Keller

Sarah Gertrude Shapiro is an Emmy-nominated producer, writer and show creator. She is most known for co-creating the Lifetime series *UnREAL*. Shapiro graduated from Sarah Lawrence College with a BA in fiction writing and filmmaking. From there she worked for shows like *The Bachelor* as a field producer, and went on to write an award-winning short film about that experience called *Sequin Raze,* which became the basis for the show *UnREAL,* starring Shiri Appleby as a TV producer who has to prove herself to her boss Constance Zimmer by doing what she does best, manipulating people. Sarah currently has an overall deal with ABC Studios.

DOI: 10.4324/9781003298229-35

There was no part of me that came to Los Angeles to get a job on *The Bachelor*. Working on *The Bachelor* was definitely a mistake. I wasn't trained to be a reality producer. I had interned at Killer Films in New York, so I was very indie film. When I came to LA, I was playing in a band and making visual art, and I got a day job on a super innocuous reality show called *High School Reunion*. And I stupidly signed all my paperwork without reading it. When they tried to transfer me on to *The Bachelor* and I said "No," I actually couldn't say no. They had unlimited, renewable options in perpetuity. At the end of every season, when I was trying to quit, they would just put a new manila envelope on my desk that said my option had been picked up. And I tried to get an attorney, but nobody wanted to take on Warner Bros. The way that I got out of my contract, finally, was that I went to my boss's office to quit, and I said, "I'm going to kill myself if you don't let me go." She actually first said, "So who coached you? Was it Mark Burnett?" I swore up and down that I hadn't been coached. She still didn't believe me. And I said, "How about if I leave the state?" And she said, "If you leave the state, then we're good." I put all my stuff in my car, and I drove to Portland. I had friends up there and loved it and had always wanted to go back, get rid of my cell phone, have no contact with the industry whatsoever, just leave. But within two weeks of being there, Nike's ad agency asked me to make a show with LeBron. And I was back in business. So, what I learned about myself was that I was actually really addicted to the work.

I wrote my short for five years because I was so busy with a day job in advertising. I think that the years of that experience on *The Bachelor*, composting and turning into something richer with perspective was also, instead of simply blaming the contractual situation, actually looking at my role in the situation. I was able to see I was hiding from my own life and feeding off of destroying other women. That was a sickness that felt like a microcosmic reflection of the greater societal sickness that was happening with reality TV, getting off on destroying real people and why that was so satisfying as a producer and why it's so satisfying to viewers, too. I'm glad it did take a long time to make my short because I think by the time I made it, I had a different perspective on myself at that age.

When I looked at my young adulthood, most of my life was spent at work. They were complicated, intimate, and dark, formative relationships with co-workers, totally non-romantic relationships, and really complex. In a capitalist workaholic society, a lot of your young adulthood is formed at work and through your relationships at work. And it's something that I felt like I hadn't seen talked about a lot, and it was something that I really was hungry to see explored more because it was such a big part of my 20s. I didn't set out wanting to make something dark. I wasn't trying to make it upsetting or unnerving. It was, "This was my actual experience with those work relationships."

208 *Sarah Gertrude Shapiro*

It felt really painful to me. When you're writing something that's based on a feeling from a moment in your life, you have no idea how it's going to resonate for anybody else. But it was physically painful for me to write about some of that stuff in the ways that I did. It was really vulnerable to paint that picture of the worst side of myself. I'm glad it took so long to make, because I had to break through that feeling of wanting to make myself the hero in my own story and really allow myself to be incredibly flawed, which was also painful at first.

I'm flashing back to my writing studio that was this horrible, rented closet in a warehouse. I had a couple of great readers in my life and one of them said, "You don't have to be the hero in the story." It was this total breakthrough moment for me because I intuitively knew that I wanted to go to those places, but I think I was scared it was going to be too dark for anyone to make it, or it would just be yucky. That shame and yuckiness around what I had done was complex to navigate. I also have a pretty severe allergic reaction to heroes who are just an anti-hero for anti-hero's sake. That wasn't my motivation at all. It was just, "Okay, face the yuckiest part of your early 20s."

I called my roommate from the time, and I said, "Can you tell me what I don't want to remember?" It's so hard to hear. She said, "I don't think you changed your clothes for like three weeks. One time I found you sleeping on a pile of dirty clothes." It was remembering terrible people I dated, if you can even call it that. I remember falling asleep with walkie-talkies on my ears, having constant ear infections, living on antibiotics, just gross stuff that you don't want to tell people or talk about. Once I realized that that was the meat of the story, I really had to think about whether or not it was worth making it because there was a high likelihood I was going to get sued. And it was uncomfortable and my life in Portland was fine. I had plenty of money and friends. I didn't need this at all. But it felt really important to me. I guess it felt like sort of my life's work. It felt like this story about women destroying other women and how we ended up destroying ourselves felt like the thing I wanted to do.

Once I decided it was important enough to do it, I developed kind of an instinct for when things felt really yucky and I felt grossed out, that was actually the story. If I was brainstorming or breaking stories, whenever I felt like, "Yuck," I knew that was probably the story. And that continued into the writers' room. It was like, "God, I don't want to tell you this," because writers' rooms are interesting because it's a cutthroat, brutal, competitive industry and I'm being ridiculously vulnerable with people who I just met. I'm telling them the grossest stuff about me and not just like physically gross, but spiritually gross, ethically gross, grossness inside of me. It became a theme that every time I sort of felt my skin crawl and I felt super ashamed and embarrassed, I knew it was probably the story. And that was where I had to write from.

Sarah Gertrude Shapiro   209

My story, the surface level is that I got trapped in a contract and I couldn't leave. And that is true. But the next layer of that story is that they wouldn't have physically restrained me from walking off set. I could have quit. I would have been blacklisted in the next job in reality TV, and they were suing people and doing all kinds of really scary things. There were a lot of reasons why I felt like I couldn't leave, but I also got to be really good at it. And I got rewarded for it financially. And attention-wise, I got a lot of pats on the head, I got promoted and I got money. And I remember going to my parents' house for a family party and my dad was a professor and my sister is an academic and everybody at the party was intellectuals, liberal, academics who wanted to talk to me about *The Bachelor*. I was the coolest person in the room. My family, too, were grossed out and thought it was so pedestrian and so, beneath my degree, beneath my family that I was doing this work, but there was a sick fascination with it. I was good at it in a way that I was really not good at my actual life. I was having zero luck dating. I had tons of social anxiety. I had put on a ton of weight. I was terrified of being in the real world. So, if I just worked 90 hours a week and slept at work, I didn't even have to think about the fact that I was unhealthy, unhappy, self-medicating for anxiety with food because people were telling me I was doing a good job. I really had to dive into why did I actually stay? And it was because I was good at it, and I was getting rewarded for it. And I didn't have to deal with depression or anxiety or just the weirdness of being 20 and trying to find relationships and love. I just worked instead.

Making *UnReal* felt worth it in such a bigger way than *The Bachelor* did. I believed in it and cared about it. And then at the end of Season Two, my dad got diagnosed with cancer and I had a huge wake up moment again of, "Oh my God, I've done it again. I'm back in this black hole of work." I haven't gone on a date in three years and the whole thing that I didn't want to be, not in terms of the show, but in terms of having my life atrophy again." I had a really sort of stunning moment of wanting to make an actual life happen for myself. And that moment, I got on dating apps, and started making myself leave work sometimes. At that point, we had a team who really understood the show. So, it became a lot easier to delegate because the people who had been there from Season One really got it. I didn't need to be doing everything. By letting go and forcing myself to show up to family events and to actually see friends and go on dates, I ended up getting married and having a baby. It happened, but it was through my dad getting really sick and actually passing away last year. So that was a big moment for me. Losing myself didn't happen again, but I had lost so many years with him, years he could have known my kids. That was painful. Very painful.

Showrunning is not a fake-it-till-you-make-it kind of thing. First, there's absolutely no substitute for experience and you can't fake it. Because so much is about your relationship with the studio and your reputation in town, and the power you bring with you when you walk in a room. I think it would have been impossible for somebody like me, coming from having a short

210 *Sarah Gertrude Shapiro*

film to having sold the show, to do it without Marti Noxon, who was the first person I was partnered with. Her capability to navigate the studio system, the network side of things, just to understand the big picture of what was happening, there is absolutely no substitute for it. I remember I had started outlining the show and I was kind of just drowning in notes. I was paralyzed because I was trying to be a good camper and respond to every piece of feedback, and it was just getting really, really mushy and scary in my head. I went over to her house, and she had made cookies and we were playing with her puppies, and we sat on the floor in her little office, and she had a whiteboard and she said, "You already know this whole thing. You know everything, I'm just going to help you write it down on this board and then you're going to go do it." It was really about her giving me the confidence in my original vision for the show, figure out the note behind the note and not get so terrified by notes. That's something that I've learned again and again and again and again in TV, is that fear is the total enemy of creativity and that when you get in that notes bog where you're trying to just go down the list and check everything off, it's when you really start ruining the soup. She taught me that. And I don't think anybody with less experience could have done that.

The other thing is that I just think there was institutionalized sexism, too. And the most pervasive and debilitating part of institutionalized sexism in the industry is the lack of assumption of confidence. The assumption of incompetence is really hard to navigate. I don't think that any young woman her first time out would necessarily be given the keys to the kingdom in the way you need to be to actually run your own show. I had an interesting experience with Sam Esmail who created *Mr. Robot*. I think it came out the same month that *UnREAL* came out, and it was in a similar situation – an interesting, darker show on a network that hadn't done that before. We had offices next to each other on the lot and ended up at a lot of things together, because we got nominated for all of the same awards that year and ended up at every single party together. And watching his trajectory versus my trajectory and the way he was treated, to me, it's really important to fight against that and that's been a lot of my life, but it's also really important to acknowledge it and not blame yourself for it. That is something that I really had to work through, too. I feel like in so many instances, if I was a guy, things would have gone a little bit differently. But it doesn't mean that I can change it by myself. And it doesn't mean it's my fault.

That's been a big, "Pick your battles, what's worth it?" kind of thing. I was very lucky to have Marti because she also had the story experience when I actually hit a roadblock to help me figure out how to fix it. I'm really grateful to have had the support, and I'm not mad about that part at all. It was just watching how much Sam Esmail was allowed to do whatever he wanted at every given turn and given every privilege and everything he could ever need. And he had basically the same credentials as I did. He was a film-maker, and he could do TV, no different. At that point there was a lot of buzz around him, and it was like, "He's going to be a big deal." So, until women start getting treated that way, you're not going to have those wunderkind kind of moments where they're like, "I know you've never heard of her, but she's going to be huge." In my situation, it was like, "I know you've never heard of her, but the show is on Lifetime," and everyone was like, "Go fuck yourself." I mean, we couldn't get the show cast to save our life because everybody was like, "I'm not going to be on Lifetime." There were some really, really important things that got done because Marti was Marti and picked up the phone. You can't fake that. It's just experience and reputation and weight in the industry.

I did so many magic tricks to get the show sold and on the air, and to get the attention that it needed to get, to get the cast we needed, to do every part of it was like backflips, magic tricks left and right. And then at a certain point, it's like, "Am I really going give all of my energy to try to gender bend my identity until I'm anointed with the privileges, because my syntax and body language has become male?" [Shapiro discusses some of this in her Ted Talk: "How to Borrow Male Privilege in Hollywood."] That just becomes so cumbersome. I don't know how much I care about trying to talk people into giving me the respect I deserve anymore. Where I have arrived is that institutional sexism is a mountain so high that I will continue to navigate it in my own way, but there has to be seismic systemic change really before one person can do all that much. When you recognize a situation is absolutely stacked against you in terms of you having a balanced, joyful life, you have a decision to make, and I just think it's better to make it with eyes wide open. When I look around the industry and I think, "Okay, which showrunners and show creators do I know who feel like their lives are pretty good?" They have enough time. They're given good opportunities. They feel basically supported. Every single person I think of is a man. I haven't run into a lot of women who have had a chill time in the industry. It's not generally very easy, right? It doesn't mean it's not worth it.

So, when I'm trying to sell a show, what I look for is passion for the project and an objective need for the material. I look at the slate of what they have and what they need, if it feels like what I am selling actually fits into where they're headed, and really feeling that they want it, to feel that you have somebody who will fight all those battles with me and really care is such an important part of my decision-making process. Getting anything on air is so brutal, arduous, challenging, and scary. Knowing that there are people that will put their neck on the line for your show, really finding that passion, I think is the number one thing. And that is something that we had on *UnREAL* in an unbelievable way. Nina Lederman, who bought the show for Lifetime, stuck her neck out repeatedly to get that thing on air. And that doesn't happen a lot. I could tell she felt something in the room when I sold it to her, and she never stopped feeling that thing. So now when I'm selling, I'm always looking for an executive who wants it enough and I believe the reasons why they want it and I believe they'll fight for it. And I just felt all of that from Nina the minute that I met her. I could just tell she felt it. I felt it. She needed it. I needed it. All those things aligned.

What I've learned over and over again is people are often self-serving, but it's very possible that your objectives can align with somebody else's. Rather than having them convince you they're going to take care of you or that they care about you, no, you take care of yourself. And if that works for what I'm doing then great. So, if I believe Nina was trying to really make a breakout hit for Lifetime, and I know that she needs it and she knows that I need it, and we need the same thing, that math equation works for me. I don't pay a lot of attention to people saying they're going to take care of me. If I believe that them taking care of themselves is going to take care of me, then that's a good partnership in my mind.

I take care of myself by taking care of my show and my vision. I'll get that part. They don't have to worry about that part of the deal. I'll always take care of that part of the deal, but if what I'm doing works for what you need to tell your boss, then we're in business. That's a good fit.

SHOSHANNAH STERN
Trusting Your Gut is The Only Way To Go

Figure 35.1 Shoshannah Stern
Source: photo by Nikol Biesek

Shoshannah Stern is an actor, writer, director and showrunner, and self-describes as a fourth-generation deaf person. As an actor, Shoshannah had groundbreaking parts on *Jericho, Supernatural, Weeds* and *Grey's Anatomy*, among many other roles. Shoshannah created, showran and wrote *This Close*, the first major American series to be created and written by deaf people and has written for Marvel's *Echo*. Recently, Shoshannah has created, written, executive produced and will star as a Certified Deaf Interpreter in the upcoming AMC thriller *Disquiet*.

DOI: 10.4324/9781003298229-36

214 *Shoshannah Stern*

I don't think I ever really saw a path as a writer until I made one of my own. But it's interesting how I've come back to the story I've told about myself, and realized it wasn't actually as accurate as I thought it was. For the longest time I've always said that I wanted to be an actor first and a writer later. But then during the pandemic I went back to my childhood home and finally had the time and stillness to clean out all the boxes of my stuff that I'd never gotten around to. A couple of them were filled to the brim with stories that I wrote throughout childhood, before I even did school plays in middle school. I think that we are defined by what we can see, and what I could see were deaf actors in front of the camera. I never saw who was behind the camera writing the stories. I guess in a way, writers often remain invisible. But also, on the few occasions I got to see them, they were almost always white able-bodied men. So I think maybe in my mind I got the impression that's who could tell these stories.

When I saw Marlee Matlin win her Oscar, that was the first time I saw myself represented on screen, and I thought, wow, I want to do that too. So I did school plays throughout middle school and high school and a lot of theater at Gallaudet. It was during my senior year there that I got my first television guest starring gig. I had just gone back to university after shooting that one when I booked my second one, and then I stayed put in LA and just never went back. I had a crazy run of good luck those first few years, but because I was starting out I don't think I realized it at the time.

Then one day, I had a really atrocious audition for a character that was written as deaf. I remember coming in really excited to show them my choices and being told that everything I was doing was wrong. I should be more stoic as well as timid, and I also shouldn't move my mouth at all because deaf people don't do that. I don't know, it's very possible I'm conflating all the ignorant stuff I've ever heard in one audition. But I could see immediately what they wanted me to play, and that was basically a hearing person's idea of a deaf person. Even though a deaf person was standing right in front of them in the room playing a deaf person, it was wrong because they'd decided that it was.

It was disorienting to try to step outside of my experience and look into it from their perspective, because the way I presented the truth of my experience wasn't actually the truth *as they saw it*. I remember saying, "I keep waiting for someone to come along and tell my story for me," like some sort of princess in a tower. Then I realized that I was doing that because I didn't think I had the right to tell my own story because I never saw anyone like me doing that.

My story was never one that I saw anyone else outside of my experience tell. I had a great childhood with an amazing family, all of whom were deaf, including both sets of grandparents. When I shared this in meetings, I always felt like I should be looking at this through a lens of sadness. While I had challenges growing up, they never came about because my family was deaf, like they expected me to say. It always came from the outside world. For example, on my first day of mainstreamed (meaning I was the only deaf person in the class) kindergarten my teacher wrote DISABLED on the board.

She said it meant something was wrong with a person, then said there was a disabled student in class today. I remember looking around wondering who it was. And then when she pointed at me I realized, "Oh wow that's how the world sees me." The thing is that she fully expected that was the way I thought about myself as a child. But I don't think kids have self-pity until people teach them they're supposed to have it. For some reason, that moment has stayed with me my whole life, specifically because of that expectation that people had that I was going to see myself the same way they do.

I realized that was exactly what was holding me back at the time of the audition. So after I realized that I was just like, I don't really want to wait anymore. So I started to write again, still in secret for a while until one day I decided not to be secret about it anymore. Soon after that, I met another deaf writer, Josh Feldman. We had a writing group of sorts where we would write separately together, but then we decided to write something for me – a story of two best friends, one of them a straight deaf woman, the other a gay hearing man. We were this close (pun intended) to selling that, but at the last minute the production company bailed. They said, "We don't understand why this character (the one we'd written for me) is deaf. There has to be a REASON." I realized I couldn't tell them the reason. I had to show them. So we decided to just shoot it ourselves, put it on YouTube and raise money for a web series. And because we were going to do that I was like, "Why don't we go balls to the walls and make BOTH characters deaf because nobody else in the world is gonna do it." It was a friendship comedy/drama. Josh was like, great, but who's going to play the other character? I just looked at him. And in that moment *This Close* was born.

At first, it was an amateur pilot on YouTube that was beige AF, with fully beige walls and a fully beige couch. We shot it in a day for like $350. For some reason a whole lot of people managed to find it on YouTube, and publications started writing about it. It was really the perfect timing because now web series on there are really professional and not beige at all. We got lucky because we were able to raise all the money we needed for our Kickstarter and then some. We thought it would come from the (deaf) community, but it came from everywhere, all around the world. Most of our donors weren't even deaf. They just liked what they saw. Then Super Deluxe (a studio) saw it and asked for a meeting. We ended up selling it to them, throwing everything out and shooting a completely different web series with them. Killer Films came on as a production company later. With them, we shot a very un-beige web series which got in the Sundance Film Festival in the only year they've ever had a web series program. Sundance Now saw it there and bought it. We threw everything out and made a season of a completely different half-hour dramedy with them. Then Season Two, SundanceTV came in like, okay, we like your show, we're moving it to our channel. It was just me and my writing partner writing all these episodes through all of this except for our stand-alone episodes, which we each wrote independently.

216 *Shoshannah Stern*

People always ask me how I created a show and had a kid at roughly the same time. I always say that there's no way I could have done it if not for having my kid. It's interesting how people just assume that motherhood is subtractive rather than additive, but it was totally the latter. I suddenly became such a better multitasker and problem solver. I understood that some days are just not going to go the way you expect them to, and in these situations there's nothing you can do except stay calm and go with it while simultaneously creating other solutions. I have been on sets where people are screaming and have expectations of how every single thing is going to go. And there are still sets like that. But I feel like as a mom I learned pretty quickly that's really not productive. I have a joke with my kid where we pretend to shriek at each other, "GO TO SLEEP NOW!" because when she was a baby I got told so often that I had to get her on a sleep schedule. Then I stared at her and was like, okay, how do I order my baby to go to sleep? Yell at her? I started laughing at the thought of it, and then I realized pretty quickly the best way to get her to sleep was to have calm, nurturing and fun energy. And guess what? She eventually got to sleep on a schedule and if she didn't, we'd do fun stuff until she eventually fell asleep. I was happy because if I wasn't, she'd immediately pick up on it, and so it was just better if we were both happy. I wanted to have a feeling like that on set for everyone, where it felt like a collaborative effort, like it was everyone's show and we were having fun doing it.

We had a crazy return rate for our crew in Season Two. I don't remember the exact statistic but I want to say it was something like 90%. They gave up other better paying work to come back to us, and I'm so, so grateful. I want to think it was because of the environment on set, the importance of fun and caring and calmness, and no screaming except the pretend kind. Real screaming won't work with me anyway. I'm not going to hear it.

I thought about it after I had my kid and realized there are so many women in the industry that I have worked with and look up to, and they've all been like that – maybe because all of them are mothers in some way too. Carol Barbee for one, kick-started my whole journey. She was the showrunner on *Jericho*. I was struggling with a scene one day when she was on set and she could tell. She came up to me and was like, "What's going on?" And I said, "I'm struggling with this scene. It just doesn't feel like something my character or really any deaf person would say." She nodded and then literally handed me a piece of paper and a pen and said, "Okay. Just write what your character would say." So, I did. Then I handed it back to her and she said, "Okay, guys we're shooting this instead." I was amazed that she trusted me enough. She didn't say anything to me about my writing at the time, because she didn't have to. She was saying implicitly, "Your words have value." I don't remember what the original lines were, but a lot of writers who aren't deaf assume that deaf people see ourselves the same way they do, like, "I feel very alone in this world of silence." That wasn't what was on the page, but it was coming from that perspective. The thing

Shoshannah Stern 217

is that I don't even know what silence is. Even if I did, it would become your norm after a very short while, so you wouldn't constantly be coming at everything through the lens of, "Oh shit, I am deaf in this moment, what do I do?"

Then I was lucky enough to be on *Grey's Anatomy*. As a result of a conversation with Krista Vernoff I had after a panel we were on together, she invited me in the writers' room, and I got to sit around and talk ideas with them all day. And she really trusted me from every stage of my character to bring my perspective to it. She even let me have conversations with the editors in post, which was amazing.

And then I met producer Jessica Rhoades (*Station 11, Dirty John, Sharp Objects*) on Twitter. Who loved *This Close*. So, I slid into her DMs and we decided to meet in LA. And that's how *Disquiet* happened. *Disquiet* was an original idea about a certified deaf interpreter who returns to the school for the deaf she herself attended after a murder occurs. My dad was a superintendent for a couple schools for the deaf. When I told him about *Disquiet*, he was a little bit like, "So you're just killing everyone at the school?" I was like, "No. Except... yes." It took him a while to warm up to the idea and then he definitely did! Now he sends me articles he finds for inspiration. I'd written it on spec, just for fun, and I ended up sharing it with Jessica. I really didn't plan to show my spec to her (or to anyone!) since it was in such an early stage. But after talking to her for ten minutes, I just felt compelled to because Jessica is just beyond. She really sees what creators are trying to do. And because she understands that vision so implicitly and fully, it leads me to believe that I can and should trust myself and my instincts the way she does.

I feel like trusting your gut is the only way to go in this business, because there are so many ways to get somewhere. Going the same path someone else has taken isn't always going to lead you to the same destination the other went. For me, almost all of my acting and writing jobs have been a result of a special connection with someone. With *Jericho*, I went in for another character and then they liked my tape, so they decided to create a character for me. Carol Barbee called me into the writers' room and had me talk to the writers about how that should go. It was absolutely lovely how collaborative and trusting that show was, especially because they had no intention of even having a deaf character on it in the first place. And because of how lovely and easy it was I told myself, "Okay, so this is going to keep happening!" And then it didn't.

So I became a professor for seven years in the meantime, teaching deaf studies, I kept writing in secret, and I did other creative work, mostly in theater. I was on the creative team for Deaf West's *Spring Awakening*, which went from a workshop to a black box to the Wallis to Broadway, starting when I was a few weeks pregnant and hadn't told anyone and ending with my five month old baby being babysat by the entire cast and creative team while we worked.

218 *Shoshannah Stern*

I was actually in New York when Robbie Thompson, who was a writer's assistant on *Jericho* and was in that room when I came in to talk, told me he created Eileen for me on *Supernatural*. That felt like a full circle moment for me, and it's beautiful when that happens. It makes me think of how we look out on a barren field and think there's nothing happening until we see the flowers starting to pop their heads out. But they've really been there the whole time, invisibly and busily growing.

What I loved about what Robbie did on *Supernatural* is that he didn't even use the word deaf at all. I don't know if they ever mentioned it in any of the seven episodes I did on the show actually. She was just this incredibly talented hunter who happened to be deaf. And that was it. I think that's what you should probably do. I think there's that fear definitely [that as a writer they're going to get it "wrong"] but there's also this assumption that everything has to be different as a result. Their "difference" has to permeate everything. It's an added layer to be sure. But I don't think most people lead lives where everything revolves around one specific part of who they are. And if they do then they're probably not that interesting. I always say my life is not about the loss of the ability to hear, just as much as it is not about the loss of the ability to be a man.

After *Supernatural* I got asked to join the Marvel room to help write and develop *Echo*, which follows Maya Lopez/Echo, a deaf Native American superhero. It was a Zoom room too which made it easier accessibility wise because we had captions and transcripts and two interpreters, who both weren't in LA, and we had two deaf writers in the room. The room was full of really talented Native American writers who were among the most brilliant writers and people I've ever met. And none of them lived in LA. It's crazy to think how we could just have missed out on them because of that. I think there's a lot of innate value in taking more non-traditional approaches to writers' rooms because you get amazing perspectives you wouldn't be able to get otherwise.

When there are interpreters and captioning present in a room, you really have to listen. I think that reminds you to stay open to doing things a little bit differently. There's a lot of inherent value in that. We typed a lot in the text chat in Zoom, so we could have a couple of conversations going on at once, and then we could save all that at the end of the day. But if you're not the type of person who's willing to wait your turn, that can be easy to exploit since because of interpreters there's going to be a lag. I get the impression that most people who hear don't like silence, so there's this inherent need to fill it up and start talking. But that sometimes means you're not allowing other people to get a word in. Maybe that's just a part of how writers' rooms are built because there are certain people who get to talk and certain people who are expected to keep their heads down, their mouths shut, and just listen to everything. It makes me wonder how people who literally can't do some of these things are expected to succeed within these institutions if these institutions don't evolve.

I'm hyperconscious, that's a big reason why I get talked over all the time. It's not easy being the only female in the room or the only deaf person in the room, particularly when you're both. I think it may be a more universal experience than it feels like it is sometimes. I was on an all-female panel with some truly amazing women like Sandra Oh and Ruth Wilson. I had literally just met them maybe ten minutes before the panel, and when we were up there, both of them immediately looked at me and stopped the conversation from going and said, "Oh, I think Shoshannah wants to say something." Then I did another panel with less fantastic people after that and I couldn't get a word in. It really has to do with having just the right kind of person around you.

Sometimes that makes me think that our experiences really aren't as specific as they feel like they are. I've noticed that the more specific I am when I write about my experience – the bigger response it gets. Maybe that's why I don't want to write about non deaf characters to tell you the truth. I'll always have characters that can hear in my stories. But I think a lot of that has to do with the belief I had for a long time that that was the only way I could ever be successful, is if I managed to erase my being deaf. As an actor I remember being told that I could only be considered someone who spoke well if I was able to "pass" as hearing. Years later as a writer, I was told by another writer that the true measure of success would only come when I sold something that had nothing to do with being deaf. And it's just like…why would I want to do either?

I love thinking of stories first. And then I think of how that story would change if there was a deaf person in it. I mean, how many cop shows are there? Why not try to write a cop show with a deaf person in it? That's actually how *Disquiet* was born. There are a lot of cop shows, and there always will be, so I thought it would be cool to show this completely different person with a completely different skill-set dropped into the kind of whodunit people know so well.

It's interesting seeing the way that people expect me to write – like how hard it is to be deaf. For me, the not hearing part is easy. It's not a big deal. But like it was for me as an actor, it's hard as a writer when you're expected to write from the standpoint that people have into my experience, when I'm expected to write as an Other, as a default from the norm. I write hearing characters all the time. It's really not that different. To me, it's just a character that uses a different language and has a different access point into things. I used to hear a lot when I was an actor that it was hard for writers to write for me. I thought that was interesting, and also, a bit lazy to tell you the truth.

Some of my ideas have just one deaf person in it. Some have many. But deaf people need other deaf people. So many shows have represented deaf people as existing in a vacuum. There's only one of them ever. In reality I'm very lucky to have other deaf creatives in my life who I can talk with, like Nyle DiMarco, who has started to produce and Marlee Matlin. It's really great to see more deaf people out there just doing their own thing. It helps that there are precedents now, something that we can turn to and say look at this, it is here, it has already been done. It's interesting because as much as they want something groundbreaking, there's always a fear that because it hasn't been done, it can't. Then once it has, people expect everything to be done the same way they were before, which is another contradiction. I think it's cool to always try to keep pushing things a little bit further. I'm still doing that, and I think I always will. But one thing I can definitely share is don't judge your worth based on what the system values. All I know is that if I had listened and waited until I sold something about hearing people or waited until I was finally hired as a writer's assistant, I would still be waiting and I'm not.

SIERRA TELLER ORNELAS
I Come from Storytellers

Figure 36.1 Sierra Teller Ornelas
Source: photo by Reginald Cunningham

Sierra Teller Ornelas is the co-creator and showrunner of *Rutherford Falls*, a Peacock comedy about the intersecting lives and histories of the Native American and Rutherford communities in a fictional north east town. Sierra is Navajo (born of the Edge Water Clan) and Mexican American, from Tucson, Arizona. Sierra attended University of Arizona and worked as an assistant film programmer at the Smithsonian's National Museum of the American Indian. She is a graduate of the ABC Writing Program, and in addition to *Rutherford Falls* she has worked on shows such as *Happy Endings, Brooklyn Nine-Nine, Superstore,* and *Loot.*

My mom says that in second grade I told my teacher that I was going to write for television. I always loved TV. My teacher told my parents that I shouldn't be living in a dream world. She said that they needed to give me some

DOI: 10.4324/9781003298229-37

222 *Sierra Teller Ornelas*

realistic paths. And my dad asked, "Do we listen to the teacher?" But my mom was like, "No, if she wants to believe that, we should just let her believe it." I had very supportive parents. My mom was an artist, and my dad was sort of a cool hippy vagabond guy. My dad always wanted to be a stand-up comedian and he really rewarded humor. If you were funny, you could get out of trouble. But my dad would try to get me to watch less television. I remember him saying, "I'm trying to make you smarter, and this is making you dumber." I explained to him that TV brings me so much joy, that he had to let me do this. And he accepted that. And now that I do write for television, he always brings up how funny it was that he was ever skeptical.

The one thing I had going for me is I just had this singular desire. I went to an accelerated high school, and I had friends who were super smart, and they all went to Harvard and had great grades. I had a lot of family issues in my teen years. So, I was kind of lost and didn't get good grades. But I still always knew I wanted to write for film and television. I would cut class and go to the library, and I'd read plays and screenplays and about the history of film.

Then there's my mother's maiden name, which is Teller. We come from storytellers. So, I say my ability to tell stories started a hundred years ago. It's sort of a natural continuation of a traditional way of Indigenous life, but also specifically my family's way of Indigenous life. When Navajos were interned at Bosque Redondo, they were given Christian names. It was like our messed up version of Ellis Island. My great great grandfather's last name was based on his job. He said, "I'm the keeper of the stories of my people." So, they named him Teller. I come from a long line of people who like to spin a yarn. Growing up, my mom would lay me on her lap and play with my hair and tell me stories dramatically like a movie. My dad, same thing, he would spin these tales. I just loved it and I think it really did lend itself to TV writing.

My grandfather worked for over thirty years at numerous Navajo trading posts. One of the big things was selling Navajo weaving. My grandmother and their kids lived at the store with him. And when tourists would show up, they'd ask, "Where's the Weaver?" And he would bring my grandma out and she would weave for them. My mom and her sister had these traditional dresses that would hang on a nail, and they would just grab them and throw them on. So, my mom wove. The way she put my dad through pharmacy school was demonstrating weaving at these museums. So, we grew up in museums, and there's just a way that you have to operate in those spaces. You don't get to be a four-year-old. Because people are going to ask you questions and you have to have answers for them. You have to quickly distill your thousands of years of culture into pithy answers. Watching her do that while also maintaining her own self-respect, her own sense of self and then having to do it as I grew up, there's a hustle to it. You're a walking ambassador to where you come from and who you are. And it's a specific kind of Native experience. I think a lot of us have it. You kind of sense it from each

Sierra Teller Ornelas   223

other. Being able to quickly articulate something while also telling people something in the most exciting way, I think it trained me to be good at staffing, to being in the writers' room, to pitching pilots and selling pilots.

There's also that hand to mouth lifestyle. Before my dad became a pharmacist, my mom would sell rugs and make enough money with one rug for us to live for two months. But she'd have to stretch that money, pay rent two months ahead of time. My mom does two Indian art shows a year, one was in August. So, in the summertime we were always super poor, until we weren't. It was feast or famine. So I knew what it was like to have a little, but I also knew what it felt like to have a lot of money all at once. And the TV writing business is very up and down. I think that kind of erratic upbringing also lent itself to this. There's something about the juice of this lifestyle that I feel built for. And whenever I talk to, especially writers of color, I always impart that we have the tools already to do this job really well. We just have to tap into it and not feel like just because we come from different backgrounds that we are ill-equipped. Because actually, we're very equipped for this environment. We have stories to tell.

We're resilient and nimble and we often carry the assumption that it's not going to just automatically work out. The belief that even when things go wrong, that doesn't mean you're going to stop. I wrote a New York Times op-ed and said that Navajos close deals, Navajos are legitimately funny and we can handle being hated. Those are three great qualities for a comedy showrunner. There's a word in Spanish, ganas, it's like the desire. There's a drive that you have. There's something about how my mother and my father raised me that just kind of made all of this feel very comfortable. I know a lot of people who are afraid of a no net situation, of just taking that leap. My dad really believed in my mom's career as an artist, and their dream pulled us out of poverty. My parents taught me you can bet big on yourself and kind of win, that on a dime, you can just throw it all away and start over. I always really admired them for that. A lot of people when I was starting out were scared. It's a big thing to move out to LA and it doesn't work out for everybody. There's the idea of like, yes, it could not go well, but that's no reason to not do it.

With my mom, a lot of people never saw Navajo weaving as art. They thought that it was a craft and something that old people did hundreds of years ago. And the weavers were all gone. And my mom and my dad both really worked hard to make people see Navajo weaving as a true artform and see her as an artist with a vision. And even now people will say, "I want this pattern or these colors." And she'll say, "You can pick a style and I will create the pattern. You can have some ideas of the colors, but I will pick the colors." This is not like you're ordering food. She's very much saying, "This is something that I do and it's homemade and it's mine, it comes from me," you know? As a woman of color, an Indigenous woman in this industry, I think seeing her do that was very influential.

224 *Sierra Teller Ornelas*

With TV, you have to really want to make art. You have to have a vision and it's just as hard to make it as it is to make art, but you also have to not be so precious with it because you have to get it made in a certain amount of time. To me that was so close to how I was raised. It's like, "That show's coming up and you've got to make those rugs." And sometimes there's a rug that you make, and you sell it because you need groceries, but then there's the rug that you make where you put everything that's ever been about you into the piece. And sometimes those rugs take you to museums all over the world. I've seen it happen with my mom. I think people have this kind of precious view of art that there's great art, and then there's trash. But the Sistine Chapel was a contract job. TV writing is very collaborative, so when you are working for a showrunner I do think your job is sort of a surrogate. I'm having this rich person's baby and it feels like my baby, cause I'm growing it. But then once it's done, I have to give it to them, and they get to raise it how they think is best. I just think that it's actually less precious than you think it is. And it's actually more precious than you think it is, if that makes any sense. I love writing. I love it. I love this job. I don't think there's any other job I am meant to have or do, but I also think that it's a slog. But that is part of the process.

For instance, being okay with a first draft being terrible is very difficult, but it always is my first step to getting a great draft. As a woman of color, you're told you have to be perfect all the time and that can make that first draft a battle because the first thing you write is always going to be at least somewhat terrible. It took me forever to do that vomit pass and be okay with that.

I'm always looking for good places to write. When I first moved to LA, I loved going to the Korean spa to write. I buy passes and it's $15. They have hot tubs. I'll write on one floor and eat Korean barbecue and write for like three hours. And then I'll think that maybe I have four jokes I need to punch up or something's not good with this act. I'll put everything back in the locker and get in a hot tub. There's a lot of languages that I don't speak being spoken. You're not trying to gossip or hear in. I used to have a lot of anxiety, and I think being in such a relaxing place, I could get my mind to wander. That's when I'm able to pitch jokes. And once I had it, I'd put all my clothes back on, go up to the patio and then just type it all out. And they're open 24 hours, so you can stay there all night. I loved it. It helped me write in so many ways. I think what helps the most is trusting the process and slowing things down a bit.

In the *Rutherford Falls* writers' room, there were five Native writers – and we all had different opinions on various Native subjects. We had Native writers who were from different parts of the US, from many different Native nations. Everyone had similar reference points, but everyone had their own specific experience. Some people lived on reservations, some people lived in the city, some people lived in the suburbs. A non-Native writer would ask a question, and you'd get five different answers from us and then we'd have to talk it out and be like, "OK, so what do we want to say in this episode?

Sierra Teller Ornelas 225

How do we want to perceive what these characters would do?" And so that to me was really powerful because when you're the only one like you in the room, you're expected to know everything, and you're also expected to confirm that your experience is going to be OK for everyone else. Shows like *Northern Exposure*, they're always told from the white guy fish out of water perspective. My show is told from a Native perspective. I'm curious how these conversations will resonate, but it's weirdly very timely. It's set in a fictional north east town. We created a fictional Native tribe because the American history is also fictional. I didn't want fake white history associated with a real tribe. And it's always going to be complicated making a show that in many ways is a first of its kind. And you can't make everybody happy, but the entire experience was pretty magical. I mean, there were more of us than any other type of writer in that room. We'd tease each other. Native humor is teasing-based. It stems from calling people out in a loving way, but it's much harsher in the best way. We are the first people of this land. Because it's all supposed to be ours so there's a bit of sarcasm to Native humor. There's a lot of immediate camaraderie, when using it. You know it when you see it.

I am incredibly proud of *Rutherford Falls*. It was made during the pandemic, during a time of pain for a lot of folks, especially Indigenous folks. I know it was a huge source of solace and fun for a lot of folks during that time. I've heard writers of color say in regards to their work that they always want to make sure they can go home for the holidays, that you made your hometown proud. I think I can go home.

We're trying to talk about this first American story of contact – first, for you guys. Not first for us, we had stories before that. And then more generally, what does it mean to be an American? What does it mean for the first people who were here? I think that that's something that's sort of difficult as someone who was raised very patriotic. But then there's just constantly the reminder of the erasure of our culture. I love TV so much. And there aren't that many positive depictions of Native Americans in the history of television. It's the feeling of, you love this thing that doesn't always love you back. I think there's something interesting in that conversation. And I think the thoughtfulness of Mike Schur, and the performances of Ed, Jana, Michael, and the entire cast are just so wonderful. I brought in my experience working in museums and what that was like, and also being friends with white people and the sort of experience of that, those genuine friendships that are surrounded by this troubled history. I don't think we're going to fix it, but I think we're going to talk about it, and as a Native person when have you ever seen that?

On both sides of my family, we're very patriotic. I grew up in Arizona and my paternal grandfather fought in World War II, and he doctored his birth certificate. So, he was 14 when he enlisted, and he was 15 when he went to the South Pacific. So part of me was raised with this idea of America as this wonderful place. My parents, my dad especially, were very much about

226 *Sierra Teller Ornelas*

patriotism and about making this more perfect union, you know? And at the same time, they protested injustices in Arizona, and saw criticizing America as being patriotic. And then I learned from my mom a Navajo POV, which is, "This is our land, separate from and predating this American concept."

In Native circles there is a conversation of Indigenizing these times. Climate change and so many other major issues affect Indigenous people first. You see it with COVID, pollution, government shutdowns and in so many ways because we're so connected to the federal government, and because we are stewards of our homelands. And I think that there is a real opportunity to Indigenize how this country is run and how we proceed. Because before white people got here, there were complex societies, with business, and technologies and science. And I feel like when you hear the term Indigenize, it means that we're all talking to "Grandmother tree" or some idealized version of my culture most people learn from bad movies. And it's not that. It's using the tools that we have, to create something that's good for the community. That we can as a community build and grow, without needing to extract and ruin our surroundings. We don't need to exploit to thrive. We can find ways to nourish instead of pillage. We don't all need to have the most. I'm patriotic about that. I think the truth and the true history of America is just a better story. It's so much more dynamic and interesting. And there's just a host of characters that don't fit into the American rebellion narrative who are incredibly interesting. We haven't told the story of America until we've told those stories.

Maybe we can come back to a place where we feel something, and we get nourishment from it. It could become this thing that actually starts to heal us.

There were so few women writers growing up that if you saw their name you just remembered them. Like Rose Marie from *The Dick Van Dyke Show*. When I saw her character, I was like, "Oh, that person is a woman and a comedy writer. I guess I'll just do that." That was like fully my plan. And then Liz Lemon. When I worked at the Smithsonian, Hulu had just come out and so I would just watch *30 Rock* on a loop. It was my first spec that I wrote and there were just these touchstones. My hope is that some Native kid is watching *Rutherford Falls* and the show is helping them figure out what they want to do and who they want to be.

SOO HUGH
Ideas are Your Insurance

Figure 37.1 Soo Hugh
Source: photo courtesy of Soo Hugh

Soo Hugh is the creator, writer and showrunner for Apple TV+'s *Pachinko*, an adaptation of Min Jin Lee's bestselling novel. Soo started writing features, then staffed as a writer on *The Killing, Zero Hour* and *Under the Dome* before she created *The Whispers* for ABC. Soo was also co-showrunner for AMC's *The Terror*. Soo is a graduate of Yale and USC Film School.

When I was growing up, the idea of being a TV or film writer, it just wasn't on my radar. It just was something I'd never been exposed to. When I started falling in love with movies, and I would see the title that says, "Written By," I was like, "Wait, that's a job!" I think growing up somewhere very, very far

DOI: 10.4324/9781003298229-38

228 *Soo Hugh*

from the industry, with immigrant parents who didn't want me to go through the hardships that they did, I never thought a career in film and TV was possible. The only way I thought about how I could break into the industry was going to film school for grad school. I just felt like I had no other choice. If I knew then what I know now, I would have told my 23-year-old self, "Don't go to film school."

But one of the things I did in film school was intern. I just wanted to learn as much as possible how the industry was run as I could. Especially because I didn't see role models that look like me or share my background. That's why I think mentorships are important, especially for women and people of color, because even if your mentor is not a woman or person of color, just having an advocate to say, "You're not crazy," is so important. I know for me, as a woman and a person of color, I was just very risk averse. You're scared because you know, deep down, how much easier it is for men than it is for women. So, having someone else say, "This is doable. You can make a life here and you're not going to go on unemployment for the rest of your life," is tremendously helpful. But after I finished school, I was pretty desperate for any job. I really wanted to be in the storytelling craft, particularly development or a production company that works with scripts. But I just couldn't get hired anywhere. So, I was really discouraged. I felt like, "Oh my god, I just took $150,000 out on loan for film school, and it may have been the wrong call. Because I can't even get a $30,000 a year job." But luckily the boss from an internship I worked for, for free, vouched for me for one of these jobs.

I encourage people to get a job in the industry as soon as possible because your bar gets reset very quickly. What I mean is when you're in film school, you're reading each other's work, and you love your fellow students, but the bar isn't very high. The minute you enter the legitimate studio environment where they're making lots of movies and TV shows and you read the scripts, you see that they are better than the student film scripts you've been reading. So, I feel really grateful that I have been championed by someone who helped me get that first job, and beyond. You're always being helped.

The belief is that the showrunner, specifically, the male showrunner, is a figure of genius and brilliance. But that's so full of shit because anyone who has been a showrunner knows it doesn't just take a village. It takes an enormous civilization to make TV shows. I think people are really afraid to admit that they've taken advice. Because it pops the bubble of "I know everything." I feel that the most successful showrunners who I learned the most from are people who say, "I actually don't know the answer to this, but that's okay. I'm going to find an answer to it."

I didn't feel safe admitting I didn't know answers early in my career. I couldn't believe someone was giving me a show to do. I felt like I was a good storyteller but had none of the experience to be a co-showrunner at that point for my first show, *The Whispers* for ABC. But I was so afraid to admit that I didn't know something, for fear that people would be like, "Why did we give this woman a show?" I didn't admit that I didn't know anything.

Soo Hugh 229

I made a lot of mistakes on that show, and it was a really miserable experience at a time when I should have really celebrated something that was really amazing. Getting a show picked up to series is really an achievement. After that experience, I made a decision to say, "I don't want to do it that way anymore." It felt inauthentic and it felt dishonest. Honestly, I don't think I made a great show, because fear really was the thing that was preventing me from doing my job well. I have been happier since I've embraced the spirit of, "No clue, let's figure it out."

And I actually think people have been more open to me because I believe it's OK to admit you don't always know the answer. That doesn't mean you cede creative control, and it doesn't mean you cede a vision. I also think it's really important not to be a pushover. But it doesn't have to be a binary experience. You can say, "I don't know how to do this part. Explain to me, give me your expertise." Then you have the resources to make the best decision possible. I always thought the term "showrunner" was very misleading. When I was first learning about the job of showrunner, I thought, "Wait, now that I've done it a few times, the job I should have is CEO." Shows cost 50–100 million dollars with P&A per year. That's an enormous business.

My first feature script was on The Black List. I broke in post-writers' strike, which was probably the worst time for people to become feature writers. I really disliked the process. The writer has become so marginalized in features. Once I did get into TV and was in the writers' room, it felt like a revelation. I learned so much from my fellow writers and the showrunners I've worked for. I purposely chose rooms with people that I heard were nice and mentor oriented. I turned down shows that were more highly regarded. Some were very prestigious shows, but because I had heard that they had very difficult rooms, I avoided them. Some people thought it was a crazy decision to turn down some of those rooms, but I know my personality, and I really do believe you just have to be true to yourself. I am not someone who thrives in an environment where I feel like I can be bullied or feels like a zero-sum game environment. So, I chose to work on shows that maybe didn't have as much critical cachet, but I knew were going to be shows where I could learn a lot, and that they were going to give me more responsibilities than an average low-level writer. I really do think that helped me with being able to rise much faster than other people. I was allowed to go on set right away. I learned production from the ground up right away. I got to be in the editing room. I got to be in mix. The amount of exposure and responsibility I got as a staff writer was pretty incredible, which I credit a lot to helping me do what I do now.

Having my first baby inspired me to create *The Whispers*, which was my first show. When ABC bought it, I had just given birth to my first daughter. She was about a month old when I sold the show. When we were editing the final episode, I went into labor with my second daughter. So that show really bookends my two children. And that's the show where, when I think about it, it's wrapped up so much with maternal guilt feelings, and the question of, can

230 *Soo Hugh*

a woman have it all? It's much easier to be a mother when you're higher up the food chain. So, I lucked out, and that's the problem that we don't address. I think the lower and mid-level writers desperately need our help. And that's not just on the corporations and the studios, it's really on the showrunner. It has to be on the showrunner to say, "I'm not going to penalize you for being pregnant. It's fine. I'll hire you." When I was pregnant and I first got my show, I was terrified. But then I felt like, "I'm the showrunner, I'm not going to hide my pregnancy. It's nothing to be ashamed of." I think people need to learn that you cannot penalize parenthood, for both men and women.

I think the room reflects the showrunner. I really do. It becomes an imprint of the showrunner's values. My rooms are very short. I do room from 10am to 3pm. After that my brain shuts down. I don't know what more you accomplish in a room, but that's also a part of it. I've been in rooms, before I had kids, that were 10am to 7pm or 10am to 8pm, and that makes having a family very, very difficult. And I just don't know what benefit comes out of it. If you can prove to me that you make better shows with rooms that run 10, 11 hours a day then, okay, fine. But I just don't buy it.

I'm always on the lookout for ideas, characters, pieces of history that inspire me. When I talk to writers and they say, "Oh, I just don't know what to do next. I can't think of an idea," I always find that very strange. People who wait for IP (Intellectual Property) to come to them are like, "What else is out there? What else can I do?" I tell people, "Think of it as a survival skill. Your ideas are your insurance." So, if you are constantly waiting for someone else to come to you with that next great idea, one day, they're going to lose your number. One day, we all fall out of fashion. This is an industry that is very much cyclical in terms of who's up, who's down. We all know this. I think the one way to ensure that you stay relevant and able to make projects that feed you creatively, is the ideas have to come from something that is really personal. That's why, if I could, I would just read all day and find ideas for the TV shows and movies. But I actually have to make them, unfortunately. So, I always tell people, you just have to always be generating ideas, because at every meeting you go to, no matter what level you are, the question that they always ask is, "So what are you doing these days? What are you working on?" You always have to have a great answer to that question.

I think each idea has its own, what I call a "Eureka Moment," when an idea becomes something more than an idea. How does it happen? I wish there was some hard, fast rule to have that happen. But in cooking all these bits and pieces that I gather over time…So many times in meetings, and this is not just for showrunners, this is for any writer who has any meetings of any importance, whether it's with a low-level executive or the studio head. They always tell you what they're looking for. Every studio, every production company, every director has sort of their list of things that they just wish they can do. For example, a studio will say, "We really want to do a buddy action comedy." When you collect all these ideas, and some of them are more specific than others, the minute someone says, "I'm interested in this," my

Soo Hugh 231

brain goes, "Oh, have you heard about this story?" Because I've collected all of them. And they're like, "Wait, what?" The minute someone says something, they become vaults that you can dig into, ideas that you can dig into. I feel like people have marveled at my ability to think on the spot of like, "Wait, did you read...?" And it's only because I've been collecting these stories for so long.

But you know, everyone chokes. There are some people who are just better in a room than others because it's the writing medium people, so people are pretty understanding about that. Follow up in an email saying, "This totally slipped my mind, but I was thinking about this after we spoke." That email gives you an informal second meeting, right away to be able to reframe your thoughts and ideas and sell yourself again. I think email is the greatest invention. I don't know what people did before email.

Verbal pitching is a very important skill though. I find I'm pretty good at that. I think it's from years of practice and years of doing these meetings, you just become flexible and elastic. I think something that's also helped is that you know your bandwidth in terms of creative interests. I can be very clear. Like, "You know what, that's of no interest to me, not that this is not a great idea, but just, I'm not the person to do it." Whereas when you're first starting in the industry, you try to just insert yourself into everything and any job. It's helpful to be able to say, "I don't think I can do a good job on that." It frees up so much of your brain cells to focus on things you are interested in. That's helpful. When I was a younger writer going in, I was so desperate to just get hired, I was a little bit more forgiving, because there's so few feature assignments. The studios make fewer movies now. So, you just end up having to pitch something you don't have to, and you don't love it. But I feel like now I know pretty quickly whether or not I'm the right person for that material. I started to have a lower tolerance for things I've seen before. In some ways, I'm looking to break the rules again, because I feel the rules have become so established. Is there a way for TV to get more nimble and bolder and more radical? I would love to find a way to do that.

I write a very full page. It's funny because I know amazing writers who, when you open their scripts, there's no sense of personality on the actual scripts, but the characters are so strong. The dialogue is amazing, and the story is really smart. I also know other writers who very much spend extra time making their scripts feel novelistic as well. And I think it just matters. I think it's determined by which process you like better. I wish I could be the former writer. I wish I could be the writer who just writes very truthfully. Someone who writes very matter of fact and is able to make the story sing. I just don't enjoy that kind of writing. Maybe it points to a failed novelist in me or something. I prefer being able to be a little bit more interpretive and editorial in the script form. I wish the script form got a lot more respect than it does. No one has won the Pulitzer for being a screenwriter, I believe. It disappoints me because I do think the script is a literary form.

232   Soo Hugh

In my career, I feel like I hit the jackpot. All of the rooms I've been in have been evenly divided between women and men. But I should say this. I've never had another Asian writer in the room with me. I'm always the only Asian writer in the room. So, on that end, the representation has been poor. But in terms of gender, I've been in rooms that have been mostly half and half. I've been lucky. I've been really supported by women in very women-friendly environments. I think I've also sought that out. I like women-heavy environments. But even when I didn't even know it, I have written like a white man. That's how systemic it is. That dominant ideology, that voice of dominant ideology. The problem is that you write like the scripts that you've read. And the only scripts that were around Hollywood when I was learning how to write screenplays at that time, was that very patriarchal voice. That's why I think it's important to have voices that fight that.

SUSANNAH GRANT
A Deeply Joyful Way to Spend Your Life

Figure 38.1 Susannah Grant
Source: photo by Don Flood

Susannah Grant is an award-winning writer, producer and director who wrote the Oscar nominated movie *Erin Brockovich*, as well as *Ever After, 28 Days, Pocahontas, Charlotte's Web, In Her Shoes*, and *The Soloist*, among others. She wrote and directed the feature films *Catch & Release* and *Lonely Planet*. Susannah was the showrunner of the award-winning Netflix series *Unbelievable* and an executive producer of Hulu's *Fleishman is in Trouble* and Apple's *Lessons in Chemistry*. Susannah is a graduate of Amherst College and the American Film Institute.

DOI: 10.4324/9781003298229-39

234 *Susannah Grant*

I believe that your family of origin is the most formative environment, at least for me. And everything else builds on that. I had incredibly strong and present women in my life who never would have thought twice about taking up all the space they needed, to do what they wanted to do with their day and with their lives. My biggest influences about how to live a fulfilling life were my mother and grandmother, both of whom worked and lived really dynamic lives and shifted where they chose to devote their energies at different phases of their lives. And they couldn't have had fuller lives. My grandmother, when she died, had a full-time job. And that was in her eighties. So making yourself useful, and making some contribution to the world that you feel like is worth a little, has always felt like one of the basic things one does in life to me.

The idea that one's gender could hold one back really didn't occur to me until I graduated from college. So that's a blessing, to have had twenty years with a strong sense that one's gender is only additive, and shouldn't ever be an obstacle. You get out into the world and you obviously encounter people who have a different worldview. And then the battle begins. I was lucky that I had as long as I did without an awareness that there even was a battle. That's a privilege, and I'm grateful for it and spending three years in an all-girls environment in high school.

I have a daughter, and she was not at all interested in going to a girls' school. And I understood that for her, but for a moment there, I felt, "Well, who wouldn't want this, who wouldn't want to live in a world where gender, when it comes to your valuation, is just a non-issue." It's only in retrospect that I realized how influential that was, but I'm grateful for that as well. It was a pretty groovy and progressive place in that regard, but it had a very proper name. It's Miss Porter's School in Connecticut. And with the name Miss Porter, it sounds like a finishing school, but Sarah Porter was, in her day, of the very forward-thinking belief that young women should have a proper education, a real education, not just be taught how to be passive.

I think the initial connection to any material, whether it's an original screenplay or something that's based on a book or something that's based on a real person is, "Do I feel that this has its hook somewhere in my heart and being?" And if it does, then I'll do the work of realizing it. But that initial connection has to be there or I'm just never going to make it through the time it takes to write a script. It takes time and work to make it something good. And that connection is just a starting point. If you try to run with only that, you'll get about five pages in, and then lose steam. So, that's where the work starts, but it's a relationship. If the initial connection isn't there, you won't have the energy to do the work, to make it really, really stand up on its feet and be something.

I've been fortunate to have mentors who taught me the importance of that connection. Nora Ephron was one. One of the first things she said to me

Susannah Grant   235

was, "Don't write what they want. They don't know what they want. Just write something great." And I have not forgotten that at all. Her sister Delia was equally generous, and Delia's husband, Jerry Kass, was my writing teacher at AFI. Jerry and Delia were just immediately surrogate parents. They were too young to be my parents, but they really absorbed me and my classmates into their worlds. One of the first jobs I had, I was working for Chris Keyser and Amy Lippman on *Party of Five*. And it was a great environment – supportive, creative, really ripe with all the fun and exploration of doing what we do. And I have been lucky enough to have a number of partnerships with people like that.

They all said things that stuck with me that they probably didn't even remember saying. My aunt was married to Herb Sargent, a writer and the brother of Alvin Sargent. And when I was starting out, Herb said, "Oh, Alvin always wants to give the money back. Alvin is always sure he can't do it. The minute he's taken a job, he says, 'I can't do it. I don't know how to do it.'" And I thought, "Okay, well, Alvin Sergent has won two Oscars, and he's written some of my favorite films. If that's his process, maybe I don't need to worry so much when I hit that stage." Just knowing that for some very fine writers, that self-doubt is just part of the process, I think made it a bit easier.

I still get to a stage with every script where it feels like I wasted two months and it will never get sorted, and maybe I shouldn't be doing this anymore. It never lasts more than two or three days, and then the good part of the work kicks back in and lasts a lot longer. I don't spend three months plagued with self-doubt – three months being an arbitrary time frame for a first draft. But I try to spend as much time as possible in that period falling madly in love with whatever I'm working on. Both the work and the product are so deeply joyful for me. I absolutely adore what I do. I love the process and I love the product, and I love the journey and I love the collaboration. I get to work with the most spectacular thinkers and creative artists. It's just a deeply joyful way to spend your life.

There are some really great stories out there and when they find their way to me, sometimes there's a great connection. And I look at the films that were so formative to me as an influence. When I was a teenager, the film industry was supporting the careers of Jessica Lange, Meryl Streep, Glenn Close, and Sally Field. You could name ten women who had a leading role in a great movie every year, and if you were a young woman, you could start to build a worldview around them. But when I was in film school in the early '90s, that was not the case. There were actresses who were every bit as good as those women, and they didn't have the parts. I thought, "Where are those parts? Where are those films?" So filling that gap felt both natural to me in terms of storytelling, but also perhaps a bit smart in terms of building a career.

I try not to get too conscious about whatever part of my unconscious is drawn to the various stories I choose to tell. I don't try to psychoanalyze that in the moment. But occasionally it will make sense to me in retrospect. I did one movie, then looked back on it two, three years later and thought, "Oh,

236 *Susannah Grant*

that's why I was so drawn to that story. I see what I was thinking about there." I could see, from a distance, how it related to my own growth. But I don't try to think about it while I'm doing it – I worry being too hyper-aware of why I'm doing something – what my own personal point is – will put me at risk of getting a little bit heavy handed. When it comes to any sort of creative work, I have faith in the power of the unconscious mind. For me, that's where my best work comes from. When I look at something I've written three hours afterward and I can't quite remember writing it, that tends to be my strongest work. Getting up really early and working when I'm still a little bit asleep, that tends to be a good zone for me. Self-doubt doesn't come to me while I'm writing, I tend to be very accepting of my work when I do it. It's only when I step away from it or hand it off to someone else that I start to think, "Oh dear, it's out in the world. Oh dear." You know, "Here is me with all my clothes off."

I think that's why I'm conscientious about not showing anything to anyone for a while, not even an idea. I don't tell people ideas for a long time because if I see a little bit of lack of interest, I'll start losing some faith in the idea – even if it's just that I haven't articulated it well – and the whole thing is really just a dance with self-doubt. I know people who don't suffer from that at all. They have to tell people what they're writing, and if they get an unenthusiastic response, that energizes them, and that's great. That just doesn't happen to be my particular ecosystem.

Before I made *Unbelievable*, I hadn't seen a lot of procedural television, so I didn't have to struggle against the genre because the genre wasn't a thing in my head. What I was conscious of – and vigilant about – was the amount of subtle or not-so-subtle rape porn that exists in our culture, and the obligation not to play into any of the tropes or familiarities of that. The normalization of assault, in ways that are violent but also sexy is poison. So once I started talking with my creative partners about how to do this show responsibly, how to dramatize these assaults, all of that was present in all our minds. I had a very instinctive insistence that there be nothing about what we were doing that could be seen as exploitation. But when it came time to write the first assault scene, I started writing it the way I had been writing everything else, which was with an objective viewpoint, and it just felt horribly, horribly wrong. I could feel that if I wrote it that way, the viewers were going to be watching a sexual assault from an outside, disconnected perspective. And there's no way, given the world we live in, given the context of the rape porn visual imagery we've all been exposed to, there's no way for something that's written that way not to feel like it tips into exploitation. And that was unacceptable. It just felt viscerally wrong. So I ended up switching to the subjective viewpoint of the survivor. And as soon as I did that, the dramatization felt right. On a gut level, I was no longer uncomfortable. I no longer felt as if I were violating some basic agreement I have with myself about how to function in the world.

We had the advantage in *Unbelievable* of having the material that it was based on – a Pulitzer Prize winning article called "An Unbelievable Story of Rape" by T. Christian Miller and Ken Armstrong, which was a treasure trove of inspiration. In that article, the detective that inspired Eric Lange's character described the day when he found out how wrong he had been – that he's ruined a young woman's life by not believing her account of being raped – as the worst day of his life. That was a key moment for me. When I read that, I thought, "Well, this isn't a guy who doesn't give a shit. This is somebody who made horrible mistakes and is the product of the society in which he was raised, the society in which he lives." As a production team, we all got obviously deeply educated on statistics around sexual assault reporting and investigation and prosecution, and the small percentages of cases that move forward toward justice at every stage of that. The numbers are so bad and so unjust that it can't just be a few shitty people who are responsible. It's not a few bad apples for those numbers to persist. It's us as a society. It's our culture, and every one of us is a part of it.

We all said on the show, let's assume that these numbers and these misapprehensions and these prejudices are ones that we all share, consciously or unconsciously. And let's make sure the same is true of all our characters. I don't think the most interesting person in the story of sexual assault is the guy who consciously thinks women deserve to be raped. That person is a monster. But the person who has somehow learned, but doesn't understand that he has learned, that women's bodies are a little bit more expendable than those of men, and doesn't even know that he has been taught that – that's interesting. Because maybe we all kind of believe that. Maybe we've all sat in our cars next to ads for jeans that imply that a woman is being violated and is getting pleasure from it. And maybe we've all internalized that, and maybe that's where the problem lies. So that was the internal conversation that we were having all through the making of *Unbelievable*. Exposing a world in which that's the case felt more interesting than one arch villain or two arch villains who just didn't give a shit about this girl.

TANYA SARACHO
We Have Been Excluded from the Narrative for So Long

Figure 39.1 Tanya Saracho
Source: photo by Jackson Davis

Tanya Saracho is a playwright who began her career as a TV writer on *Devious Maids, Looking* and *How to Get Away with Murder,* before creating and showrunning *Vida* for Starz. Tanya is one of the founders of the Untitled Latinx Project and co-founded the Writers' Access Support Staff Training Program. Tanya created the Ojala Ignition Lab to create and promote Latine voices and narratives. She has an overall deal with Universal Content Productions to create new shows.

DOI: 10.4324/9781003298229-40

Tanya Saracho 239

I worked for Walgreens doing the voice of Special K in Spanish for ten years. That's Chicago, that's just what you do. That's where I was able to start a theater company. I had gone to school at Boston University and on the weekends, I would visit my New York friends and I would see how they were struggling. No shade, but I was not going to choose LA for theater, but New York of course was a possibility. But starting a theater company in New York was cost prohibitive. And I had a couple of friends that went to visit Chicago because they wanted to start a theater company, too. There was some kind of anniversary for Steppenwolf and they were like, "You can go to Chicago and start your company and it'll go really well for you." So I moved to Chicago, having never been there before, with two suitcases. We found a place that first weekend, and then I stayed in that apartment for sixteen years. Chicago is my heart's town. I miss her every day. She truly saw me as an artist. She nurtured me.

My theater company was small and only my executive director and I were paid, and only just a little bit. We were doing everything: directing, getting the grants, doing the box office. In Chicago I made a real living from voice-over acting. But a decade in, when it started to go well for me, I started to get distracted – and there was drama. It was ten Latinas all in our early thirties, but we started to become divided. I saw that as the right time to leave, and it was the best thing that could have happened. Because then a guy from UTA (United Talent Agency) took me out to lunch and told me that I could write for TV. I just had to take meetings. So I took those meetings while I was rehearsing for a play, and they worked out. I came out to LA and got a gig almost right away.

I was on *How to Get Away with Murder*. Out of nine people, I think six were of color. And I want to say there were half women and half men. That was powerful to see, that it could be a mostly BIPOC room and women of color had such agency. And it was right before *Vida*. I was only working in TV three years before I got *Vida*. It was amazing, but it was also an incomplete education. Three years was not enough time to know all the tools. I don't know what the hell people are talking about when it comes to business. I think it's important to note that the reason why that happened is that the executive who "found me" protected the shit out of me. There were battles that she fought that I will never be privy to, but I could feel them because I felt her protection. So I never got a note about having an all Latinx writers' rooms, all Latinx directors, all female editors, all female department heads, never. I think she was fighting these battles.

Having an all Latinx room keeps you honest. Because you can say, "That's not how we say it or that's not how it's said." It's regionalism. And you do it in white culture and not question it. If you're doing a show in Mississippi, you try to approximate a Mississippi slang. So it's the same thing if you want to approximate an East LA slang. But also, historically, we haven't respected the different Spanish accents within the Latinx community, like what a Salvadorian, Cuban, Chilean accent and so on sounds like. For the most part,

240 *Tanya Saracho*

showrunners of the dominant culture and gender have been at the helm and they have the privilege of not having to care. So unfortunately you get these generic representations of yourself. It's so toxic to consume yourself through the prism of the dominant culture because then you start to believe that, "Wait, am I a thief and a prostitute and a maid?" We can be those things, but they do it with no nuance. It's the same thing with language. Tongue is nuanced and we're trying to honor an East LA accent. Like, you wouldn't do *Peaky Blinders* without a Brummie accent, and you'd criticize it if it wasn't coming out right. And Ser Anzoategui, who does the role of Eddy, their pronouns are they/them, and it's hard sometimes because they grew up in East LA, but their real accent has different syntax because they're Argentinian. However, other characters, the two sisters, don't have to do that same accent because the point is that they've Americanized their tongue. That's the point of them, but the rest of the people around them are supposed to sound accurate to East LA.

I don't like stuff that's subtitled because when you go to Boyle Heights, nobody's subtitling you walking down the street. I think that it should be that same experience when you're watching. I got such shit in the theater around this when I did talkbacks. People just wanted to yell at me like, "Do you want to alienate us? We didn't understand 40% of this." I'm like, "You are not missing anything. You're not missing any story. You might miss a joke, but it's not that important. You never miss a story. You never miss a feeling." What monolingual people hate the most is when somebody laughs at something they don't understand. It's so funny because when I'm around people who are laughing at something in their own language, I don't get threatened in the same way that monolingual people get threatened. These audience members, especially the older ones, have to yell at me about not using subtitles or translating it. Here's what I say: "The feeling of otherness isn't pleasant, is it? It's not nice to be marginalized." In the theater, you can do that exercise with language and audience expectations. It worked for me for what I was trying to do.

In *Vida*, it's not just word choice, or accent, it's also cultural. For example, the meaning you might have taken from the character of Señora, the witch for lack of better terminology, is as a story device, but culturally, those people believe in that. To those of us that do believe in that practice, it means something else. A lot of people are like, "Oh my God, my aunt is one of those ladies like that," or "My mother used to take me." You don't miss anything by not having had that experience personally in your life, but what it does is enhance your representation from seeing it represented well. It doesn't take away from someone who doesn't understand it because the story still stands. We have been excluded from the narrative for so long. Our details, our quirks, our stories. Just to see ourselves represented that way, there's an alchemy to that. A person from the dominant culture cannot understand the alchemy about a recognition. It's like, "There I am, I exist, I am." It's the holiest, most metaphysical prayer. And we haven't been

Tanya Saracho 241

allowed that because for so long, we've been told "they" are those people, but to be a full "I" am, in whatever flawed way, is a gift. One example is the flan thing in the show. People who've been to these funerals, they were like, "Oh, the flan, yes." Showing up with flan. That pulls in an old legacy. There are small moments in the story, but breaking bread, eating flan together, became huge. Also story-wise, whoever didn't grow up doing flan, the fact they were breaking bread together, basically, you got right away. But them sharing the flan made it deeper and more profound.

We know there's a problem of representation, and so we're trying to solve that problem, but it needs to be more muscular. It's sometimes cosmetic. Money talks and money is support. So produce us, yes, and then stick by us, let us learn and fail sometimes. You've let other people of the dominant culture and gender fail. And then market us. Because that's the second part of the support. That's how we die. The network or the studio doesn't stand behind the product and let it sort of play until it finds an audience, until it doesn't anymore. Money is support in this industry, unfortunately. I wouldn't say that money is support in the same way in theater, here it's mostly transactional in that way, which is fine. This is the business, but we can't forget that it's also an art form and it needs to be nurtured.

It is a budget, but it's also a vision. For us, we have never had a prime cable Latinx theme show on television before *Vida*. So you have to convince a culture, meaning millennial Latinx, to come and consume prime cable, which they haven't been, they've been doing the streaming and stuff. How an audience, I mean especially the Brown millennials, consume television now, they really like binge watching and streaming, from what I understand. And so to go on this model of prime cable is not in their budgets. I think in the second season, we were mostly watched by middle-aged white men or something. It was interesting, but also that's mostly what audience they have. But also, we increased their – they call us Hispanics in their data – but the Hispanic usage. More Hispanics came for the show than they've ever come for any of their other shows. But it was a very big battle there. I guess we ultimately lost, but I can't say we lost after having three seasons. But also, you're fighting a battle that's bigger than you.

I would have loved for the story to keep going. We had more story to tell and then they cut me down to six episodes the last season, and with a smaller budget. So in a way that was a loss, but it's also a win because we have three seasons of a story and we got to tell it the way we wanted to for the most part, except for when they took away things. But that's the business, I guess. It would have been great to keep telling the story not just because I think we have way more story to tell, but because I love employing all those Brown people and all those queer people, and they loved being represented on screen and not just working on the show.

But during production, we weren't always welcome. It was a small faction of the community. They started protesting us when we did the pilot, so they hadn't seen anything, but it was just like pedigree that I'm not from Boyle

242 Tanya Saracho

Heights. That was the first offense, and I say that with no irony. I actually understand why they protested us. So I'm not defensive about it. I get it. How many times have people come in there, represented their neighborhood and what have they represented? Mostly graffiti and cholos and "eses" and gangs. And they come in with their trucks, which is a little bit oppressive and a little bit of an occupation. Hollywood trucks are oppressive. They're loud, take over blocks, and people's lives are disrupted, which is what gentrification is.

So, we go in there and then for it to be helmed by me, the queen gentrifier of it all, who has no right to their stories because I am not from their neighborhoods. They're not wrong about that. I'm not from their neighborhoods. The complaint was that I am benefiting from their struggle which, again, is also valid, but it's so complicated. I tried to portray it as a complicated way, through all points of view. We started our first day of shooting at 7 AM and we got our first online protest at 11 AM. They called me "whitetina," which was offensive. They called me "sell out" in Spanish. I immediately went up to Chelsea Rendon, who plays Mari, and told her to change some of the "putas" in the script to "whitetina." She went, "That's so mean," and I'm like, "Yeah, exactly." She would have rather said "puta" than "whitetina." I was like, "That's exactly why we need to say it." So she said it the day I got called that and I feel like it's almost like a comic thing. Art mimicking life and vice versa.

Then they snuck into our base camp. That was creepy. They were taking pictures of us having dinner. That made me feel protective over my crew. Then there were threats to some of my writers. Some of my writers are from the area, that's the whole reason why I hired them. So Starz did step up the security a little bit, which is not what you want. You don't want more cops. It's like, "Fuck, this is exactly what they're talking about, by bringing the cops." But these were more politicized activists who were feeling this way. The whole neighborhood didn't feel that way. Some people were really welcoming of us.

Going forward, I'm trying to bring more people into the industry with the Untitled Latinx Project. I got eighteen ladies together, including my bestie, Gloria Calderón Kellett. I wanted to do like a supper club of Latina badasses who are showrunners or about-to-be showrunners. I just wanted for us to be friends and mentors for each other. We became sisters and have been there for one another. Then Untitled Latinx Project partnered with The Black List to do a Latinx pilot list. One of our members/sisters, Lindsey Villarreal, who was on *Vida*, works with The Black List. It's beautiful because hundreds of scripts came in, and we'd all read the semi-finalists together. And the talent is here. I already have my eyes on a couple of them. They get script deals at Hulu and the writers have access to us, which is so good that we were able to do this as sort of big sisters in the community.

I think we're a very different community than the generation before us. I don't think the generation before had as much solidarity. We all have different talents. I don't have Sierra's (Teller Ornelas) comedy skills. And Glo

Tanya Saracho   243

(Gloria Calderón Kellett) has like comedies with heart. I'm a jaded person who likes flawed women who have sex. And there's a room for all three of us. The dominant culture has never been limited as to what narratives they've been able to tell. For a while I would always get offered stuff for cartel or domestic workers, but those have stopped now. Listen, we are cartel people, and we are domestic workers, but it's just the point of view that has been exhausted. And the immigrant trauma, that shit, the dominant culture loves immigrant porn. And I'm from the Texas-Mexico border, so everything was that. But I'm glad that's stopped for me. But now I've gotten so many hypersexual things. I don't know when I became hypersexual. So, it's a fine line because I'm like, "You're not watching *Vida* the way I need you to be watching it if you think that this is all I do." Somebody offered me a sexy soap. And I felt like, "You did not watch *Vida* because there's no gratuitous sex scenes on the show." It's all character stuff that adds to the thing.

In upcoming projects, I want to decolonize magic from Hollywood because it's been centered in European belief systems for so long. Images of witches are all wearing like Victorian garb. There is never representation of where Palo and Santeria and Voodoo come from, or Curanderismo, which comes from Indigenous belief systems in Mesoamerica. Or Michica and Aztec traditions, which are way older than the European traditions. But because of who has been at the helm, images of *The Craft* and *Practical Magic* and *Charmed*, is all like *Harry Potter*. It's all castles and it's almost like a little British boarding school. It's almost not even Eurocentric, it's just British. I grew up with Grandisimo. In Hollywood, it's like dead chickens and weird zombies. It's just that it's a Brown people, a Black people, a poor people religion, and it's a colonized religion. I feel like those religions carry our colonization with us, for good or bad. So, if I ever get to do a show about brujas, I hope I would decolonize magic once and for all, and sort of center us as these, especially women, wise women, who have been holding onto this torch of tradition and we brought it to the Americas and kept it alive. We've pulled this matriarchal knowledge with us, even though they've tried to beat it out of us.

TRACY OLIVER
Know What You're Worth

Figure 40.1 Tracy Oliver
Source: © Elisabeth Caren

Tracy Oliver is a writer and producer, known for writing the hit movies *Girls Trip, Little* and *The Sun is Also a Star*. She starred in and produced the web series *The Misadventures of Awkward Black Girl* and wrote for *The Neighbors* and *Survivor's Remorse*. Tracy created and showruns the TV shows *First Wives Club* and *Harlem*.

A few years ago when I was doing *Girls Trip*, that was the first time that I realized how little people value the writer in a project and how much you do. You're shaping the entire world. In your mind, you're dreaming up characters. You're dreaming up dialogue and situations to put them in. You're writing a hundred plus pages. So, when you're in the trenches like that, you really get a sense of how valuable you are to the project. Then it takes on a life of its own. And it does really well and that's fantastic, but I

DOI: 10.4324/9781003298229-41

had no ownership over it whatsoever and don't see any of the profits and success of it. And because it was a Black project, they wanted to keep the budget low for everything, but particularly for the writers. It was an extremely low amount of money, but I was so eager to write that movie and so excited to do it, that I was like, "Yeah, I'll do it for whatever." It's just one of those life lessons that you learn. I created something that was in my mind and I worked really hard on it and I didn't really have equity in it. I had no ownership comedically over what happens and also financially.

And so now whether it's TV or film, I approach it differently. I am very cognizant of deals and what's written in them, and I ask for points and backend and producing credits. So now I won't write a movie without also producing and working out a separate deal structure so that I'm connected to it and its success. TV is more of a writer's medium, but even with that, you have to know what you're worth and be willing to walk away from something. The industry is set up to be fear-based and you feel if you don't take this not-that-great offer, maybe nothing else will come along. You have to bet on yourself and know the value and know how good the product is that you have and turn stuff down that's not favorable to you. So that's really important to me now.

You have to defend writing the most because it's so invisible. When you're an actor and you're on set doing long days and long nights, people see it. When you're a director, you're saying "Cut" and you're giving notes. And so people come in, they're like, "Wow, the director and the actors worked so hard," but we sit in an office space for months on end. However long the shoot took, writing took way longer. But it's not visible because people aren't watching you work. Even though you guys were on set for six weeks, I wrote this for a year.

I was kind of in a similar boat as Adele Lim in the sense that my quote off of *Girls Trip* was so low because no one predicted it was going to make $150 million. They thought, "Maybe we can make this movie for like nineteen million and hopefully get it back." That was kind of the attitude about it. And so, my quote on it did not reflect the quality, the time, or the success. And then when they come back for the next movie, I do think that my quote went up, but not nearly as much as some white male writers that haven't even had $150 million movie come out. This is now me speculating, but I think it's that they feel better about spending their money on a Colin Trevorrow than they do with the Adele Lim or me. To them it feels like a safer bet or a better investment. It kind of undoes what you accomplished because you're still "a risk." I personally know white writers, some of them my friends, so no judgment there, but they'll go in and the idea of the movie or show that they're pitching is not any less risky than mine. But because it's coming out of a white male mouth they say, "OK yeah, I think we can put money on that," and, "Yeah, it's really interesting." So, I always feel like I'm still trying to earn the right quote and the right fee.

I think approaching writing like a job helps. I have a couple of friends who are always asking me, "How do you write so much?" And I tell them,

246 *Tracy Oliver*

"Because I like to make money and earn a living." And they say, "Well, I do too." And I say, "You don't like it like I like it then." I really treat it like a job. And I think that helps take out a lot of the emotion out of it, too. Because some of it is art, but a lot of it is what you do for a living. I make goals for myself, show up, and do what I said I would. I'm better when I'm super regimented. I'm such a Gemini that if I'm not super regimented, nothing will get done. I usually write a little through the weekend too, Monday through Saturday. I know what those days are and it's usually done by themes that I want to do. I can't write more than about four hours at a time. I've met writers who write from nine to five like it's a regular job. God bless you, but I cannot do that. But for those four hours I'm doing nothing but that. I don't go online or go watch something. I try to hyperfocus for four hours and then I have the rest of the day to do whatever.

I'm always writing about friendship and girlfriends hanging out, and there is nothing harder and worse than trying to do four different voices. It takes so much mental work to capture four different voices and be funny and put in a set piece at the same time. But I do try, even in the first draft, to look for funny things or try to think of funny scenarios to put people in and think of funny jokes. But I try not to get too hung up on it because then you won't get through it. I'm not like, "Is this the best joke?" I'm more like, "This is fine for now." And then I keep moving. There's a lot of things that I've had to learn to get through it. One is to stop judging it. When I was a slower writer, it was because I was agonizing over if what I was writing was good. And you're just really just prolonging the process. And so I just had to tell myself, "No matter what I write, it is good enough today."

In the first draft, now it's not the time the judge, you're just figuring it out. Let that art go. Something I actively had to train myself to do was to be kinder to myself in my writing. Rewriting is kind of fun. Then you're refining it and deepening and finding new layers. But that first draft always kind of kills me. Like I have to mentally prepare and the sense of like, "I'll be okay, alright, I got this, you can do it."

I'm looking for feel-good, funny, binge-worthy entertainment right now but also heartfelt and meaningful. But I still try to land in a place that's a place of love. I'm not as attracted to so much dark stuff because the news is dark enough. I want women to feel good about themselves when they watch it. I never want to do something that tears us down. There was a string of shows for a second that were deliberately being unlikable to the point of I would hate this person in real life. I'm going in the opposite direction. I want these women to really like each other. They can have spats, but it's all rooted in love and forgiveness at the end. I'm big on that. And even when I go into other genres, it's still pushing that agenda. It's still female friendships or love stories within horror, within sci-fi, within whatever the genre is. When I come up with things that I want to write, it's always rooted in what I am interested in watching. If I don't want to watch this, I'm definitely not interested in writing it.

Tracy Oliver 247

I always start from the heart, the core. I started there for sure with *Girls Trip*. That was the one thing I had, even from the pitch, was that end monologue. Everyone at Universal said that that's literally why I got the job. That monologue. Even with all the silly set pieces, they said it was the heart of it. And I think what I try to do is think about a group of people that are normally not given the platform and the opportunity to say something. What attracted me to *First Wives Club* was women over 40 feeling invisible and feeling powerless and what that's like if you're a woman of color over 40. We're told that we don't matter a lot and we're always fighting against that. There was a conversation initially, in this new version, of, "Do we age the women down?" I was like, "Absolutely not. I am not interested in it if we're not saying something deeper that resonates with me emotionally." I will sugarcoat it with comedy and hijinks and stuff. I wanted people to tear up a little on *Girls Trip*. You don't have to be full on sobbing, but I wanted it to emotionally land.

The comedic stuff comes from me drinking a lot and being a very silly person. A lot of it is because I spent the majority of my twenties partying really hard, a lot. And I was almost thirty when I got *Girls Trip* and the funny thing was, I didn't pitch it. It wasn't my original, I mean the cast, the characters in the plot were original, but it was a writing assignment. It was funny because at least five different people saw in the trades that the movie was like a party hardy movie with Black women. Everyone said, "There's nobody better than you to write this," because I just had so many dumb things happen, from living life, traveling, and hanging out with my girlfriends. Some of my friends said, "I can't believe you put that in the movie." It was just drawing from real life. I definitely drank too much or did molly one time in Vegas. My friend and I were hallucinating. I thought a bird was talking to me. And she said, "Oh my God, I see it." And none of it made any sense. But I had to write it down.

I think to write comedy in that way, you have to live a life. I think on the drama side, you could probably get away with being brooding and introverted. But I think to write these party movies and friendship stories convincingly, you do have to go out with your friends. It's genuine for me. I think people can kind of tell, but I love hanging out with my girlfriends and I love traveling and going to parties and stuff with them. It's coming from an authentic place. What I'm learning because I'm now having to become more mature, is that I really have to not drink as much if I have to write the next day.

It's definitely gotten easier than when I was first pitching stuff. When I first started out I wasn't selling anything. But then from *Girls Trip* to *First Wives Club* and the Amazon show, it has absolutely gotten easier. However, you still kind of fight the same battle where they don't pay you as much for those things. And they also don't give you the type of budget that they'll give a more mainstream project. I was just talking to a friend yesterday and I am ashamed to admit I had a very cynical conversation, but I will literally tell you what happened. I said, "Do you think I would make more money if I just

248 *Tracy Oliver*

stopped writing about Black people?" And he said, "Yeah." Writing is really hard. Writing Black people isn't easier. It doesn't take less time, but the money doesn't measure up to other creators I know who are not working on Black stuff. Before it was if you want to make money, period, you need to write white characters. And now it's like, "I'm making money, but if you want to make more money or the type of money that your peers are making then you might need to diversify." It's still a little heartbreaking when I think about that. But then also, I guess that's just the reality that I'm in. I'm at a different crossroads now of figuring out if I should start writing more mainstream stuff and I might, you know, it sounds crazy to say that, but I might cause you do want to make more money for as hard as you work.

I acted throughout childhood up until college and in my twenties with the web series I did with Issa Rae. Talk about fear-based, I realized that I didn't want to be at the mercy of someone else all the time to get a job. This is why Issa and I did *Awkward Black Girl* because everyone told her she didn't look like an actor. And we were like, "Says who? Well, then we'll create an opportunity where you can look like an actor." I liked the power of being able to create something. And with the Stark program I did at USC, you get more connections than in the MFA program. You learn how to make stuff. You learn how to do the business aspects of it and not just the creative, the best of both worlds. I think it really was helpful to do that. It was the reason I could put together the *Awkward Black Girl* web series. I learned how to do that and used the same crew that I met at USC to shoot that. People are always surprised I jumped from a low-level writer to a showrunner really quickly and part of that is because a lot of writers don't have production experience. I just had a lot of life experience going to Stark and running a successful web series. Showrunning to me is, I have more money to do what I was always doing when I was trying to make it. Now there's a whole department that does that. That used to be all just me because I used to be craft services, the one that would run around and get the food. I would line produce, get the props, do so much work. We didn't have any money. We were so broke then. And I'm borrowing $2000 from my mom to help with craft services. And she was like, "When are you going to get a job?" Little did she know that was actually preparation for what I do now. The assistant route, that's the traditional path. That's the path that I would say 99% of my classmates took. They were on a desk and they were learning directly from a boss and they weren't in this really scary place that I was in. I don't even know if I would recommend what I did to most people because it took a huge leap of faith, but I just knew I wanted to make stuff and get out there.

Now I try to cut through and get people opportunities because Hollywood doesn't bring in diversity if you don't make the extra effort. I do my own outreach. And that's where the community really helps. Issa, Amy Aniobi, we're all sending each other stuff and trying to help usher in new people at the same time because we have the power. Even when I was starting out, I don't think there was that community. There was Shonda and there weren't

Tracy Oliver 249

that many Black women or opportunities to work for people of color. It didn't exist honestly. I did an initiative in 2020 with BET to specifically find new comedic voices. And we got a lot of submissions. Had I not done that initiative and opened it up wide you may not have met those people. I'm really trying to find new people and expand beyond just LA. I'll be honest. Sometimes it's a fight. There's always the experience argument, like, "Why does it have to be this show we're experimenting?" Well, because I don't know, maybe this is my last show. I treat every show that I'm on like it's my last job. So, I'm like, "We all coming through on this one." I try to get as many new people to break in as possible because I may not be in this position next year.

VEENA SUD
Blasting Away the Sacred Cow of Motherhood

Figure 41.1 Veena Sud
Source: photo by Angela Lewis

Veena Sud got an MFA from NYU's Graduate Film Program, then worked at MTV as a director, before moving to Los Angeles and working her way up as a TV writer, starting on CBS's *Cold Case*, and moving up to showrunner. Veena created and showran the Emmy-nominated American television adaptation of *The Killing*, and then created, wrote, and showran the Emmy-winning limited Netflix series *Seven Seconds* and *The Stranger*. Veena also wrote and directed the features *The Salton Sea* and *The Lie* (Amazon).

I was one of a majority of female directors on MTV's *The Real World*, where my boss was willing to take risks on new talent and didn't exclude anyone based on what we looked like, or what we had in our pants. I just got my MFA in film at NYU on a scholarship, which was like being on this ridiculous luxe vacation because I didn't have to work full-time to support my son. All I had to do was watch movies, go to class and learn everything about the craft of filmmaking. I even brought my 4-year-old son, Kumar, to some of my classes. I had always wanted to be in and around film. Before film school, I had made some short films while I was working at Third World Newsreel. That's when I felt my life began, at Third World Newsreel, where people of color like me were making films, showcasing our communities' history in films. It was there I got the courage to make films myself. I always knew I wanted to pursue film, but I couldn't do that because I was a single mom... who was going to pay the bills? NYU gave me a wonderful, very generous scholarship and living stipend so I was able to just do that full time and not have to work at night. I'm very grateful.

At *The Real World*, it was six months of cinema verité because *The Real World* is, or was, weirdly strict in their documentary filmmaking style. I learned a lot just by observing human nature for ten or twelve hours a day. It actually informed *The Killing*. One scene in particular towards the end of the pilot was hugely influenced by what I witnessed while working on *The Real World*. People repeat themselves when they fight, I learned. They keep saying the same thing: "You cheated on me. No, I didn't. Yes, you did. I hate you. Let's get divorced. Ok, fuck you. You cheated on me. No, I didn't..." The energy's up and then it comes down and then it goes up again, then down. It's circular. So you would run in with the camera and get your close ups. This was round number one. And then round number two, drop back and get your medium shots. By the time round five comes around, you're thinking, what else am I going to shoot? They're just saying the same thing, over and over. But I noticed—because we had cameras all over the house— that the people who are listening to the fight are actually more powerful than the people who are fighting, because they're the ones who are just reacting. So, we would go downstairs and shoot them listening to the fight, having all sorts of emotional reactions. I did something similar on *The Killing*. At the end of the *The Killing* pilot, the mom is on the phone, and she's discovered that her daughter's body's been found in the trunk of the politician's car. One of the most powerful images in the pilot is the reaction of her two young sons as she's screaming and crying. They're standing outside the kitchen, listening to their mom, not saying a word, just watching, and their whole world falls apart. That came from being able to observe a house of people and how they reacted towards one another in times of conflict. Observing our lived behavior is a critical part of being a writer, a storyteller.

Writing for *Cold Case* was so different from *The Killing*. It's heartbreaking how on commercial broadcast (network TV) you have to keep cutting page count because of commercials. I don't remember the page count for a *Cold Case* episode, but my tendency is to write very little dialogue. I'm not talky, or quippy, or joke-y. I'm much more interested in the physical and the visual telling of the story. Meredith (Steihm) writes that way too, and I learned so much from her on *Cold Case*. I started as a staff writer there and then, a mere few years later, I inherited running the show from Meredith, who's so amazingly generous and supportive to let me take care of her baby for two

252 *Veena Sud*

years as a showrunner. Then I created *The Killing* and ran that for four seasons. Then I took a bit of a break, did research, filled the well, traveled, read, saw the world, tried to live as much as possible so I could have something else to say.

Over the course of four seasons on *The Killing*, I tried to showcase a woman who is as flawed as any male hero on television, blasting away the sacred cow of motherhood, being the type of woman we never get to see on television. We do see that more now, thankfully, but I hadn't seen a woman like that before with the exception of Helen Mirren in *Prime Suspect*. There weren't many or any women in dramas, especially procedural dramas, who looked like homicide detectives I had met, who wore shoes they could run in, who didn't wear make-up, who just did their jobs with as much ambition as any male character. There's this nod to girlishness on TV—incessant talk of men and children and waxing and clothes—it's ridiculous. I like women who are angry and ambitious and passionate and forces of nature to be reckoned with. We don't have to be soft. We don't have to be safe. And Sarah Linden wasn't soft or safe. I think that pissed some people off. And made a lot of women very happy.

The Killing was originally a Danish series created by Søren Sveistrup. I was delighted to build on his version of Sarah Linden and create my own heroine: a fierce, obsessive, destructive, self-destructive, committed, passionate homicide detective and human being. He provided a lot of material to play with, certainly for a season. But there's a difference between merely transcribing a show into English and actually, as writers, walking in the shoes of those characters. We had to understand the characters from the inside out, and to create new backstories for all the characters that resonated with us in our version of *The Killing*. It was like planting two trees next to each other. Their limbs, their branches, will start in the same place but over time, grow in different directions. That's what happened with the American version of *The Killing*.

Season One was very much influenced by the Danish version. But then again by planting different notions and ideas about who the characters were, they started to branch out into a different story, and it was radically different from the Danish version in Season Two. By the time we got to Season Three, we started with a whole new world with street kids, which is just something I've been fascinated by for many years. I'm obsessed with Mary Ellen Marks and her photographs. And I think I saw *Streetwise* when I was about twelve or so, talk about getting scarred at a young age! Then again, my parents who were immigrants never censored what I watched. It was such a powerful documentary, and especially in a city like Seattle that has such a huge street population of kids and teenagers, it felt like that story needed to be told and I wanted to tell it. I also wanted to tell a story about the death penalty and the prison system. For Season Three, we partnered with Netflix. Netflix and AMC both were partners in distributing and broadcasting the show. And then our last season, Netflix was so gracious to come in and give us a chance to say goodbye to Sarah and Holder and finish the story, which we really needed to do.

Veena Sud 253

This is a new golden age of television for a reason. Before there were three outlets, way back in the dinosaur age, right? And now there's multiple outlets and not just a five hundred station cable monster. Now there's money and interest, as well as a bigger appetite for good storytelling. Audiences—who are really smart—are now, finally, given good material, and they're hungry for more. In this new age, television is finally showing our heroes can be women. Our heroes can be people of color. Our heroes can be transgender. Television has the potential to become this great equalizer, to show the truth of who America really is. But it still has a long way to go in really telling all of our stories. Qualifying that still, the majority of shows are about the white straight male hero, with writing staffs staffed with guys, white guys. So, there's still a long way to go, even more so with directors. If I didn't ask specifically for agents to submit women directors, I'd get a bunch of dudes. This industry overall needs more women and more people of color in every position—agents, the agencies, the executives at the network, the studios, and the showrunners, the press. It's not just who creates the shows, it's who greenlights the shows, who publicizes the shows, who believes in the shows. We just have to keep fighting for an equal playing field.

I broke into the industry through the ABC Disney program, which is a diversity program. I understand why some people of color in the industry say that now diversity programs can sometimes be a bit of a trap. It's shocking and infuriating that a lot of lower-level writers who are BIPOC are still getting regurgitated at staff writer level for multiple years, over and over. On my shows, we bump people up if they stay on the show, but I'm seeing that revolving door pattern in writers I'm hiring. I know we're all trying to pinch pennies to make the shows that we want to make, but as a woman, as a person of color, as someone who went through the prejudices of this industry myself, having staff repeat levels over and over is problematic because it's so clearly based on gender, and it is based on race.

My feeling is there's been a small incremental change in the industry. It needs to speed up. We need more female executives. We need more executives of color. I can pitch so many different stories and I have pitched stories, but if people aren't buying them, it doesn't matter. I've pitched stories with all the leads being detectives of color—they didn't sell. So, I felt very lucky to have Sarah Linden as this female detective who was very different from what we were seeing on television at that point in terms of female detectives. But I had to really fight to keep her flawed. There was nervousness around how bad of a mother she was. Could she be softer? No fucking way. That's not who she is. We've got enough of the soft moms on TV. There's a lot of moms out there who are conflicted, overworked, exhausted, a disappointment to their children, to themselves—as they try their best to hold up the whole damn world. There's nothing more maddening to me than to see the perfect mom on TV flipping pancakes at breakfast and she's also a neurosurgeon and her hair is perfectly curled. Come to my house. No one's getting pancakes. No one's hair is being curled. Like the homes and the lives of so many working moms I know, it's far more complicated than *Leave It To Beaver*. Whose reality was that anyways? Not mine or my mother's or any woman I know. Maybe it's time for TV to catch up to the real America.

WINNIE HOLZMAN
See the Beauty of It

Figure 42.1 Winnie Holzman
Source: photo courtesy of Showtime

Winnie Holzman is the creator and showrunner of *My So-Called Life*. She also wrote the book for the musical *Wicked* and the screenplays for the forthcoming *Wicked* movies. In television, she started out as a writer on *Thirtysomething*. She developed and ran *Huge* with her daughter, Savannah Dooley, has been the co-showrunner for *Roadies* created by Cameron Crowe, and, as an actress, has done cameos on *Curb Your Enthusiasm, Jerry Maguire,* and others.

DOI: 10.4324/9781003298229-43

256   *Winnie Holzman*

I was the creator and showrunner of *My So-Called Life*. It came about because these two incredible men, Marshall Herskovitz and Ed Zwick, from the second I met them, on *Thirtysomething*, were mentoring me. They had a huge impact on my life and my writing. With *My So-Called Life*, there were times when it was genuinely a collaboration and there were other times when they were letting me just do my thing. A major part of that collaboration, though in a different way, was with Claire Danes. Because Claire is such an incredible artist. This is an overused word perhaps, but she was a muse to me during that time, and still is. Her influence on me as a presence and as an artist can't be overstated.

When you work in television, you have this group of actors that gather together, and you work with them not just on one two-hour script, like a movie or a musical with a limited timeframe. You travel through time with them and you often don't know for how long. In my case I've only been involved with TV in very short bursts, I haven't had long ones, but it's still a longer amount of time than a movie (or a musical) would be. So, you keep being influenced by the way they're relating to each other and by the way they relate to you and what you observe about them. I find that thrilling. You're coming back week after week to make a new story, with basically the same group of people, and they're often fascinating people, exceptionally sensitive and intuitive.

Any time you're working with actors, in a play, in a musical, in a movie, they are your collaborators. They're your collaborators before you even know what actors you've got. Because you're writing for people to play these parts. If you're writing with the hope that actors are going to come into those parts, you have to ask yourself, at some point, what it would be like to play those parts. That's not unique to TV, that's unique to writing for actors. But it gets a little more intense with TV because they don't go away. You may live with them for years. I tend to choose actors who have some comedy ability. My background is in comedy. People may think of me as being a drama writer, and I do write about emotions, but I use humor a lot. Humor unlocks everything and makes all the emotion possible.

With *My So-Called Life*, the casting process fell into place almost effortlessly. The person who actually found Claire for us is a woman named Linda Lowy, who casts pretty much all of Shondaland, I think. We knew the biggest issue was: Who is this young girl going to be? Linda said to me, "Winnie, I know this girl in New York. Her name is Claire Danes." That was the first time that Claire's name had ever been mentioned. Linda knew her work, and she said with complete authority: "That's going to be the person. That's who you need." I was so relieved, because, of course, one of my fears was, what if we can't find this girl? I had even said to Ed at one point, "What if we don't find her?" And he said, "If we don't find her, we won't do the show." Which was an incredibly comforting thing to hear. And then he said: "But we will find her, and you're going to fall in love with her." And he was right.

Winnie Holzman 257

When it comes to my work, I'm interested in looking at somebody on the surface and then coming to understand them in a deeper way. TV is well suited to that. I'm also interested in what it means to be a good person. That's something I'm constantly exploring. *Wicked* is all about that. *Wicked* is to some extent about who is good and who is wicked, and what goodness really is, rather than what it appears to be. Surface appearance versus the deeper truth. The young women in *Wicked* find their individual ways to do good in their world. Their lives take dramatically different directions but in their respective ways, they end up finding a way to do good and to be good people. And even though one of them will be, for the rest of time, thought of as a wicked person, it doesn't matter, because she finds a way to do what she knows is right.

Writing is a mysterious process. My experience is that for most of the writing process there's so much you don't know. Slowly things become clearer and sometimes there's things that never become clear. Every project has its own reality and its own sense of itself and its own life. There isn't one way that I approach anything because it really depends on what the project is and who I'm working with. Whoever I collaborate with will influence me, and you end up doing things together that neither of you would ever have done by yourselves.

I'm introverted, but I sort of turned into this extrovert person as a teen, when I started acting. But I still remain secretly an introvert. That's one of the hardest things for me about showrunning, because being a writer, I do like to be alone a lot. I don't always want to interact with huge groups of people. Then you take on this job where you're basically in charge of a huge group of people. The job itself taught me a lot about communication skills and handling other people's needs and listening and all of those basics of taking on a leadership role. I've learned things showrunning that I could have never learned otherwise. When you're a showrunner, you become like a parent figure. It's inevitable. You have to manage that too and figure out a way to still be yourself.

It can be a very challenging job because it's all about the creative process. You're trying to figure out: how best I can make this show happen? I think that's why people love to work with people that they've worked with before because there is a sense of trust and a shorthand that will give you some ease and confidence. There's so much writing you've got to do in a short amount of time.

When I created *My So-Called Life*, Marshall and Ed had just come off of *Thirtysomething* and they were really respected in the industry, specifically at ABC. So, the network kind of left us alone. They had problems and worries that they did express, but I wasn't forced to follow their directives. My alliance with Marshall and Ed empowered me. I didn't have to take all the network's suggestions. You know, there's an aspect of doing something for the first time, called beginner's luck. You literally don't know how much can go wrong. I was like that when I was doing *My So-Called Life*. I was a beginner, and it worked in my favor. I just kind of didn't know how wrong things could go.

258 *Winnie Holzman*

Back then the way you did TV was you never had unlimited time. You always had a very short amount of time to do a lot of episodes. The lack of time made it easier for me to depend on my own instincts, trust myself. You get into a rhythm with it. And Marshall and Ed had modeled a kind of confidence in their own instincts doing *Thirtysomething*. They did their show the way they wanted to. I was very influenced by that. With *My So-Called Life*, they stepped in and took a lot of the heat for me. They shielded me from a lot of the most negative network interactions. By the end it became pretty clear to all of us, oh, the network really isn't into this and they're looking for reasons to cancel it. A few months after we got canceled, I saw the beauty of it. And I certainly do now. All these years later I see how it was just perfect the way it was. I don't need it to have lasted one minute longer than it was.

When you have a peak experience, you end up just being grateful that you had the experience. You don't focus so much on, "How come it didn't last another year?" You had it, and it was really precious. I got it on the air, and my show has communicated with a lot of people. I had an amazing experience with two truly brilliant men who really supported me and gave me a platform. And I had an incredible actress to work with, and that amazing supporting cast.

Being grateful for what you've been given is very important. It's really everything. *My So-Called Life* has had its own charmed life.

Printed in the United States
by Baker & Taylor Publisher Services